Valenti, Patricia Dunlavy, 1945-

To myself a stranger.

$29.95

DATE			

10/91

To Myself a Stranger

To Myself a Stranger

A Biography of

Rose Hawthorne Lathrop

Patricia Dunlavy Valenti

LOUISIANA STATE UNIVERSITY PRESS
Baton Rouge and London

Manufactured in the United States of America
First printing
00 99 98 97 96 95 94 93 92 91 5 4 3 2 1

Designer: Patricia Douglas Crowder
Typeface: Linotron 202 Bembo
Typesetter: G&S Typesetters, Inc.
Printer and binder: Thomson-Shore, Inc.

All photos courtesy of Archives of the Servants of Relief for Incurable Cancer.

LIBRARY OF CONGRESS CATALOGING-IN-PUBLICATION DATA

Valenti, Patricia Dunlavy, 1945–
To myself a stranger : a biography of Rose Hawthorne Lathrop / Patricia Dunlavy Valenti.
p. cm.
Includes bibliographical references and index.
ISBN 0-8071-1612-2
1. Lathrop, Rose Hawthorne, 1851–1926—Biography. 2. Authors, American—19th century—Biography. 3. Dominican sisters—United States—Biography. 4. Cancer—Patients—Long term care—New York (N.Y.)—History. 5. Hawthorne family. I. Title.
PS2231.V35 1991
362.1'96994'0092—dc20
[B] 90-23670
CIP

The paper in this book meets the guidelines for permanence and durability of the Committee on Production Guidelines for Book Longevity of the Council on Library Resources. ∞

For my parents,
Francine Alessi Dunlavy and Alfred Rankin Dunlavy

'Tis Scarcely Spring

But yet one wild Rose came,
Our wild, New England Rose,
And twined her vines round all our hearts,
And threw their sprays in all old haunts,
Lighting up dark and shady nooks
And opening buds in sunny spots.
The fragrance of this eglantine
Was like naught else but love itself—
For what more subtly sweet?
Perfume wakes memories
Long eclipsed by time and care
And with these dance back youth and Hope
That had slumbered and died not
Ever ready to live again,
Summoned by the gifted young
Who make youth immortal
Showing us that Hope cannot die.
Our wild Rose loves to death old age,
Wreathes it in smiles, makes it forget long past joys
And bathes the future in love's light
To make each moment as it passes sweet.
This is the task of our wild Rose
And she has gone again,
    to sweeten other homes.

—[Mary Tyler Peabody Mann?]

Contents

Illustrations

Preface

I SUSPECT that all biographers begin with some knowledge of the broad outlines of their subject's life. Like many other people, I originally knew of Rose Hawthorne Lathrop because of my knowledge of her father, Nathaniel Hawthorne. She, his last child, was overshadowed not only by the magnificence of her father's literary productions but also by her two older siblings and even her husband. Rose's sister, Una, whose life was characterized by illness and loss, continues to be the subject of attention because she figured in Hawthorne's portrayal of Pearl in *The Scarlet Letter.* Rose's brother, Julian, who had a prolific if not always distinguished literary career, is the subject of a biography by Maurice Bassan entitled *Hawthorne's Son: The Life and Literary Career of Julian Hawthorne.* Rose's husband, George Parsons Lathrop, enjoyed respect as a writer and as editor of the Riverside Edition of *The Works of Nathaniel Hawthorne* during the last quarter of the nineteenth century. Rose, heretofore eclipsed rather than illuminated by the brilliance of her family, more than deserves to be the subject of extensive biographical attention, for her life, worth telling because of its intrinsic narrative appeal, both embodies and transcends elements of the American culture in which she lived.

Born in 1851, Rose pursued a literary career for twenty years of her adult life, never approaching the success or satisfaction in that arena obtained by her father, brother, and husband. Her successes and satisfactions were to be obtained in another arena entirely. In 1891, at the age of forty, she converted to Roman Catholicism. Five years later, in an even more radical departure from her past, she took an apartment on the Lower East Side of Manhattan—then, as now, a violent slum area—and ran an ad in the newspaper inviting indigents dying of cancer to live with her and be cared for by her until their death.

This kind of move in midlife is hard to imagine, even more amazing when we realize that cancer was probably more dreaded in the late nineteenth century than AIDS is today. The tubercule bacillus had recently been identified, and bacteriology was a burgeoning science. Informed and rational people thus made the logical (but incorrect) assumption that cancer, too, was contagious. Rose, however, had the unfaltering intuition—and intuition it must be called—that cancer was not contagious and that its victims, regardless of their class, race, religion, or sex, should not be ostracized and abandoned in their final moments. Thus she began a work that would be supported by a rapidly growing network of donations, and she immediately attracted other woman adherents to her cause. She founded a group of religious women called the Servants of Relief for Incurable Cancer, who to this day nurse those dying of cancer who do not have financial or, at times, emotional support.

Rose's intuition about cancer defied current assumptions. Her work with medical outcasts functions as a paradigm now in a culture ridden with hysteria about AIDS. Caring for the dying, a social responsibility distinct from curing the sick, continues to confound American institutions, which focus on saving lives to the exclusion of caring for the terminally ill. Rose's acceptance of death as both a natural and a spiritual reality suffused her care of the dying with love and dignity.

Rose was remarkable not only in her desire to alleviate economic and physical suffering but also in her commitment to poverty as her own elected way of life. Other women at the turn of the century—Jane Addams, for example—also addressed the needs of the poor, at Hull House and other settlements. These women who possessed the vision of a better society, coupled with administrative, organizational, and fund-raising skills, have begun to assume their rightful place in history. But Catholics and non-Catholics alike continue to undervalue or ignore altogether women in religious sisterhoods who made a tremendous impact on social institutions and provided neglected but indispensable services to society.

Rose's adoption of Roman Catholicism and religious sisterhood, however, was not primarily for the purpose of redressing a particular societal wrong. Confronted with the religion of her forebears, Rose negotiated her own path through and eventually out of their beliefs. From the paternal side, she had imbibed the distillations of Puritanism. She knew about human frailty, its propensity toward evil, and the guilt that ensues. The Unitarianism of her maternal relatives, on the other hand, was a religion of reason, common sense, and social justice propelled into action. These aspects of Puritanism and Unitarianism are both reflected in her election of Roman Catholicism. But like others at the turn of the century such as T. S. Eliot and Henry Adams, she was drawn to Catholicism for emotional as well as doctrinal reasons. This was a church where ritual, pageantry, and tradition added a decidedly feminine warmth to the despair of guilt and the chill of reason.

Previous books about Rose have essentially been hagiographies written for Catholic audiences: Katherine Burton's *Sorrow Built a Bridge* (1937), Theodore Maynard's *A Fire Was Lighted* (1948), and Marguerite Vance's *On the Wings of Fire: The Story of Nathaniel Hawthorne's Daughter Rose* (1955). These works have not utilized the abundant manuscript material available, nor have they assessed Rose's literary career or placed her life and work for the cancerous poor within the larger (non-Catholic) context of American culture—its medical mores, its socioeconomic assumptions, its religious trends. These heretofore neglected areas of literary and cultural assessment are what I attempt in this book.

I have chosen to refer to my subject by her given name, Rose, throughout the book. Although some people find the use of first names for women patronizing, especially because men are typically referred to by their last names, I find it equally problematic to refer to a woman by a name acquired through her father or husband. Furthermore, to call Rose "Hawthorne" would confuse her with the other Hawthornes: Nathaniel, Julian, Sophia, Una. To call her "Lathrop" would confuse her with George, and the purpose of this biography was *not* to perpetuate the commingling of her identity with that of her relatives or husband. I also decided to employ first names for members of her family—unless to do so would cause confusion—and for a few close associates.

Indeed, during the research and writing of this book, a core to Rose's identity emerged that was separate from her associations with family and distinct from the several phases in her development. The various names by which she was known naturally and neatly delineated these phases, and I have decided to use them as chapter titles. Yet Rose became for me an individual with a unified identity that transcended its transient manifestations; hence my decision to call her "Rose" throughout the text.

In the use of unpublished and published material, I have been faithful to the author's text even if it does not conform to current correct usage. I have kept the use of *sic* to a minimum. So often, the idiosyncracies of spelling and grammar, for example, suggest a sense of personality that might be lost if corrected or dissipated if called to the reader's attention by *sic.* I have documented manuscript material as fully as possible.

In the narrative of this remarkable woman's life, I have attempted to evoke the context in which she lived. I realize that my decisions to include, omit, emphasize, and celebrate were conditioned by my intellectual starting point, as is true of any biographer. I have not written this biography in an ideological vacuum. I recognize, too, that my relationship to my subject is at this point no longer detached, for I have come to know someone whom I admire and who has enriched my life immeasurably. Thus I wish to echo the sentiments expressed by George Parsons Lathrop in the first chapter of his study of Nathaniel Hawthorne: "Sympathy, after all, is the talisman which may preserve even the formal biographer from giving . . . injury."[1]

1. George Parsons Lathrop, *A Study of Hawthorne* (Boston, 1876), 17.

Acknowledgments

I WISH to acknowledge my indebtedness to many persons who assisted me—both directly and indirectly—in completing a project that grew well beyond what I had originally envisioned. I am, first and foremost, grateful to my husband, Peter L. Valenti, who early recognized the potential of this study, purchased our word processor, and endured life with a woman who chose to add writing a book to the pressures of family life. I am grateful as well to the community of Hawthorne scholars, particularly John Idol, whose interest has been a source of great encouragement. Librarians of numerous manuscript collections have helped with their prompt, thorough attention and their interest. I particularly wish to thank Herbert Cahoon, at the Pierpont Morgan Library, New York; the late Lola Szladits, of the New York Public Library; Richard Fyffe, of the Essex Institute Library, Salem, Massachusetts; Susan Boone, of the Neilson Library, Smith College; and Susan Ravdin, at the Bowdoin College Library. I also appreciate the help of Debbie Smith Gordon, whose sense of humor assisted me through the preparation of this manuscript.

I wish to thank the New York Public Library for permission to publish extracts from the correspondence and other manuscript materials of Rose Hawthorne Lathrop, George Parsons Lathrop, and Sophia Hawthorne in the Henry W. and Albert A. Berg Collection, and in the Alfred Williams Anthony Collection, the R. R. Bowker Papers, the Century Company Papers, and the William Conant Church Papers, Rare Books and Manuscripts Division, New York Public Library,

Astor, Lenox, and Tilden Foundations. I am also grateful to the following institutions for permission to publish excerpts from correspondence and manuscript materials: Archives of the Archdiocese of New York; Archives of the Servants of Relief for Incurable Cancer; Concord Free Public Library; Essex Institute Library; Houghton Library, Harvard University; Massachusetts Historical Society; Neilson Library, Smith College; and the Pierpont Morgan Library, New York, MA 3400.

The extract from Mother Deschamps' letter to George Parsons Lathrop is published with the permission of the Grey Nuns of Montreal. Sophia Hawthorne's letter to Henry Bright is located in the Collection of American Literature, Beinecke Rare Book and Manuscript Library, Yale University, and is quoted with permission. The extract from George Parsons Lathrop's letter to Horatio Bridge is published with the permission of Bowdoin College Library. Extracts of letters from Rose Hawthorne to Annie Fields, from Sophia Hawthorne to Annie Fields, and from Rose Hawthorne Lathrop to Thomas Wentworth Higginson located in the American Collection, Boston Public Library, are published by courtesy of the Trustees of the Boston Public Library. Sophia Hawthorne's letter of January 19, 1865, to Julian Hawthorne is located in the Ulysses S. Milburn Collection, Owen D. Young Library, St. Lawrence University, and is quoted with permission. The extract from Nathaniel Hawthorne's letter of [March 14?], 1856, to Rose Hawthorne is reprinted with the permission of Ohio State University Press from Nathaniel Hawthorne, *The Letters, 1853–1856,* ed. Thomas Woodson, James A. Rubino, L. Neal Smith, and Norman Holmes Pearson (Columbus, Ohio, 1987), 451.

Both the beginning and the completion of this book were assisted by grants. The National Endowment for the Humanities provided a Travel to Collections Grant in the spring of 1984 that enabled me to commence research at various manuscript collections, and Pembroke State University awarded me a Faculty Development Grant in the form of released time during the spring, 1989, semester so that I might complete the preparation of my manuscript.

My largest debt of gratitude goes to those who not only helped me but were a source of admiration. I thank and profoundly respect Mother Anne Marie, O.P., Superior General, Mother Bernadette,

O.P., and all members of the Servants of Relief for Incurable Cancer, who extended their generosity to me while I spent time with them doing research for this book. Their daily lives are an inspiration to all who come to them for comfort. I would also like to mention two friends who will never read these acknowledgments. As I wrote the final chapters of this book, Carol O'Sullivan and Patricia Koehne died of cancer. Each was a woman in the prime of life, raising a family when overtaken by illness and death. Both women, however, were fortunate enough to die at home, surrounded by family and friends whose faith, support, and consolation embodied what Rose Hawthorne Lathrop brought to those whom she would not relegate to despair and loneliness in their final moments.

Abbreviations

AANY Archives of the Archdiocese of New York, Yonkers
AGNM Archives of the Grey Nuns of Montreal
ASRIC Archives of the Servants of Relief for Incurable Cancer, Hawthorne, New York
BCL Bowdoin College Library, Bowdoin College, Brunswick, Maine
BPL Boston Public Library
BRBML Beinecke Rare Book and Manuscript Library, Yale University, New Haven, Connecticut
CFPL Concord Free Public Library, Concord, Massachusetts
EIL Essex Institute Library, Salem, Massachusetts
HL Houghton Library, Harvard University, Cambridge, Massachusetts
MHS Massachusetts Historical Society, Boston
NL Neilson Library, Smith College, Northampton, Massachusetts
NYPL New York Public Library, New York City
ODYL Owen D. Young Library, St. Lawrence University, Canton, New York
PML Pierpont Morgan Library, New York City

To Myself a Stranger

I / Rosebud

WHEN Rose Hawthorne Lathrop reviewed her youth, she saw a "girlhood [that] made me seem to myself a stranger who had come too late." Perhaps she was right, at least regarding her relationship with her father.[1] By the time Rose was born, on May 20, 1851, Nathaniel Hawthorne had twice experienced the joys of paternity. Una, who was then seven, had awed and fascinated Nathaniel with her babyish antics, and she provided him with a fund of observations that crowded his notebooks. Julian, then the perfect specimen of a five-year-old boy, basked in the attention given by a father to his only son, and the two had already enjoyed many special outings together.

Nathaniel greeted Rose's arrival in the world as something of an anticlimax. He announced her birth to his sister Louisa the day of its occurrence in one brief paragraph of a long letter: "You have another niece. She made her appearance this morning at about three o'clock, and is a very promising child—kicking valiantly and crying most obstreperously. Her hair, I understand, is very much the tinge of Una's. Sophia is quite comfortable, and everything is going well." Nathaniel went on at much greater length in this letter chiding Louisa for not writing and particularly for her silence on his newly published novel, *The House of the Seven Gables*. Although Nathaniel thought of Rose, his last child, as "the daughter of my age—the

1. Rose Hawthorne Lathrop, *Memories of Hawthorne* (Boston, 1897), 213.

comfort (at least so it is to be hoped) of my declining years," he continued to remark upon her birth and infancy with detachment. In July, Nathaniel announced Rose's birth to William Pike: "We have another daughter, now about two months old. She is a very bright and healthy child, neither more nor less handsome than babies generally are." That month he also wrote to Louisa that Rose "grows prettier, but cannot be called absolutely beautiful."[2]

Sophia, however, more than compensated for her husband's restraint even in advance of Rose's birth. Living in Lenox, Massachusetts, she had attempted to withhold the fact of her pregnancy from her mother, Mrs. Elizabeth Palmer Peabody, who lived in Boston. Having at one time been convinced that her daughter would forever be an invalid, unfit for marriage or childbearing, Mrs. Peabody worried incessantly about Sophia's health. Sophia hastened to write about the expected "little flower" when Mrs. Peabody did become aware of her pregnancy. "I thought it would save your fear," Sophia assured her mother, "if I should not let you know anything till I could write you that I had multiplied my powers of loving you by a whole new soul in a new form." Indeed, the baby, nicknamed Rosebud, with her blue eyes, rosy cheeks, curling reddish hair, and droll expressions, was the joy Sophia had anticipated.[3]

Sophia found the daily routines of walking in the woods and playing with her child on the shores of the Stockbridge Bowl to be intense experiences of maternal love for which she could not find adequate utterance: "How wonderful is this love for which there is no mortal expression, but which we can only shadow forth by death and destruction." Julian's solicitude toward his baby sister also pleased Sophia. Watching Julian hold Rose on his knee, Sophia reflected that she would "as soon expect an angel from the sky to descend to a rough scuffle with a desparado as for Julian to disturb or annoy the little Rosebud."[4]

2. Nathaniel Hawthorne, *The Letters, 1843–1853,* ed. Thomas Woodson, L. Neal Smith, and Norman Holmes Pearson (Columbus, Ohio, 1985), 433, 464, 453, Vol. XVI of William Charvat, Roy Harvey Pearce, and Claude M. Simpson, eds., *The Centenary Edition of the Works of Nathaniel Hawthorne,* 22 vols. projected.

3. Julian Hawthorne, *Nathaniel Hawthorne and His Wife* (2 vols.; Boston, 1884), I, 394, 469, Vols. XIV and XV of [George Parsons Lathrop, ed.], *The Works of Nathaniel Hawthorne,* 15 vols.

4. R. H. Lathrop, *Memories,* 169.

Perhaps the contrast between mother's and father's reactions to the new baby was caused, in part, by the fact that Rose's infancy coincided with the most prolific period in Nathaniel's literary career. *A Wonder Book for Girls and Boys* was published shortly after Rose's birth, and between December, 1851, and April, 1852, Nathaniel wrote *The Blithedale Romance;* in the fall of 1852, he wrote *The Life of Franklin Pierce,* and the following spring he finished *Tanglewood Tales.* These four major publications undoubtedly prevented him from giving Rose the kind of attention he had been at leisure to focus upon Una and Julian at their births.

All of this writing took place during a series of moves. Nathaniel had never liked the Berkshires, and when Rose was just six months old, the family put its few possessions in an old farmer's wagon and spent a bleak day traveling to West Newton to the house of Sophia's sister, Mary Mann. The Manns were then in Washington, D.C., vacating for the Hawthornes' winter use a small, white frame house in what Julian would recall as a "dismal and unlovely little suburb."[5] Notwithstanding the financial contraints under which the Hawthornes lived, they were soon able to purchase from Bronson Alcott a home in Concord surrounded by about twenty acres of fertile, wooded land. On June 6, 1852, the family moved into the Wayside, which was to be the only real home Rose ever knew and one in which she would experience some of the most significant and tragic moments of her life.

The Hawthornes arrived at the Wayside in the midst of a heat wave. Sophia nevertheless lost no time in making decorative additions to the house, though no structural alterations were made during this period of their residence. She created minor transformations by putting up wallpaper, laying a rich, lapis-lazuli-blue carpet, and hanging her painting of Endymion in Nathaniel's study. In this environment the family entertained as many visitors as Nathaniel's reclusive nature could bear, and Rose was included in some of these gatherings. With maternal pride, Sophia observed Rose attending to the Emersons' conversation "in perfect sobriety."[6]

Rose flourished at the Wayside. During the summer of 1852, she

5. J. Hawthorne, *Hawthorne and His Wife,* I, 429–30.
6. *Ibid.,* I, 435; R. H. Lathrop, *Memories,* 190, 196.

learned to walk, stumbling at first in the grass. Then, in Sophia's words, waving "her hands like wings she set forth. To fall down seemed a new joy." Sophia, amused by her mother's suggestion that she spread a rug for the baby, wrote to Mrs. Peabody: "I should as soon think of keeping an untamed bird on a rug as a baby. I assure you that since she has had the use of her feet she does not pause in the race of life." Rose was intrepid and mischievous, laughing with delight when she caused consternation by covering herself with molasses, and digging, hoeing, or raking in the yard with the heaviest tools she could manage to lift.[7]

It is no wonder that Sophia regarded the Wayside as the "sweetest place," notwithstanding the personal losses her family sustained there. In July, 1852, for example, the Hawthornes received news of Louisa's death. The steamer on which she was traveling down the Hudson River caught fire, and after jumping overboard to escape the flames, Louisa drowned. Only a few months later, Sophia's mother died.[8]

The family was still grieving when, in March, 1853, thanks to U.S. president Franklin Pierce, Nathaniel was confirmed by the Senate as consul to Liverpool. Sophia felt at home at the Wayside and regretted having to leave it, but she knew that the older children would regard the move as an adventure, and as for "Rosebud, what matters it to her whether she stand on one hemisphere or the other, so long as Papa, Mamma, Oona, and Dulan are within sight?" Nathaniel's major inducement to accept this post was financial; he felt assured that his position as consul would provide him with the means to secure his children's future. Consequently, the Hawthornes left their newly established home, and on July 7, accompanied by their two maids, Mary and Ellen Hearne, they boarded the *Niagara* for Liverpool.[9]

The steamer, with 140 passengers aboard, left Boston and stopped briefly at Halifax, Nova Scotia, where, instead of the typical two-gun salute, a long cannonade send-off honored the consul and author Nathaniel Hawthorne. This was the first of many shows of privilege

7. R. H. Lathrop, *Memories,* 201–202, 208, 211.

8. R. H. Lathrop, *Memories,* 211; J. Hawthorne, *Hawthorne and His Wife,* I, 454–56.

9. J. Hawthorne, *Hawthorne and His Wife,* II, 12–14; R. H. Lathrop, *Memories,* 218; Raymona Hull, *Nathaniel Hawthorne: The English Experience, 1853–64* (Pittsburgh, 1980), 9–10.

and status that characterized the Hawthornes' English experience from the start. When Sophia complained about the diluted milk that Rose was given to drink during the crossing, the steward allowed the Hawthornes to avail themselves of the cow on board, and Sophia noted: "It is very convenient to have rank with these English people. It commands good service."[10]

The *Niagara* was a 250-foot-long vessel propelled by paddle wheels, upon which Julian and Una climbed during the abundant calm weather that blessed the voyage. So tranquil and agreeable was their journey that Sophia felt it to be more like a pleasure excursion on a lake than a 3,000-mile voyage away from her family in New England.[11]

On July 17 the Hawthornes arrived in Liverpool, and they stayed at the Waterloo House for ten days. The children were fascinated by their first experience in a hotel, especially by the elegant, four-postered, canopied beds in the rooms. The kitchen was run by a friendly cook who allowed them to nibble tidbits off a long skewer; eating in the dining room, however, was quite another affair. The head of the Waterloo House, Mr. Lynn, saw fit to preside over the pouring of soup with great seriousness and ceremony. He was the essence of formality, "resembling one's idea of an ancient duke,—dressing with elaborate elegance, and with the finest ruffled bosom. . . . This homage diverts Mr. Hawthorne so much," wrote Sophia, "that I am afraid he will smile someday."[12]

The Hawthornes then moved into Mrs. Mary Blodgett's boardinghouse, a different but equally pleasing experience because of the genial proprietress who set such a hearty table. Here they lived while they looked for a house, which they found within a month in the suburban community of Rock Ferry. On September 1 the family moved into 26 Rock Park, an ample, three-story gray stucco house with a large garden full of fuchsias, carnations, and roses. The house was in a row of villas "mended on to each other," as Sophia described it, "in castellated form," and situated on a road protected by a manned gate. The rental agent originally wanted to charge £200 annually for this furnished house, but when he discovered that Nathaniel Hawthorne, United States consul, wished to live there, he reduced the fee

10. Hull, *Nathaniel Hawthorne*, 9–10.

11. Julian Hawthorne, *Hawthorne and His Circle* (New York, 1903), 79; R. H. Lathrop, *Memories*, 221.

12. Hull, *Nathaniel Hawthorne*, 13–14; R. H. Lathrop, *Memories*, 224.

to £160.[13] No such consideration had ever been granted Nathaniel Hawthorne, author. Indeed, living in England promised to be financially advantageous.

The Rock Ferry home figured in Rose's earliest memories—remembrances that had a fairy-tale quality. She imagined her father, who traveled daily to Liverpool to fulfill his office as consul, as working in "an ogre's lair, though the ogre was temporarily absent, while my father, like a prince bewitched, had been compelled by a rash vow to languish in the man-eater's place for a term of two years." Rose, assuming that her father could not consider her a suitable companion, was awed and silenced by his presence when they met by chance in the large house. Looking back, she realized that Nathaniel must have been at greater leisure to share his powerful presence with Julian and Una before she was born. At this period of her life, Rose later wrote, she believed that she had to be "satisfied with a glance and a smile, which were so much less than he had been able to give my brother and sister in their happier childhood days."[14]

Just as life in England made Rose's father seem distant, it removed as well the familiar image Rose had of her mother. Consular responsibilities required the Hawthornes to entertain on a scale that had been unknown to them in New England. As an adult, Rose recalled that a "delightful peep at the glitter of little dinner-parties" revealed a surprising change from the home she had left in Concord: "Down the damask trooped the splendid silver covers, entrancingly catching a hundred reflections from candle-flame and cut-glass and my own face as I hovered for a moment upon the scene while the butler was gliding hither and thither to complete his artistic arrangements."[15]

Sophia enjoyed playing her new role as elegant hostess. One evening she went to Rose's bedside to kiss her child good-night before she departed for a party. Because Rose should have been asleep she pretended to be, but her furtive glance caught her mother for the first time in a ball gown: "Her superb brocade, pale-tinted, low-necked, and short-sleeved, her happy, airy manner, her glowing though pale

13. J. Hawthorne, *Hawthorne and His Circle,* 118; J. Hawthorne, *Hawthorne and His Wife,* II, 22–23; Nathaniel Hawthorne, *The English Note-Books* (2 vols.; Boston, 1883), I, 443, Vols. VII and VIII of [George Parsons Lathrop, ed.], *The Works of Nathaniel Hawthorne,* 15 vols.; Hull, *Nathaniel Hawthorne,* 33.

14. R. H. Lathrop, *Memories,* 281, 215, 217, 213.

15. *Ibid.,* 263.

face, her dancing eyes, her ever-hovering smile of perfect kindness, all flashed upon me in the sudden light." Rose pretended to rouse herself, and "insisted upon gazing and admiring, yet I ended by indignantly weeping to find that my gentle little mother could be so splendid and wear so triumphant an expression." Sophia surmised, "She is frightened at my fine gown!"[16]

Notwithstanding Rose's dismay, such elegance was an indulgence that Sophia thoroughly enjoyed, and a dream come true. She spent a good deal of money on ornate clothing at this time.[17] The Peabodys had always lived under financial constraints in spite of their place in New England society and her father's renown as a dentist. As Nathaniel's wife, too, Sophia had in the past needed to be frugal, but now she enjoyed the comforts and elegance that naturally should have—but had not—attended prestige.

Sophia took her children to church for the first time while they were in England, thus fulfilling another dream. "How very singular," she wrote, "that this dream of mine, like so many other[s] . . . is coming true!" She had wanted the children to worship "in a grand, old cathedral, so that their impression of social worship might be commensurate with its real sublimity," and their visit to Chester Cathedral gave them this experience. The manifestations of the British social order pleased Sophia, who regarded English society as agreeably "stereotyped, crystallized. . . . In this old civilization there seems to be no jealousy, no effort to alter position."[18]

The old friends and new acquaintances who visited the consulate also enriched the Hawthornes' lives. Their appearances were filtered through the distorting lens of Rose's childhood perceptions, which typically focused on isolated physical details. Henry Bright, who had been introduced to the Hawthornes in Concord, was their most frequent visitor in England. Because he was a Unitarian, he had not been granted a degree by Trinity College. The details of his face were what Rose particularly recalled about him: His nose was "a mountainous range of aristocratic formation; and his far-sweeping eyebrows of delicate brown, his red lips and white doglike teeth, and his deeply cleft British chin were a source of fathomless study." Rose re-

16. *Ibid.*, 264.
17. Hull, *Nathaniel Hawthorne*, 36–37.
18. R. H. Lathrop, *Memories*, 244, 256.

membered his particularly sonorous rendition of Alfred, Lord Tennyson's "The Brook," and later attributed to Bright her adolescent taste for the English poet laureate.[19]

The Hawthornes had also been introduced to the actress Charlotte Cushman in Concord, and when she dined with them, Rose was fascinated with the gems dangling from her watch chain. Another visitor was James Buchanan, U.S. minister to Great Britain, who arrived dressed unappealingly in an overly large black cloak with a crooked white choker. He persuaded Rose, who stared unflinchingly at his swollen joints and ragged fingernails, to sit on his lap, and then he played peekaboo with her until her solemn gaze was transformed into laughter. William Henry Channing, who had known the Hawthornes in New England, moved to Liverpool with his family about this time. He was installed as pastor of the Renshaw Street Chapel, which Sophia attended as often as she could, praising Channing's sermons. Julian was a constant playmate of Channing's son, Frank, and it was Channing who baptized all the Hawthorne children in January, 1857.[20]

John O'Sullivan and his family stayed with the Hawthornes en route to Lisbon, where O'Sullivan had been appointed United States minister. Although O'Sullivan's friendship with Nathaniel was longstanding—O'Sullivan, as editor of the *Democratic Review,* had years earlier invited Nathaniel to become a contributor for the fee of five dollars per page—the seven-week-long visit created a strain. O'Sullivan's mother was frequently sick, and soon after the O'Sullivans' departure, the entire Hawthorne family came down with whooping cough. Sophia had no time to attend to the older children's lessons, and the Hawthornes' maid Ellen Hearne reacted to being overworked by becoming ill-tempered, the consequence of which was her dismissal. Mary Hearne, too, had fallen into disfavor with the family, for although "efficient" she had, according to Sophia, "great faults and was not true."[21]

The new maid was Fanny Wrigley, who was to become an integral part of Rose's memories of her childhood European experience.

19. Hull, *Nathaniel Hawthorne,* 22–23; R. H. Lathrop, *Memories,* 225–26.

20. J. Hawthorne, *Hawthorne and His Circle,* 138–40; Una Hawthorne to Elizabeth Palmer Peabody, January, 1857, in ASRIC.

21. Robert Cantwell, *Nathaniel Hawthorne: The American Years* (Ann Arbor, 1979), 374; Hull, *Nathaniel Hawthorne,* 48–49, 250.

Fanny, or Fancy as the children called her, was twenty-five when she was hired, and she stayed with the Hawthornes throughout their sojourn in England. She was "sterling stuff," Julian would recall, with her "brown hair, vaguely massed on top of her small head, hairpins insecure, and strands escaping. . . . She had innumerable little special knowledges and aptitudes—plain sewing, making tea, child-care (indulgence, rather), dusting furniture, boiling eggs, making responses at Church of England services, household medicines, handling of invalids; she was the victim of endless timidities, mostly irrational; and was heroic before dangers on behalf of those she loved."[22]

Since Fanny had never before been in service—her father was a cotton manufacturer who had lost his fortune—Sophia soon concluded that the young woman was not suited for her work, being frail and unaccustomed to it. By the winter of 1854, however, Fanny had settled into the job and constructed a daily routine for the older children's activities: lessons from ten to noon, followed by a walk; lunch at one-thirty; exercise, then a change of clothes to receive their father; and a visit with the adults until dinner. Fanny then played with Rose until she went to bed. Rose spent a lot of time with Fanny each day and was often left with her when the rest of the family went on excursions; thus the two developed a close, fond relationship.[23]

During the summer of 1854, the Hawthornes spent several weeks on the Isle of Man. Later that year they vacationed on the Welsh coast, at Rhyl. During these trips Nathaniel would commute back and forth to the consulate in Liverpool. The children and Sophia still had traces of whooping cough, and Sophia seemed to have the greatest difficulty keeping healthy in the damp English climate.[24]

Sophia's continual ill health was one of the first indications that the Hawthornes' experience in England was not to be the realization of family aspirations. Sophia wrote to her father that she regretted having expected so much from England. Life there had soon become far more expensive than she had anticipated; "I am rather disappointed to be so circumscribed," she stated. She was angered that one English publisher had sold 35,000 copies of *The Scarlet Letter*

22. Hull, *Nathaniel Hawthorne,* 53–54.
23. *Ibid.*
24. J. Hawthorne, *Hawthorne and His Circle,* 49, 57.

with no royalties going to Nathaniel. Without an international copyright Nathaniel reaped little financial benefit from his popularity: "Is it not provoking that the author should not have even one penny a volume?" Nathaniel had hoped to save about $30,000 from a combination of salary and fees derived from his work as consul. But his expenses were many: annual living expenditures, his clerks' salaries, and donations or loans to needy persons who came through the consulate. Also eroding his hopes of accumulating savings was the congressional decision in the spring of 1855 to do away with the fees consuls received in favor of a flat $7,500 salary.[25] The Hawthornes were as constrained financially at this point in their lives as they had been at any other.

Nathaniel, like Sophia, had originally been happy in England. On Christmas Day of 1854, he recorded: "I think I have been happier this Christmas than ever before,—by my own fireside, and with my wife and children about me,—more content to enjoy what I have,—less anxious for anything beyond it in this life." This joy colored Rose's recollections of holiday celebrations, which, despite the absence of a Christmas tree or Saint Nicholas, were made memorable by small gifts that gave pleasure because of the care Nathaniel exercised in choosing them. "All his presents were either unusual or of exquisite workmanship. The fairy quality was indispensable before he chose them," Rose would later recall. "How easy it is," observed Sophia, "with . . . small thing[s] to cause a great joy."[26]

The work of the consul, however, soon became demoralizing. Nathaniel was constitutionally unsuited to public life, which left him no time or energy for his fiction: "I am sick to death of my office,—brutal captains and brutal sailors; continual complaints of mutual wrong, which I have no power to set right on either side; calls of idleness or ceremony from my travelling countrymen, who seldom know what they are in search of at the commencement of their tour, and never have attained a desirable end at the close of it; beggars, cheats, simpletons, unfortunates so mixed up that it is impossible to distinguish one from another, and so, in self-defense, the Consul distrusts them all."[27]

25. R. H. Lathrop, *Memories*, 269–70; Hull, *Nathaniel Hawthorne*, 55; J. Hawthorne, *Hawthorne and His Wife*, II, 30–31.

26. N. Hawthorne, *English Note-Books*, I, 549; R. H. Lathrop, *Memories*, 297–98, 305.

27. N. Hawthorne, *English Note-Books*, II, 68–69.

By the spring of 1855, Nathaniel's dissatisfaction with his position, his poor finances, and Sophia's failing health forced him to consider resigning his post. The family could travel on the Continent before returning home later that year, he reasoned. John O'Sullivan's invitation to Sophia, Una, and Rose to spend the winter with his family in Lisbon presented another, more palatable option, however. This arrangement would allow Nathaniel to continue as consul, provide Sophia with a climate more conducive to good health, and diminish the Hawthornes' living expenses. Thus, as their lease on the Rock Park house neared its expiration, the Hawthornes moved their belongings to Leamington and then toured the English Lake District before Nathaniel took Sophia and the girls to London in September. In the Lake District, the Hawthornes visited William Wordsworth's home in Rydal. Once in London, they prepared for the journey to Lisbon.[28]

During the month that Sophia and the girls were in London, Nathaniel traveled back and forth to Liverpool, seeing to consular matters and establishing a place for Julian and himself at Mrs. Blodgett's boardinghouse. When in London, Nathaniel spent time with his older children, taking them to the zoological gardens and leaving Rose in Fanny's care as he had during his outings with the rest of the family in the Lake District. Then the Hawthornes proceeded to Southampton, where, on October 7, Sophia, Una, and Rose boarded the steamer *Madrid* for Lisbon. The parting was emotional, for Nathaniel and Sophia had never before been separated by such a distance during the thirteen years of their marriage. Nathaniel recommended Sophia and the girls to the special care of the captain, and amidst everyone's tears, the ship departed.[29]

Rose was an inquisitive, talkative, and sometimes mischievous four-and-one-half-year-old child during her stay in the American embassy in Lisbon. As always, Sophia had words of praise for her little Rosebud. In a detailed letter, Sophia described to Julian an incident in which Rose cut her finger when Una grabbed a brooch from her hands. Rose refrained from telling Una that her finger was cut for fear that her sister might be sickened by the sight of blood. Wasn't this the "essence of Benevolence," "the Attar of Rose?" queried

28. J. Hawthorne, *Hawthorne and His Wife,* II, 64, 66, 62, 70.
29. Hull, *Nathaniel Hawthorne,* 63, 66, 69.

Sophia. Yet this little girl who could reflect a "pure and peaceful expression" when dressed up as Mary of the Angels could also don a visiting monseigneur's black beaver and run about the embassy in it. One evening at bedtime, Rose confessed a childish fear to the maid: What if she awoke with toads in her room? The maid assured her that God would take care of her, whereupon Rose retorted: "I am not at all afraid of God. If I were in a room with him, I would go quite near him. If I knew God was naughty, I would get somebody to kill him." Rose was not to be persuaded by the maid's logic in other areas either. When told that the rain washed the earth, she countered with obvious empirical evidence: "I see and know that rain makes mud."[30]

Several of Nathaniel's letters to Rosebud, or Pessima, as he began to call her, suggest that at least he had reason to believe she was not altogether well behaved.

> I hope you are a very good little girl; and I am sure you never get into a passion, and never scream, and never scratch and strike your dear Nurse or your dear sister Una. Oh no! my little Rosebud would never do such naughty things as those. It would grieve me very much if I were to hear of her doing such things. When you come back to England, I shall ask Mamma whether you have been a good little girl; and Mamma (I hope) will say: "Yes; our little Rosebud has been the best and sweetest little girl I ever knew in my life. She has never screamed nor uttered any but the softest and sweetest sounds. She has never struck Nurse nor Una nor dear Mamma with her sharp little nails; and if there was a little angel on earth, it is our little Rosebud!"[31]

By February, 1856, Sophia was able to write her husband that her health was much improved, and in June she and the girls returned to England. Upon their reunion Julian discovered that his little sister had grown into a "big girl baby." During this phase of their English experience, the Hawthornes did not establish a permanent residence. At first they stayed at Mrs. Hume's, a Southampton boardinghouse that Julian in particular disliked, for he thought Mrs. Hume attempted to starve her guests with the petty portions she served. They then moved to Blackheath, where they spent the summer in the

30. Sophia Hawthorne to Julian Hawthorne, October 12, 1855, Sophia Hawthorne to Nathaniel Hawthorne, 1856, both in ASRIC.

31. Nathaniel Hawthorne, *The Letters, 1853–1856,* ed. Thomas Woodson, James A. Rubino, L. Neal Smith, and Norman Holmes Pearson (Columbus, Ohio, 1987), 451, Vol. XVII of William Charvat, Roy Harvey Pearce, and Claude M. Simpson, eds., *The Centenary Edition of the Works of Nathaniel Hawthorne,* 22 vols. projected.

home of their friend Francis Bennoch. Although Nathaniel believed that he was experiencing some of his happiest moments since leaving the United States, he also recognized that "Bennoch's house [was] not so big as his heart." Thus in September the Hawthornes moved to Southport, where they eventually found a fairly inexpensive, private home to rent while Nathaniel commuted daily to Liverpool.[32]

Sophia complained about the dullness of life in this seaside resort community. Her boredom was no doubt accentuated by doctor's orders to walk no more than half an hour a day. One deviation from the monotonous routine was, however, unpleasant. One night, as the family slept, two men broke in and stole some of Nathaniel's clothing and small items of silver plate. The men were caught almost immediately and sentenced to prison. Although Nathaniel laughed at the incident, such an occurrence could not have endeared the Hawthornes to their stay in Southport. Finally, the itinerant life had begun to wear. Una wrote to her aunt Lizzie: "Here I am, writing to you from still another place; for, poor wanderers that we are, we cannot count upon where we will be for a day, and do not know but that the next week may find us in Jericho."[33]

In Southport the Hawthornes made an addition to their household in the person of a governess. Miss Browne, the first true governess that they had employed, had been recommended for her character and her ability to instruct in mathematics and languages. She was, as Julian recalled, "barely five feet tall, and as thin and dry as an insect . . . and her ignorance . . . was . . . if possible, greater than our own." Indeed, Sophia was soon disappointed in Miss Browne, as she was with all those employed to care for or instruct her children. Nonetheless, both Una and Rose were left with Miss Browne and Fanny when Nathaniel, Sophia, and Julian toured Lincolnshire, York, and Manchester.[34]

In July, 1857, the three left Southport for the Manchester art exhibit. This event was certainly a high point in Sophia's sojourn in En-

32. J. Hawthorne, *Hawthorne and His Circle,* 209; Hull, *Nathaniel Hawthorne,* 88; J. Hawthorne, *Hawthorne and His Wife,* II, 126–27, 132–34.

33. R. H. Lathrop, *Memories,* 324; Hull, *Nathaniel Hawthorne,* 111–12; Una Hawthorne to Elizabeth Palmer Peabody, n.d., in Hawthorne and Lathrop Collections, MA 3400, PML. Sophia's mother and sister were both named Elizabeth Palmer Peabody.

34. J. Hawthorne, *Hawthorne and His Circle,* 227; Hull, *Nathaniel Hawthorne,* 108–109; J. Hawthorne, *Hawthorne and His Wife,* II, 137.

gland. Before her marriage, Sophia had demonstrated the considerable talent and seriousness of a professional painter and sculptor. By seeing firsthand the great masterpieces of art, some of which had been the subjects of her copies, she fulfilled a dream she had had for almost thirty years. Nathaniel, however, did not enjoy the exhibit as did his wife, and their accommodations in Manchester were uncomfortable. Moreover, the industrial atmosphere of that city proved to be hard on Sophia's health, so the realization of a dream gave way to yet another disillusionment.[35]

In September the Hawthornes again took up a brief residence in Leamington, a locality that promised to be kinder to Sophia's health. There they were joined by Ada Shepard, who replaced Miss Browne as governess. Ada became fond of the children, noting that Una was "most remarkably developed" and Julian was "Hercules in miniature," but that Rose was "less remarkable, evidently, than the other two." As a recent graduate of Antioch College, Ada had come highly recommended by its president, who was also Sophia's brother-in-law, Horace Mann, and although Sophia had to admit that Ada was more successful in teaching Rose to read, write, and cipher than had been her predecessor, she was critical of Ada. The new governess spent too much time away from her young Hawthorne charges writing to her fiancé, Clay Badger, said Sophia, who informed Ada that she had never left her children "even long enough to go out to tea" before coming to Europe, for it was a "mother's duty to devote herself to her children first of all." According to Nathaniel, Ada had "imbibed . . . all the women's rights fads and other advanced opinions of the day," a flaw that classified her with Sophia's relatives who espoused liberal causes. Ada's arrival coincided almost exactly with that of a tract on abolition by Sophia's sister Elizabeth Palmer Peabody, which had been mailed to the consulate. Nathaniel withheld the tract from Sophia and sent it back to Elizabeth, who in turn mailed it across the ocean again. Nathaniel finally relented and allowed Sophia to see the work, which he deemed "not very good; not worthy of being sent three times across the ocean." When Sophia read the tract, she was appalled that Elizabeth thought Una should be informed about the horrors of slavery: "As to displaying before the great innocent eyes of a girl like Una all the horror of a slave-

35. J. Hawthorne, *Hawthorne and His Wife*, II, 142–43.

auction—a convent is better than such untimely revelations."[36] Despite Ada's association with the liberals in Sophia's family and the Hawthornes' criticism of her, she stayed with their household until the conclusion of their travels on the Continent.

In the fall of 1857, Nathaniel resigned his post as consul in Liverpool, and the family moved to London. When Fanny's father drowned in December, she left to live with her grieving family. The Hawthornes departed for Paris after the children recovered from a bout with measles, and they arrived in cold, rainy weather on January 5, 1858. They managed in France with the help of Ada's linguistic abilities and were joined there by one of her companions at Antioch, Maria Mitchell. Reluctant at first to acquire another traveling companion, the Hawthornes later found this plain, middle-aged New Englander, who was the foremost female astronomer of her time, to be a delightful addition to the group. Together they arrived in Rome after a long, cold carriage ride during which Rose nestled, dozing, against her mother's bosom.[37]

Life in Rome was of singular importance to Rose because her "first frequent companionship" with her father began there. Rose and her brother and sister went for regular walks with Nathaniel on Sunday afternoons on the Pincio hill, pausing to sit on the benches and play a game with stones. Happy though these occasions were for Rose, her memories of them evinced the pathos of a child eager to please and awed by someone she regarded as remote: "When one game was finished, I trembled lest he would not go on with another. He was never fatigued or annoyed—outwardly. He had as much control over the man we saw in him as a sentinel on duty . . . my father peacefully breathed, in half-withdrawn brooding, either pursuing our pebble warfare with kindest stateliness, or strolling besides lovely plots of shadowed grass."[38]

Rose enjoyed an affectionate relationship with Ada, even though she did not like the schoolwork the governess attempted to impose on her. Ada was able to claim success only in teaching Rose to print nicely and spell a little. Rose, however, was receiving a broad, if not formal, education in Rome. She sometimes accompanied her mother

36. Hull, *Nathaniel Hawthorne*, 132–33, 179, 229–30; R. H. Lathrop, *Memories*, 337, 358.

37. J. Hawthorne, *Hawthorne and His Wife*, II, 169; Edith Garrigues Hawthorne, ed., *The Memoirs of Julian Hawthorne* (New York, 1938), 202; R. H. Lathrop, *Memories*, 352.

38. R. H. Lathrop, *Memories*, 352, 361.

to such sites as the Temple of Peace, the Colosseum, the Caelian Hill, and the Forum, where she was disgusted by the dirty ruins. She wrote succinctly to her aunt Lizzie: "Forum has got columms all tumbled down." Rose enclosed in this letter a piece of glass she had found amidst the rubbish.[39]

While in Rome the Hawthornes saw a good deal of the American artists William Wetmore Story, Hiram Powers, and Cephas Thompson. Their presence must have reminded Sophia of her youth in Boston in the early 1830s, when Thomas Doughty, Washington Allston, and Chester Harding had been her mentors. Surely this contact with art and artists was the realization of yet another dream, as she visited their studios and the galleries where the art of the ancient world and the Renaissance was housed.

Rose did not have quite so positive an impression of the artistic milieu. She remembered most vividly the studio of Cephas Thompson, which was a large, shadowy, low-ceilinged room. Rose was delighted by the aroma of his paints, but appalled when she was required to sit extremely still on a stool while he painted her portrait. Added to this unpleasantness was the fact that she was, for the first time, left alone without another member of her family or household. "Although I was by that time a perfect recluse in disposition," she later recalled, "I was under the impression that I was being punished by the invisible powers, which I was conscious of eminently deserving."[40]

Rose's impressions of Italy took on a penitential and morose coloring. She had seen England through enchanted eyes. Her father travailed in an ogre's lair, her mother was transformed by a ball gown, and they were visited by one person with a mountainous nose and another with ragged fingernails. The greatest evil of which Rose was aware was the meager portions served by a stingy boardinghouse proprietress. The English experience impressed with Dickensian eccentricities; Italy, however, took on the horrific images of a Gothic novel.

The family visited the catacombs together, and Sophia thought that Rose was not alarmed by the "profound darkness that swallowed

39. Hull, *Nathaniel Hawthorne,* 154; Sophia Hawthorne, *Notes in England and Italy* (New York, 1870), 293–94; Rose Hawthorne to Elizabeth Palmer Peabody, n.d., in Hawthorne and Lathrop Collections, MA 3400.

40. R. H. Lathrop, *Memories,* 372.

up our tapers" as the child held tight to her skirts. What Rose later recalled from this experience, however, was her "first impression of death that really was death." The skulls and unburied bones, the monks who scurried about with their faces "covered with hoods . . . two holes permitting the eyes to peep with beetle glistenings," the chants that accompanied burials—all these images converged to form a gloomy picture in Rose's mind.[41]

After four months the family moved on to Florence to escape the summer Roman fever. There the Hawthornes eventually occupied Casa Del Bello, the ancestral estate of Count da Montauto, whose straitened finances forced him to rent his castle. The lovely weather in Florence after the unrelenting chill of Rome and the castle's garden abundant with figs should have been a happy change for Rose, but such was not the case. She despised the figs, which were so popular with everyone else, and the castle itself was a "morose experience." Its garden was damp, "full of green things and gracefully drooping trees, doubtless, but never embracing a ray of sunshine." Shortly after their arrival Julian caught a lame bird, which Nathaniel wisely observed should be left to "Dame Nature." Despite Julian's attempts to revive the bird, it died; henceforth Florence became "intolerable" to Rose.[42]

The castle was inhabited by huge spiders, which looked to Rose like enormous plums with numerous legs that "spread and brought their personality out to the verge of impossiblity." There were rooms at Montauto that she avoided: A "forlorn cavern of a parlor" and the oratory she eschewed as the fearful domains of returning spirits. The resident maid, Stella, who fed Rose melon seeds, presented a gruesome image kneeling in her room before a crucifix. "I thought her temporarily insane to pray so much," Rose later recalled.[43]

Life in Florence was punctuated by what should have been more pleasant moments. Sophia took Rose to the Boboli gardens, where they watched the swans and Rose jumped rope. Together with her mother, sister, and Ada, Rose attended the races and annual pageants. She was allowed to visit Elizabeth Barrett Browning, who normally did not receive guests until the evening; since Rose would be asleep by then, Mrs. Browning made an exception and saw her in

41. S. Hawthorne, *Notes,* 255; R. H. Lathrop, *Memories,* 375–76.
42. J. Hawthorne, *Hawthorne and His Wife,* II, 189, 198; R. H. Lathrop, *Memories,* 383.
43. R. H. Lathrop, *Memories,* 404, 392–93.

the early afternoon. Indeed, the Brownings were a welcome addition to the Hawthornes' life both in Florence and upon their return to Rome. Mrs. Browning, a spiritualist, induced Sophia to attend a table turning in a neighboring villa in Florence, and on this occasion Sophia and Ada claimed to have summoned Mrs. Peabody's voice.[44] This incident could only have added to Rose's impression of Gothic extravagances in Florence.

In October, 1858, the Hawthornes returned to Rome. There Nathaniel intended to finish a romance, which he could then have copyrighted in England before returning to America. While in Rome they lived around the corner from the Trevi Fountain in a house that Cephas Thompson had engaged for them. At the beginning of their stay at 68 Piazza Poli, the children remembered their father as a cheerful companion who would play euchre and old maid with them in the evenings when the Brownings, Horatio Bridge, or one of the members of Rome's American artist community did not call. Because there were no kitchen facilities in this house, prepared meals were brought in daily in large tin boxes. Julian, for whom eating was always a notable event, enjoyed the food, which was cooked in the French style. Other members of the family, however, lamented the "perpetual rice pudding" and quickly realized that life in Rome was going to be quite expensive.[45]

As fall moved toward winter, Rome became chill and damp, and so uncomfortable that Sophia's fingers were sometimes too cold even to hold a pen. The entire family became ill with what at first seemed to be colds; soon all but Una returned to health. But what had been for Rose macabre images of death became a terrifyingly real possibility. Sophia, who enjoyed sketching Roman sites with Una and Ada, recorded in her notebook that she had abandoned sketching a bridge at sunset, fearing that the still waters were unsafe at that time of day. But because the night air was assumed not to be dangerous after October, Ada and Una stayed out past six one evening to sketch a ruin. Soon after, Una was taken ill, and in November the Hawthornes knew that she had contracted the dreaded Roman fever.[46]

44. S. Hawthorne, *Notes,* 449, 410–11, 361; R. H. Lathrop, *Memories,* 397–98.

45. R. H. Lathrop, *Memories,* 356–57, 363–64; J. Hawthorne, *Hawthorne and His Wife,* II, 200, 203–205.

46. R. H. Lathrop, *Memories,* 354; S. Hawthorne, *Notes,* 535; J. Hawthorne, *Hawthorne and His Wife,* II, 206.

Una's illness hung on day after day and steadily worsened. Social calls ceased, but as Rose realized, "everyone who had seen Una in society or anywhere came to ask" about her. The American minister came frequently, and great bouquets of flowers were delivered. Mrs. Browning brought broth; Mrs. Story brought jelly. Franklin Pierce visited as often as three times a day to sympathize with his old friend Nathaniel.[47]

After two months Una could not leave her bed. Sophia had no time for Rose, for she attended constantly to Una. Never robust herself, Sophia did not go to bed for thirty days and nights, resting instead in a chair next to her older daughter's bed. "No one shared my nursing," Sophia recalled, "because Una wanted my voice and my touch." All letter writing ceased; Nathaniel laid aside his notebook. Never did their father look slimmer or so serious as he did now, thought Julian and Rose, "but as long as he could play cards, there was no danger of an evil issue of the fever." Then the card playing stopped. Routine life was suspended.[48]

By April 5, 1859, Una was on the brink of death. Dr. Franco, the attending physician, diagnosed "quick consumption" and broke the news that Una might not live through another day. Within four days, however, the course of her illness had changed, and she was on the road to a lengthy recovery—a recovery complicated by the lasting ill effects of the massive doses of quinine that Una had been given to abate her fever.[49]

The memories of Una's long illness and subsequent recovery became inextricably intertwined for Rose with memories of the Roman Carnival. As Una languished, the "untrammeled bonhommie" and "hurly burly" of the carnival gave way to Lenten rituals, which Rose observed that spring from her window. In the square beneath her rooms were stands where cooks with white caps and aprons fried "countless flat pancake-looking pieces of dough" in olive oil. "I watched this process," recalled Rose, "until I grew to regard Lent as a tiresome custom."[50]

In May, Una was sufficiently recovered for the family to leave Rome. When they arrived in Le Havre, Ada joined the Thompsons,

47. R. H. Lathrop, *Memories*, 370–71.
48. *Ibid.*, 370–71, 357; J. Hawthorne, *Hawthorne and His Wife*, II, 207–208.
49. Hull, *Nathaniel Hawthorne*, 165–66; J. Hawthorne, *Hawthorne and His Wife*, II, 210.
50. R. H. Lathrop, *Memories*, 377, 380.

who boarded the *Vanderbilt* to return to America. The Hawthornes embarked on the steamer *Alliance,* bound for Southampton, where they landed in late June, 1859. Nathaniel had arranged with the English publishers Smith and Elder to pay him £600 for a projected romance; consequently, the Hawthornes needed to find a place to reside that would be conducive to Nathaniel's writing.[51]

They first alighted in Whitby, which was memorable for Rose only because she hurt a knee and an elbow during one of her outings there. Nathaniel found that this seaside resort did not promote composition, so the family moved briefly to London, where Una soon began to fade. In July, Fanny Wrigley rejoined the Hawthorne household, and the family moved to Redcar, another English watering place, where they found an inexpensive house to rent. Fanny and Rose shared a bedroom, and Nathaniel had a room to use as a study.[52]

Redcar provided the tranquil backdrop necessary for Nathaniel to write, which he did routinely each morning and early afternoon until the family had dinner at one-thirty. Then he would often take a walk with Julian. Rose enjoyed the outdoor life that Redcar offered, and during the "uninspired hours when there was no father" about, she made the acquaintance of a little girl named Hannah King. Although Rose originally disliked the girl because of her first name, eventually she became attached to Hannah, and the two played imaginary games of grocer's shop, using the sugary sands as their store of food. Yet Rose believed that her father regarded this child's play as "useless, time-frittering amusement, which I already knew was withering my brain," and she consequently felt guilty about her innocent association with Hannah. When the summer season was over and inclement weather began, the Hawthornes once again moved to Leamington. Deprived of the only friend that she seems to have made during her itinerant childhood in Europe, Rose fell back on a readily accessible companion, imagination: "I had night-vigils which were delightfully entertained by a faculty for hearing quite splendid music,—music that my imagination composed with a full orchestra of admirable brilliancy; and I was also able to see in perfect distinctness a splendid bazaar, filled with any quantity of toys, which I could summon at

51. Hull, *Nathaniel Hawthorne,* 168–70.

52. R. H. Lathrop, *Memories,* 350; J. Hawthorne, *Hawthorne and His Wife,* II, 225; Hull, *Nathaniel Hawthorne,* 171.

will. . . . In the course of several months this charming capacity [imagination] was modified to that of being able to evoke most clearly scenes where imaginary characters, more real than actual companions, leaped into being, and talked and moved to any extent."[53]

Only Christmas in Leamington was a sufficiently vivid experience to compete with such an active imaginative life. Rose remembered this celebration, not for extravagant gifts—for, as always, the Hawthornes had to adhere to a strict budget—but for "those luxuries which would gather the least rust" and the retrospective appreciation of "hours spent in toughening the sinews of endurance."[54] She delighted in the few handmade gifts that she received from Una and from her beloved Fancy.

Nathaniel concluded "The Romance of Monte Beni" in the spring of 1860. Published under the title *The Transformation* in England and *The Marble Faun* in America, the book did not receive the enthusiastic reviews that had been accorded to his earlier novels. Fatigued by England and by his own lack of desire to write, Nathaniel and his family began in March to look for a place to live until their ship sailed. They decided that Bath would be a better place for Sophia than Liverpool, although as Nathaniel had noted grimly, "There is no air in England fit for her to breathe."[55]

The Hawthornes spent their first few nights in Bath at the York House Hotel, a grand establishment that Sophia feared would cost "a year's income," with its "lordly sitting room, hung with crimson" and its "solid richness." Luckily for Rose, her friend imagination transformed Nathaniel and Sophia into the duke and duchess of Maine; Julian became Lord Waldo; Una, Lady Raymond; and, finally, there was Lady Rose. The dining room attendants were dubbed the Sublime and the Pensive: "Their footfalls were descending snowflakes, their manner devout, solemn, and stately. It was really quite delicious, just for a short time; and it was impossible not to be convinced that we at least came over with William the Conqueror."[56]

53 Hull, *Nathaniel Hawthorne,* 173; J. Hawthorne, *Hawthorne and His Wife,* II, 227, 230; R. H. Lathrop, *Memories,* 351, 341.

54. R. H. Lathrop, *Memories,* 342.

55. J. Hawthorne, *Hawthorne and His Wife,* II, 238, 242.

56. R. H. Lathrop, *Memories,* 343, 344.

Within a few days, however, reality was reclaimed in the form of a modest house that the Hawthornes rented at 13 Charles Street. For Rose, the days of waiting to return to America seemed filled with meaningless routines such as attending church, which she found tiresome. Even her ninth birthday lacked festivity in her mind because her father was absent for the occasion. She wrote plaintively to "my dearest Papa. . . . cannot you stay with me today its my berthday."[57]

Rose had many times before missed her father's attention, but for the first time in her life, she seemed to lament the lack of young companions. She wrote her aunt Elizabeth Hawthorne that she liked some girls better than others, and that Hannah was one girl she liked very much. Now she missed Hannah terribly. But Rose wrote Hannah that when she returned to America, she would be surrounded by friends and live in a house with a big garden. It appears as though Rose was beginning to think of America as a promised land that would supply her with the social contacts she had only recently begun to crave. Eagerly anticipating life on the other side of the ocean, Rose looked beyond "the shipping"—with her fears of seasickness, high winds, and drowning—to thoughts of a happy homecoming.[58]

57. Rose Hawthorne to Nellie Hill, n.d., in ASRIC; Rose Hawthorne to Nathaniel Hawthorne, May 20, 1860, in Henry W. and Albert A. Berg Collection, NYPL.

58. Rose Hawthorne to Elizabeth Hawthorne, April 4, 1860, in Berg Collection; R. H. Lathrop, *Memories,* 421–22; Rose Hawthorne Lathrop, "Memories" (MS in Hawthorne and Lathrop Collections, MA 3400).

II / *Pessima*

THE Hawthornes' ten-day voyage to America was mercifully uneventful for Rose, though, as Julian later noted in his memoirs, the controversial Harriet Beecher Stowe was also on board. The Hawthornes arrived in Concord on an oppressively hot June day. Unfortunately, the Wayside did not fulfill Rose's high expectations, and the next few years stretched before her as a lonely and boring time. "I distinctly remember," she later recalled, "the ugliness of the un-English landscape and the forelornness of the little cottage which was to be our home. Melancholy and stupid days immediately followed." Rose was annoyed by trivial matters such as the unpicturesque presence of sand in the flower beds and the "delinquencies" of the Hawthornes' lone servant.[1]

Even more distressing to Rose was her virtual lack of playmates. Rose wrote to Annie Fields, who had taken a special interest in her, that although she had a doll, she did not play with it because "it seems so desolate to play alone. . . . I never have anyone to play with me." Rose continued to miss her English friend Hannah. "I am in Concord now, and long to see you again, but I suppose that is useless to think of," Rose wrote her gloomily; "I am going out after my lessons to have a good time. —A very good time to be sure, for there [is] nothing but frozen ground."[2]

1. E. G. Hawthorne, ed., *Memoirs of Julian Hawthorne,* 281–82; R. H. Lathrop, *Memories,* 421.

2. Rose Hawthorne to Annie Fields, 1861, in American Collection, BPL; R. H. Lathrop, *Memories,* 422.

From time to time, Rose later recalled, she attempted "to bring the stimulus of great events into the Concord life" by employing the imaginative faculty that she had developed so keenly in England. Now she used her creativity to write stories. One afternoon she was entertaining a little girl in the neighborhood with a "thrilling denouement." The two children were "standing beside the sweet-clover bed, not dreaming of anything more severe than its white bloom," when her father appeared, hovering, as Rose remembered, "dark as a prophetic flight of birds." He bellowed, "Never let me hear of your writing stories!" in what Rose thought was the greatest display of anger she had ever witnessed from him. "I forbid you to write them!"[3]

The motives behind Nathaniel's angry injunction are not absolutely clear. Nathaniel had considered the women authors of his day a "d——d mob of scribbling women," whose novels gave him "no chance of success [in the marketplace] while the public taste is occupied with their trash." Sophia had escaped his opprobrium by exercising her creativity through painting and sculpting—which he thoroughly encouraged—rather than through writing. She steadfastly refused to write for publication and money until economic necessity gave her no other option. Nathaniel had also attempted to dissuade his son from writing for a living.[4] Perhaps Nathaniel wanted to caution Rose as well as Julian against the uncertainty of writing as a means of income, or maybe he simply could not abide his daughter's entry into the ranks of Harriet Beecher Stowe, Margaret Fuller, Maria Cummins, and Elizabeth Palmer Peabody. In any case, neither Rose nor Julian heeded their father's advice.

Nathaniel's prohibition against writing, Rose later remembered, "only added a new attraction to authorship, agreeably haunting me as I beckoned imaginary scenes and souls out of chaos." Yet Rose temporarily laid aside the writing of stories, and her idle time at the Wayside was punctuated with an assortment of other activities. Going to school for the first time, she attended the East Quarter Public School, directed by a woman. Meanwhile Julian attended Franklin Benjamin Sanborn's coeducational institution.[5]

3. R. H. Lathrop, *Memories,* 422–23.

4. N. Hawthorne, *The Letters, 1843–1853,* 304; Maurice Bassan, *Hawthorne's Son: The Life and Literary Career of Julian Hawthorne* (Columbus, Ohio, 1970), 59.

5. R. H. Lathrop, *Memories,* 423; Margaret Mulford Lothrop, *Wayside Home of Authors* (New York, 1940), 112.

William Ellery Channing and Horace Mann had highly recommended Sanborn's school for both Nathaniel's son and his daughters, but Nathaniel, who could not have approved of Sanborn's involvement in the John Brown incident, was "chary" of entrusting Una and Rose to the perils of coeducation. Julian, however, thoroughly enjoyed the school. There he associated with two of Henry James, Sr.'s sons, Wilkie and Bob, as well as with the Emerson and Alcott children. "There never was and never will be such a genial Concord," Julian recalled.[6]

While the school's frequent dances, picnics, and other "jollifications" delighted Julian, they made Sophia uneasy. She wrote to Sanborn: "Pray that you will see fit to forbid all committees for providing 'good times' . . . Mr. Hawthorne and I are quite appalled by this FLARING OPEN of girlhood and boyhood, when they ought to remain delicately folded up in quiet, reserved manners."[7]

Rose would undoubtedly have enjoyed the social nature of Sanborn's school, for that seems to have been the only redeeming aspect of formal education to her. She wrote to her aunt Ebie that she only went to school in the afternoons because she wanted to be with other girls. Activities other than reading and mathematics, she remarked, were far more appealing to her. She enjoyed drawing, tracing John Flaxman's figures, and creating—according to her mother—"wonderfully . . . recognizable portraits of Mr. Bennoch" on the chalk board before she had even turned ten.[8]

Rose also enjoyed a trip to the theater with the Fieldses and had some instruction in music from Una, who judged her sister to be a receptive pupil. Rose, on the other hand, thought that Una was off-key as far as "the south from the north." Rose made friends with a girl named Patty, and the two made paper dolls and planned Rose's birthday party, an annual high point for the honoree.[9]

The unrivaled social event at this period of Rose's life, however,

6. E. G. Hawthorne, ed., *Memoirs of Julian Hawthorne,* 120; J. Hawthorne, *Hawthorne and His Wife,* II, 264–67.

7. Franklin Benjamin Sanborn, *Memorabilia of Hawthorne, Alcott, and Concord* (Hartford, 1970), 7.

8. Rose Hawthorne to Elizabeth Hawthorne, March 16, 1862, in ASRIC; Sophia Hawthorne Diary, December 31, 1862 (Hawthorne and Lathrop Collections, MA 3400, PML); R. H. Lathrop, *Memories,* 426.

9. Rose Hawthorne to Nathaniel Hawthorne, n.d., Rose Hawthorne to Elizabeth Palmer Peabody, April 11, July 18, 1861, all in ASRIC; Rose Hawthorne to Patty, March, 1863, [April?] 1863, both in Hawthorne and Lathrop Collections, MA 3400, PML.

was a masquerade ball at which Rose, at the tender age of ten, was the belle. In a short, full dress, covered with silver spangles, she was disguised as Titania, wearing a crown and carrying a gold and silver wand. Because her father was away, Rose was accompanied by Julian, who disguised himself as the duke of Buckingham. Sophia praised Rose's appearance as "airy, sparkling, and lovely." Rose, like her mother—who wrote to Annie Fields that the Hawthornes would "remain hidden if their wardrobe is not fit for court"—thoroughly enjoyed the finery and wore this costume as often as she dared. Even at this young age, however, Rose's desire for fine things and her mother's awareness of the family's financial constraints caused minor conflicts.[10]

Rose's various lessons and social engagements were interrupted from time to time by more serious endeavors. Aware of the ongoing Civil War through the return of prisoners, Rose and other young women made efforts in behalf of the Union soldiers. Rose wrote to Fanny Wrigley that she was to go to the town hall to "sew and nit for the soldgers," and she was able to sell her drawings from Flaxman for ten dollars each to raise money for the war.[11]

In general, however, the grim reality of the war did not intrude upon such daily activities as gathering chestnuts with her cousin Georgie Mann and berrying with Abby Alcott. The more lively the activity, the better Rose seemed to like it. In August, 1862, Rose wrote to Patty that she could never go canoeing because she was too restless to stay still for more than a second, and her preference for horseback riding and ice-skating was clear. Rose skated with Julian as often as she could, lamenting the thaws and skating to the point of becoming lame on a number of occasions.[12]

In addition to her skating injuries, Rose, along with her sister and brother, suffered through colds, influenza, fever, stomach upsets,

10. Una Hawthorne to Elizabeth Hawthorne, March 16, 1862, in ASRIC; S. Hawthorne Diary, March 13, 1862 (Hawthorne and Lathrop Collections, MA 3400); Sophia Hawthorne to Annie Fields, April 11, 1862, in American Collection; Rose Hawthorne to Elizabeth Hawthorne, February 23, 1861, in Henry W. and Albert A. Berg Collection, NYPL.

11. Rose Hawthorne to Patty, 1862, in Berg Collection; Rose Hawthorne to Fanny Wrigley, May 16, 1861, Una Hawthorne to Elizabeth Hawthorne, February 24, 1864, both in ASRIC.

12. Rose Hawthorne to Edith, 1862, S. Hawthorne Diary, January, February, August, October, 1862, and Rose Hawthorne to Patty, August 13, 1862, all in Hawthorne and Lathrop Collections, MA 3400; Rose Hawthorne to Annie Fields, January 1, 1864, in American Collection.

and mumps, and the children endured as well the homeopathic remedies of mercury and arsenic with which Sophia treated these ailments. Unfortunately, not all of Una's illnesses were amenable to such cures. Upon the family's return to the Wayside, Nathaniel's fear about Una's "unsound condition" was confirmed. What was described as a recurrence of the Roman fever was treated in Boston late in the summer of 1861 by Mrs. Rollins' "medical electricity." Una was again seriously ill in the fall and winter of 1862–63; this time the problem was diagnosed as the aftereffects of the excessive quinine administered to her in Rome. At the invitation of her aunt Elizabeth Hawthorne, Una went to Beverly, Massachusetts, with the expectation that the change of scene would restore her health. The visit was temporarily beneficial, but in the spring of 1863, Una's health was once more precarious.[13]

Una apparently suffered from some type of emotional or nervous disorder, which may or may not have had its origin in the Roman fever or the medication used to fight it. Her poor health affected the entire family; "the least mischance to Una wrung her father's heart," Julian noted. Rose had grown to enjoy her sister's company and was pained by her absences from home; Rose was also distressed by the attention that her sister absorbed and the alterations in family life that Una's illness necessitated. Yet Una received many fond letters from her sister, some of which demonstrate an interesting variety of spelling and diction. Rose signed one letter "your afecshanet sister Rose," and in another letter she told Una that her "amiable letters made us all exceedingly delighted." Rose grew to confide in Una through these exchanges, requesting on one occasion that if Una loved Rose, she would not show her younger sister's correspondence to anyone.[14]

Rose grew fond of Julian during these days at the Wayside and missed him greatly when he was on trips with their father and after his departure for Harvard in the fall of 1863. "O I do MISS you so," she wrote to him, adding, "I do not know whether that miss is

13. S. Hawthorne Diary, November, 1862 (Hawthorne and Lathrop Collections, MA 3400); Sophia Hawthorne to Annie Fields, March 13, 1863, in American Collection; Rose Hawthorne to Una Hawthorne, March 31, 1862, in Berg Collection; J. Hawthorne, *Hawthorne and His Circle,* 274; Hull, *Nathaniel Hawthorne,* 199; J. Hawthorne, *Hawthorne and His Wife,* II, 324.

14. J. Hawthorne, *Hawthorne and His Wife,* II, 324; Rose Hawthorne to Una Hawthorne, 1861, in Hawthorne-Manning Collection, EIL; Rose Hawthorne to Una Hawthorne, March 30, 1862, January 3, 1863, both in Berg Collection.

spelled right or not. . . . I wish that I could write an interesting litter [*sic*], but I can only say that kitty smells as if she had been eating mice or rats." In another letter to "my dear Jue," she described the cat as giving "a sort of groul (I am afraid I have put this rong)." Elsewhere she expressed her hope that her roaming brother had not had "any perolous adventures, have you?"[15]

Notwithstanding Rose's affection for her siblings, her relationship with them was characterized by a normal dose of animosity, engendered, perhaps, more by their absence than by their presence. Such feelings occasioned the following fledgling attempt at poetry, presumably a permissible genre to use as a mode of imaginative release.

Una & Julian have gorn away
And I am left to wander about
Una & Julian don't like me
And if they do, it you shall see
Unas a tirant
And Julians a bore
And thats the way for ever more.
The sun peeps through the trees at me
And as to my sight it blindeth me
I'v got a kitten as black as soot
And Benj'y my cousin says he'l her shoot
The girls they are walking all round
But as to the place there's not a sound[16]

Rose's relationship with Una and Julian, however, was not nearly as significant at this point in her life as was her relationship with her father. Upon the Hawthornes' return to the Wayside, she sensed with a child's timorous accuracy that "the first notes of the requiem about to envelope us fell through the sound of our daily affairs, at long intervals, because my father, from that year, began to grow less and less vigorous." Rose noted that her father spent many hours walking upon the hill behind their house.

His dark, quietly moving figure [passed] slowly across the dim light of the mingled sky and branches, as seen from the large lawn, around which the embowered terraces rose like an amphitheatre. . . . A cord of wood had been cut upon the hill, and he deliberately dragged it to the lower level of his

15. Rose Hawthorne to Julian Hawthorne, [1861?], June 26, 1860, November 5, 1863, all in Berg Collection.

16. Rose Hawthorne, untitled poem (MS *ibid.*).

dwelling, two logs at a time, by means of a rope. Along the ridge and down the winding pine-flanked path he slowly and studiously stepped, musing, looking up, stopping to solve some point of plot or morals; and meanwhile the cord of wood changed its abiding-place as surely as water may wear away a stone. But his splendid vigor paled, his hair grew snowy white, before the end.[17]

Nathaniel had returned to Concord a man out of tune with his times and his own creative genius. Financial worries continued to plague him. He renovated the Wayside to better accommodate his family and his writing, but the estimated five-hundred-dollar cost of the renovation was far less than the actual two thousand dollars he had to pay in the spring of 1861. In addition, the tower-study was not as conducive to his writing as he had hoped; he worked on, but could not complete, the manuscripts of three romances: "Septimius Felton," "Dr. Grimshawe's Secret," and "The Dolliver Romance."[18]

In the fall of 1862, Nathaniel began *Our Old Home,* based upon his English experience. In gratitude to the man who had made that experience possible, and contrary to the advice of a number of people, he dedicated the book to Franklin Pierce. This act bore witness to the long-standing friendship between the two men, a friendship to which Pierce was as yet to bear his final testimony. Nathaniel avowed that to withdraw the dedication because Pierce was in political disfavor for his stand against the Civil War and abolition "would be a piece of poltroonery. . . . If [Pierce] is so exceedingly unpopular that his name is enough to sink the volume, there is so much the more need that an old friend should stand by him." Nathaniel's gesture was veritably heroic, demonstrating the fidelity of his nature and a generous disregard for his own financial welfare. But his sympathy with Pierce set him apart from the intellectual currents of Civil War Concord, and his position was excoriated by Emerson, James Russell Lowell, Stowe, and his own sisters-in-law, Mary Mann and Elizabeth Palmer Peabody.[19]

Adding to Nathaniel's burdens at this time was his failing health, for which the family prescribed numerous changes of scene. During the summer of 1861, Nathaniel used Julian as a pretext for traveling

17. R. H. Lathrop, *Memories,* 433–34.
18. Hull, *Nathaniel Hawthorne,* 199.
19. Randall Stewart, *Hawthorne: A Biography* (New Haven, 1948), 232–33.

to the coast of Massachusetts for several weeks. In the spring of 1862, Nathaniel went to Washington, D.C., ostensibly to ascertain first-hand the course of the war, but the family hoped that the trip would restore his waning vigor. Later that year he and Julian spent several weeks together in Gouldsboro, Maine. Again in the fall of 1863, Nathaniel traveled to the seaside, this time with Una.[20]

Rose never accompanied her father on these trips, and she compensated for his absence by writing to him often. Her letters recount daily events—putting her cloak on inside out ("that was a bad sine"), dining on nothing but soup and "raisons," feeling ill because of a heavy thunderstorm—as well as her greater concerns. In one letter Rose told her father that she hoped he would "not sail about too much, for fear that you will get drowned," and elsewhere she remarked how nice it was to have a pet that appreciated her. She also observed, "It is about time for this family to collect itself together." Invariably these letters were signed "BBB" or "Baby Bab Bad." Evidently Nathaniel's earlier name of Pessima for his daughter had been translated into an alliterative tag. Rose curiously persisted in using this name for herself when writing to her father, even though she had told her aunt Elizabeth Hawthorne in July, 1861, how much she disliked being called "Baby," especially in front of strangers.[21]

By the end of 1863 and the beginning of 1864, Nathaniel's health was alarmingly fragile. In April, his old friend William Davis Ticknor took him to New York and Philadelphia, and wrote to Sophia often about the condition of "our patient." During this trip, Rose, always happy when she was the exclusive recipient of her father's attention, wrote to thank him for a letter: "I got your delightful letter this morning. Mama is very jealous I know, and I hope you will continue to write me that Mama may feel as badly as possible."[22] But this hopeful journey took a disastrous turn when Ticknor died unexpectedly in his sleep. Thus added to the burden of Nathaniel's own ill health was his grief over the passing of a good friend and the responsibility for overseeing the return and burial of Ticknor's body.

Almost immediately, Franklin Pierce sought to comfort Nathaniel

20. J. Hawthorne, *Hawthorne and His Wife,* II, 282, 315, 331.

21. Rose Hawthorne to Nathaniel Hawthorne, n.d., March 25, 30, 1862, all in Berg Collection; Rose Hawthorne to Nathaniel Hawthorne, July 30, 1861, in Hawthorne and Lathrop Collections, MA 3400; Rose Hawthorne to Elizabeth Hawthorne, July, 1861, in ASRIC.

22. J. Hawthorne, *Hawthorne and His Wife,* II, 342–43; Rose Hawthorne to Nathaniel Hawthorne, April 4, 1864, in Hawthorne and Lathrop Collections, MA 3400.

by escorting him on yet another trip, this time to Plymouth, New Hampshire. Rose watched her father depart: "I cannot express how brave he seemed to me. The last time I saw him, he was leaving the house to take the journey for his health which led suddenly to the next world. . . . Like a snow image of an unbending but an old, old man, he stood for a moment gazing at me. My mother sobbed as she walked beside him to his carriage. We have missed him in the sunshine, in the storm, in the twilight, ever since."[23]

Nathaniel died early in the morning on May 19, 1864, in Plymouth, one day before Rose's thirteenth birthday. "Cannot you stay with me today its my berthday," she had written him four years earlier. Now his many temporary absences had been replaced by a permanent one. Years later, however, she would in a sense regain her father's presence as her memory selected and magnified certain facets of his character.

On May 23 James Freeman Clarke, who had celebrated Nathaniel's marriage to Sophia twenty-two years earlier, officiated at his funeral in Sleepy Hollow Cemetery in Concord. Sophia demonstrated remarkable resilience born of a transcendental faith. She wrote to Annie Fields: "Oh blessed be God for so soft a translation—as an infant wakes on its mother's breast so he woke on the bosom of God and can never be weary any more." In this letter Sophia also alludes to an event that had taken place in an almshouse in England that Hawthorne had recorded in *Our Old Home,* not identifying himself as the "gentleman" who hugged a leprous child. Sophia describes "a tenderness so infinite—so embracing—that God's alone could surpass it. It folded the loathsome leper in as soft a caress as the child of his home affections. Was not that divine! Was it not Christianity in one action—what a bequest to his children—what a new revelation of Christ to the world was that!"[24]

Leaving his family with an uncertain financial future, Nathaniel had nonetheless bequeathed to his children a tremendous legacy. Sophia had correctly identified the nature of her children's inheritance.

Rose's admiration for Julian grew during the years immediately following her father's death. Julian, who enjoyed good health and an attractive physique, took up weight lifting at Harvard, much to the

23. R. H. Lathrop, *Memories,* 480.
24. Sophia Hawthorne to Annie Fields, n.d., in American Collection.

chagrin of his little sister. Rose wrote him: "When you last went away your shoulders were getting improportionally big. When you sat at the dinner table your shoulders would hang over the side of your chair in the most shocking manner. I am very sorry that you persist in doing what is so very hurtful to you. . . . The dumbbells that you have at present are a great deal too heavy." Sophia sought to reaffirm the advice "Little Ecclesiastica" had given her brother about his "bicepts": "I do not desire to see you a big jointed, thick armed man, but rather more Greek of contour." Notwithstanding this and the other atrocious changes Rose thought her "dearest Herculian Boy" had made in his appearance—he had grown a moustache, for example, which she believed made his mouth look like a frog's—she declared her fondness for him in a letter as she denied having a crush on Eliot Clarke: "You will see that I must necessarily be desperate if I like anyone to surpass my BOUNDLESS love for you, my boy."[25]

On one occasion Rose confided more troubling matters to her brother. She had dreamed "of a little niggar girl that Aunt Mary wanted me to buy. But she had such horrid hands, that it was imposs'—she was awfully ugly too. She kept taking hold of my hand and making me perfectly miserable. She had two too many fingers . . . on one hand and they were no bigger than knitting needles and no bones in them. I guess I dreamed it because I saw a boy at dancing school who had two fingers off, and in chassizing I had to take hold of it. It was torcher."[26] Perhaps Rose was aware of how her father had acted in a similar situation, and knew that as his heir she should have accepted the disfigured hand of the boy or of the phantom slave, just as her father had folded the leprous child in his embrace. Was the discrepancy between the ideals that had been bequeathed to her and the reality of her adolescent life what caused the next few years to be particularly painful for her?

No one knew better than Una the turmoil Rose experienced, for Rose saw Una as the only one who could "open up my secret doors." Unfortunately, Una's poor health persisted, necessitating frequent trips, so Rose's intimacy with her sister grew largely through corre-

25. Rose Hawthorne to Julian Hawthorne, January 18, 1865, December 22, 1864, both in Berg Collection; Sophia Hawthorne to Julian Hawthorne, January 19, 1865, in Ulysses S. Milburn Collection, ODYL.

26. Rose Hawthorne to Julian Hawthorne, December 22, 1864, in Berg Collection.

spondence. In addition to writing "Nona" for reports about "sailor boys and blue eyes," Rose confided in her sister day-to-day distresses: She was "dying" to go to a party, for she hadn't "been in ages"; and she had attacks of "nausea" as a result of Una's teasing her about a certain Mr. Longworth. Rose also unburdened herself to Una of greater problems: "I hate anyone tending to the other sex. It is not comfortable to love what one hates." Rose's disappointment in the subjects of her adolescent crushes sometimes grew into a general despair about life.

Everybody is false and I need somebody substantial like you. . . . I think Julian is the highest man; but he doesn't come up to my idea. In short, I hate men as cordially as I love you. As much as they scorn us . . . however much they love us, they think us inferior. And that shows a homely mind. You turn up your nose? Do then, and pack as the rest of my acquaintances have done. For if I am foolish, it comes from the bottom of my heart, and is all I have. Thus it ought to be respected.[27]

In another letter Rose told Una that her life was "nothing but torment. I never shall have that rare pleasure of being loved infinitely, that is what makes a person the noblest and highest they can dream of." Was Rose comparing her transient infatuations with the ideal relationship her parents had manifested? If so, the comparison must have left her own life the more unsatisfactory. "I have tried to believe that we can ourselves be sufficient for ourselves (under certain circumstances)," she wrote to Una, but, she continued self-deprecatingly:

I am not strong enough to have my self respect keep me from falling if I stumble. . . . Just because heaven does not choose that I should be a genious, I am miserable and sour. . . . I know what I should do, but I don't, and I say, can't. I know that life is a wonderful chance—not to be wasted and lost but earned. . . . I think that a person should devote himself to others, forgetting himself, not thinking that he must perfect himself, and as he helps others to be good, he suddenly finds himself good. . . . I see how good Mama is; but it don't make me good.[28]

With Julian and Una both away so frequently, Rose spent much of her time alone with her mother during the two years immediately

27. Rose Hawthorne to Una Hawthorne, July 21, October 11, 1867, December 13, 1865, January 13, February 5, May 4, October 4, 1866, all *ibid.*

28. Rose Hawthorne to Una Hawthorne, July 15, 1866, *ibid.*

following Nathaniel's death. Sophia began to loom as another impossible ideal of human behavior, one whom Rose resented strenuously at times. At an earlier age Rose had exclaimed to Sophia amidst hugs and kisses: "Oh, darling Mamma, I wish I was like you, and then I would do everything I did not want to!" Perhaps in an attempt to emulate her mother, Rose showed a great interest in drawing and painting, one that she did not manifest in her schoolwork. Sometimes Rose and Sophia would paint together; at other times Sophia would read to Rose from her father's fiction while Rose painted.[29]

Attempting to offset the desultory nature of Rose's education, Sophia placed her in Dio Lewis' boarding school in Lexington during the fall of 1866. Sophia's choice of this school is surprising inasmuch as Lewis was an educational innovator, not by fostering coeducation like Sanborn, but by emphasizing physical education for young women. Julian obviously admired Lewis, a "chunky but not obese man" with thick yellow hair and beard. Holding his head erect with chin down, Lewis looked to Julian "like a horse bridled." Lewis, with grace, flexibility, and well-developed muscles, exhibited feats with dumbbells that prompted Julian to view him as the "Greek ideal." Lewis' pedagogical philosophy of doing "good to the mind through the judicious cultivation of the body" had led him to purchase an old hotel in Lexington, which he remodeled as a school. To it he attracted about three hundred female students from throughout the United States. These girls, wearing a uniform that consisted of a blouse and knee-length Zoave breeches, allowing, as Julian recalled, "a charming revelation of stockings[,] . . . would tramp all over the neighboring country, educating the inhabitants as they went."[30]

Despite Rose's enjoyment of physical activity, she did not like this school. She immediately had difficulty getting along with her roommate, Bessie: One girl wanted to put more wood on the fire and to stay up later in the evening than the other. Rose wrote to her mother: "The ridiculous goose's affection for me disappeared. . . . She probably knows what a shallow puddle of dish water she is. I thought we should have a healthy fight which would warm us up beautifully, not that she would be so doubly mean." Sophia attempted to placate Rose by observing that affection does not necessarily flee when two

29. R. H. Lathrop, "Memories" (MS in Hawthorne and Lathrop Collections, MA 3400, PML); Sophia Hawthorne Diary, *passim,* 1866 (ASRIC).

30. E. G. Hawthorne, ed., *Memoirs of Julian Hawthorne,* 138–39, 141.

people quarrel, but her advice did nothing to mollify Rose. According to Rose, Bessie was a gossip, tattler, and busybody. Sophia wrote to her daughter that such behavior should have taught Rose herself "NOT TO SPEAK OF THE AFFAIRS OF OTHERS. . . . When you must speak, you must run to the cars and come home." Worse yet, one of the girls' instructors, Mr. Weld, gave Bessie the enigmatic message that they must make Rose more "demonstrative." Rose declared, "If he pricks me any more, he will be unpleasantly surprised for I will knock him over."[31]

Adding to Rose's unhappiness was her constant lack of money in a situation where other girls could spend freely, especially on clothing. Rose wrote her mother: "I have nothing to wear, and am in an awful pickl [*sic*]. . . . You can't do anything without money." Sophia's attempts at economy in making Rose's dresses and repairing them—adding scalloping to a frayed hem, letting out the waist of a dress that had become too tight—did not offset the frustration Rose felt at being obviously poorer than her companions. On more than one occasion, Sophia generously acceded to Rose's demands: "Yet if you will not be happy unless [your jacket] be trimmed with silk, I will not refuse you. I do not wish you to make any sacrifices about it, dearest, but merely think whether you want it very much or not."[32]

Rose also resisted the regimentation of boarding-school life, and this was nowhere more obvious than in her dislike for mandatory church attendance. At home she could avoid going to church. As she wrote to Aunt Ebie one Sunday from Concord: "Every one is going to Church to hear our stupid old minister, excepting ourselves, who are the only sensible people in Concord." At school she could not exercise such liberty. She had asked her mother for a letter excusing her from attending church with the other girls, but Sophia refused to oblige her. She wrote Rose: "I wish you could go, not with a critical spirit but with an intention to derive all the good possible, and to make the kindest interpretation of the preacher. It is disorderly not to attend church with the others, at a school, and I wish you would try it—and see whether a teachable state of mind will enable you to bear

31. Rose Hawthorne to Sophia Hawthorne, November 4, 1866, in Berg Collection; Sophia Hawthorne to Rose Hawthorne, n.d., January 14, 1867, both in ASRIC; Rose Hawthorne to Una Hawthorne, December, 1866, in Berg Collection.

32. Rose Hawthorne to Sophia Hawthorne, November 4, 1866, in Berg Collection; Sophia Hawthorne to Rose Hawthorne, November 4, 19, 1866, January 26, 1867, May 10, 1867, all in Hawthorne and Lathrop Collections, MA 3400.

it." Later Sophia wrote even more emphatically on the subject; Rose must obey the rules "or you cannot stay, and one is wise to submit with grace. I am sure you will if you think about it."[33]

Perhaps it was these disputes about churchgoing that caused Rose to fear James Freeman Clarke's disapproval. When she wrote to thank him for all he had done and to tell him of her high regard for his sermons, she concluded the letter thus: "You must see how unworthy I am of being liked." So troubled was Rose by the possibility that Clarke thought her mean that Sophia found it necessary to write her twice to assure her that this was not the case and to add her own maternal observation: "I have never discovered a grovelling tendency in you my princely child."[34]

The experience of Lewis' school only added to Rose's adolescent frustrations and doubt about her own worth. Rose resolved to "stick it out because they were so good to let me stay such a long time" (Sophia had been unable to pay the tuition), and she feigned enthusiasm when she wrote Aunt Ebie that "life is such a jolly shift after all, and boarding school not so bad a discipline as some anxious mothers fear." Yet she did not return to the school in the fall of 1867.[35]

Rose's position at Lewis' school must have been particularly awkward, obliged as she was to appear grateful for an experience that she disliked. The complex feelings accompanying indebtedness were ones with which the Hawthornes became all too accustomed at this time. Although Franklin Pierce was paying Julian's way at Harvard, this fact did not motivate Julian to industry. The young man's excessive absences prevented him from returning to Harvard in 1866, and he never graduated.[36]

The Hawthornes were also the beneficiaries of the Fieldses' largesse. Annie Fields gave Rose many items, among them a subscription to *Young Folks* and a dyed opera mantle. The most substantial aid that James Thomas Fields could give Sophia was an income. Al-

33. Rose Hawthorne to Elizabeth Hawthorne, February, 1867, Sophia Hawthorne to Rose Hawthorne, n.d., November 13, 1866, all in ASRIC.

34. Rose Hawthorne to James Freeman Clarke, June 1, 1867, in Perry-Clarke Papers, MHS; Sophia Hawthorne to Rose Hawthorne, n.d., in Hawthorne and Lathrop Collections, MA 3400; James Freeman Clarke to Rose Hawthorne, June 11, 1867, in ASRIC.

35. Rose Hawthorne to Una Hawthorne, January 28, 1867, in Berg Collection; Rose Hawthorne to Elizabeth Hawthorne, March 30, 1867, in ASRIC; Theodore Maynard, *A Fire Was Lighted* (Milwaukee, 1948), 142–43.

36. Bassan, *Hawthorne's Son*, 42–43.

most a decade earlier in England, he had suggested that she become a correspondent for the *Atlantic Monthly.* She had rejected the offer then, asserting that only starvation would force her to write for a magazine. The time had come, however, when she could not disdain such an offer. Putting aside her scruples about authorship and with Fields's help, she published twelve installments of Nathaniel's note-books in 1866, and then went on to publish *Passages from the American Note-Books* in 1868 with the expectation that her children would thus be free from the pinch of close economy. But the financial pattern of her life was not to change; and when even Sophia's publications failed to increase her family's income significantly, her relationship with the Fieldses turned sour. Sophia became convinced that they were cheating her and cut the ties of friendship with them. Losing such steadfast friends under Sophia's suspicion of their dishonesty must have been painful for the entire family.[37]

Rose's life continued to be supported by the beneficence of others. In the fall of 1867, Sophia's cousin Mary Loring enabled Rose to attend yet another school, at 17 Chestnut Street in Salem. Mary paid Rose's tuition and gave her free room and board, and thus Rose lived under the same humbling conditions that had characterized her life at Lewis' school. Her mother had less money than ever to provide Rose with anything but the bare necessities at a time when Rose seemed less able than ever to bear the financial constraint. Clothes were still important to her, and even Una acquiesced in her sister's whims when she agreed to use an old parasol so that Rose could buy a new one that would, as Sophia described it, "be lady like but not gorgeous." Often Sophia's only solution to Rose's problems regarding clothing was good advice: "Resist all swelly proceedings (as you cannot afford expensive dress). . . . You must feel independent enough not to try to equal rich folks in your clothes."[38]

Sophia had to justify every expense, from concert tickets for Rose to the envelope and writing paper she used. More than once Sophia had to tell Rose to borrow money from Mary, even for necessities such as books. Indebting herself to Mary must have particularly

37. Rose Hawthorne to [Annie Fields?], October 16, 1867, March, 1866, both in American Collection; Hull, *Nathaniel Hawthorne,* 181–82; James R. Mellow, *Nathaniel Hawthorne and His Times* (Boston, 1980), 585.

38. Maynard, *A Fire Was Lighted,* 143; Sophia Hawthorne to Rose Hawthorne, April 20, 30, 1868, in Hawthorne and Lathrop Collections, MA 3400.

galled Rose since she disliked her cousin. Sophia reminded Rose that she was probably overlooking Mary's good points and added firmly, "You are indebted to Cousin Mary for going to a very superior school." As their financial situation grew more and more acute, Sophia continued to hope that things would improve; but she had to urge Rose to keep a careful accounting and to acknowledge the receipt of money from home, reminding her daughter that she could not send money indefinitely.[39]

While Sophia sympathized with one daughter tormented by the embarrassment of unfashionable attire and by the requirement of cordiality to her benefactress, she knew that her other daughter suffered from much more severe problems. Una's health was still precarious; and her engagement to Storrow Higginson, a nephew of Thomas Wentworth Higginson, only accentuated the fluctuations in her emotional stability. Storrow, a former army chaplain and a Harvard graduate, intended to make his fortune in Brazil before their marriage. On one occasion Sophia wrote to Rose that with Storrow present, "Una the sad, the weary [was] hitherto sad, weary no more." Yet on another occasion Sophia wrote that Una's excitement at seeing her fiancé caused the return of her fever.[40]

Una and Storrow's relationship eventually crumbled under pressure from the Higginsons, who apparently persuaded the young man that he was unworthy of his fiancée. This vacillation in Una's situation affected her well-being and added to Sophia's responsibilities, for she waited upon her daughter constantly. Una's ill health also put obligations upon Rose, who was enjoined never to say a sharp word to her sister. "Una suffers incalculably," Sophia told Rose, "and we are bound to shelter her from every possible hurt."[41]

Una's deteriorating condition, Julian's floundering about after his departure from Harvard, and the Hawthornes' gnawing financial problems led Sophia to plan a change of scene to help her family. She

39. Sophia Hawthorne to Rose Hawthorne, April 16, 1866, in ASRIC; Sophia Hawthorne to Rose Hawthorne, April 20, 23, May 13, June 12, 1868, all in Hawthorne and Lathrop Collections, MA 3400.

40. Raymona Hull, "Una Hawthorne: A Biographical Sketch," *Nathaniel Hawthorne Journal,* VI (1976), 101; Sophia Hawthorne to Rose Hawthorne, May 3, 13, 1867, both in Hawthorne and Lathrop Collections, MA 3400.

41. Hull, "Una Hawthorne," 101; Sophia Hawthorne to Rose Hawthorne, April 16, [1868?], in ASRIC.

began to search for someone to buy the Wayside so that she and her children could move to Dresden. There, Sophia thought, the family could live cheaply while Julian pursued courses in engineering and Rose cultivated her art.[42]

The prevalence of difficulties had at least one positive result, and that upon Rose's character; her adolescent narcissism began to yield to the first signs of maturity. She began to realize that she was not the only Hawthorne with troubles, but this recognition engendered a guilty awareness of her own failings. "I know," Rose wrote Una, "that I am only a girl, but I have come to feel the responsibility of my own life—not mine, but given to me in trust. I suppose there is nothing which is so little a man's property as himself." Yet this sense of responsibility did not preserve Rose from actions that she had grown to deplore. She wrote to her aunt Elizabeth that while she read her father's works she felt moved: "So deeply do I love him that I must always be guided by him, I think, as if he were to speak to me and I were to see his face. But I am pitiably moody and unself-controlled, so that I shall never come off well in the world." She concluded, "I despise my foolishness and sinfulness," no doubt believing that she had more than earned the epithets of Pessima and Baby Bab Bad.[43]

Rose felt particularly guilty with regard to her mother, who had undergone so many trials in her behalf. Rose lamented her selfishness and desire for silk and fine ornaments. Sophia, in turn, tried to assure Rose that this was merely the fancy of youth and "no proof of selfishness." Now that Rose was older, Sophia observed, she had become conscious of her faults, and thus they seemed to overwhelm her. "When we know ourselves, we can be kinder to ourselves, as well as more severe," was her maternal advice.[44]

Birthdays and anniversaries had always been sacred occasions in the Hawthorne household, and Sophia consecrated the event of Rose's seventeenth birthday with an eloquent testimony to her love for Rose and her faith in her daughter's character. Demonstrating sensitivity

42. Hull, "Una Hawthorne," 101; Sophia Hawthorne to Rose Hawthorne, April 20, 1868, in Hawthorne and Lathrop Collections, MA 3400.

43. Rose Hawthorne to Una Hawthorne, July 21, 1867, May 18, 1868, both in Berg Collection; Rose Hawthorne to Elizabeth [Hawthorne?], February 1, 1868, in ASRIC.

44. Sophia Hawthorne to Rose Hawthorne, May 20, 1868, in Hawthorne and Lathrop Collections, MA 3400.

to Rose's bruised psyche and prescience of the course her life would take, Sophia's letter was the finest birthday gift she could have given her daughter.

I think you inherited from Papa this immitigable demand for beauty and order and right. & though, in the course of your development, it has made you sometimes pettish and unreasonable, I always was glad you had it, because I knew the impatience and crossness it often caused, would prove a transient phase. I knew that religious principle and sentiment would surely render you at last gentle and charitable to the shortcomings of your fellow mortals. . . . And this will lead you to hieghts [*sic*] of being at last. Whereas if you were easy and indifferent, you might deteriorate, and lose the exquisite felicity which comes with the exquisite pain of a noble fastidiousness. I have never doubted your most profound and tender love and devotion to me, in the worst paroxysms of your impatience, and so my heart was never seriously wounded. . . . You have to suffer because GOD has given you the perilous gift of genius. With it you are to become greater and lovelier than your less gifted fellow beings.[45]

While this letter, with its expression of Sophia's love and confidence in the superiority of her younger daughter's character, must have boosted Rose's self-esteem immeasurably, another letter, written to Rose the day after her seventeenth birthday, indicates one more reason why Rose would have begun to see herself in a new light. On May 21, 1868, Mary Betts wrote to Rose, chiding her: "Not tell me about your friend in Germany? Indeed, I should like to know all about him. What joy for you, little Rose, to know yourself so beloved! . . . with that heart of yours beating so fast with his, over the seas. I wish you every happiness, the truest love, the noblest life in bright companionship."[46] Thus, not quite two years after Rose had written to Una despairing of ever experiencing the "pleasure of being loved infinitely," Rose seems to have confided to Mary Betts that she had those feelings that "[make] a person the noblest and highest they can dream of."

Rose was undoubtedly experiencing many conflicting emotions when in October, 1868, Sophia and her children left the Wayside for Dresden. Rose was seasick for the duration of the voyage, and when she arrived in Dresden, she missed the Wayside terribly and asked her

45. *Ibid.*
46. Mary Betts to Rose Hawthorne, May 21, 1868, in ASRIC.

cousin Robert Manning to write her about every detail of her home, including each weed that had sprung up in her absence.[47]

As the months passed, however, Rose shared in the many diversions Dresden offered. She enjoyed the warm weather, the operas, and the bands; and she went on a variety of expeditions, including one to Weisen Hirsch and another to a chocolate factory. She took German lessons, and she observed the handsome horseback riders in the park. When Sophia found the right teacher for Rose, she began art lessons.[48]

Julian, Una, and Rose particularly enjoyed the other young people in the American colony in Dresden. There Julian met Minne Amelung, whose German grandparents had established a glassworks company in Maryland, and he became formally engaged to her in July, 1869. Another American family in Dresden was the Lathrops. Sophia had already made the acquaintance of Dr. George Alfred Lathrop ten years earlier, as her 1859 letter to Henry Bright indicates. Dr. Lathrop had been head of the Marine hospital in Honolulu, serving also as United States consul there at approximately the same time Nathaniel was consul in Liverpool. Sophia did not like Dr. Lathrop and wrote to Bright with uncharacteristic vehemence: "I am not surprised that you do not quite like Dr. Lathrop because I cannot endure him myself. . . . He is not only earthly, but earthy—and I will say it, though I agree with you about not being censorious on paper."[49] Notwithstanding her opinion of the elder Lathrop—who does not appear to have been with his family in Dresden—Sophia, her daughters, and Julian became constant companions of Mrs. Frances Lathrop and her sons.

The older son, Francis, had been born aboard ship on June 22, 1849, while his parents were en route to the Hawaiian Islands. George Parsons Lathrop was born in Oahu on August 25, 1851. After returning to the United States briefly, Frank and George had gone to Dresden to study in 1867. It is entirely possible, therefore,

47. Rose Hawthorne to Robert Manning, June 13, 1869, in Hawthorne-Manning Collection.

48. Rose Hawthorne to Eliza Clapp, March 23, 1869, in Hawthorne and Lathrop Collections, MA 3400; Rose Hawthorne to Mattie L. Stearns, 1869, in Berg Collection.

49. Sophia Hawthorne to Henry Bright, September 12, 1859, in Collection of American Literature, BRBML.

that George was the young man who set Rose's "heart . . . beating so fast with his," but it was not until September 11, 1869, that Sophia's journal mentions George in conjunction with an outing he, Frank, and Julian had made.[50] From that date through the spring of 1870, Sophia, as well as Una and Rose, made frequent entries in her diary about the numerous occasions when the Lathrop gentlemen called for tea or dinner. Frank and Rose shared an interest in painting; George and Julian soon became great friends. So close did these expatriate families become that they celebrated Christmas of 1869 together.

George's visits were especially noted. He paid Rose special attention, on one occasion giving her a carved napkin ring, and on another, having her fan mended. Later, after thanking him, she noted in her diary: "He looked so *good* and held out his hand across mama to shake hands for good bye kindly." In April, 1870, George departed for the United States to commence his study of law at Columbia University. Perhaps Rose was projecting her own distress when she remarked, "Mrs. Lathrop is disconsolate."[51]

Rose had briefly attended Miss Rintze's boarding school in Dresden, but after about a month, she had had a falling out with the headmistress and left the school, declaring in a diary entry, "I shall not stay after such treatment."[52] In addition to hurt pride, Rose may have had a monetary motive for returning to her family, for Sophia had overestimated the ease with which her family could live in Dresden.

Adding to Sophia's financial difficulties was the expense of treating Una's recurrent ill health. Sophia, too, succumbed to illness—a cold, bronchitis, influenza, and finally a bad cough, which she treated with arsenic. Perhaps it was these illnesses or the medications that caused Sophia to dream that Nathaniel beckoned her to plunge into a frigid lake. In her dream she obeyed her husband's invitation and discovered that the lake was soothingly warm.[53]

To remedy her ever-growing problems, Sophia once again at-

50. *Dictionary of American Biography,* VI, 14–16; Sophia Hawthorne Diary, September 11, [1869?] (Henry W. and Albert A. Berg Collection, NYPL). This diary does not indicate the year of entries, only the day and month. Although it has been cataloged as Sophia's Diary in Dresden for the year 1868, the date of the Hawthorne family's arrival in Dresden indicates that this diary is for the following year.

51. S. Hawthorne Diary, November 25, [1869?] (Berg Collection); Rose Hawthorne Diary, January 10, April, 1870 (ASRIC).

52. R. Hawthorne Diary, February 14, 1870.

53. S. Hawthorne Diary, February 23, 1869 (Berg Collection).

tempted a change of scene. On May 11, 1870, she and Una left Dresden for England, leaving Rose and Julian behind. This was the hardest thing she had ever had to do, Sophia told Rose, abandoning her younger daughter, as it must have seemed, to the rigors of poverty in a foreign land and with the responsibility of keeping house for her brother. But Sophia believed that the change of scene would "save Una's life by giving her something to look forward to."[54]

In England Sophia once again became optimistic about her family's finances. She had published *Passages from the English Note-Books,* and she began to work on *Passages from the French and Italian Note-Books.* She also renewed her friendship with the Bennochs and wrote to Rose from Blackheath about all the good things that life in England could provide. Art had come to be a subject of great concern to Rose, as clothing still was, and in England, Sophia wrote, you "will have every possible advantage in art. . . . Clothing is far cheaper than in Dresden, even. And it is LIFE here. It is the very centre of the world! I think Mrs. Bennoch can find us a perfect servant, like her own, and we will have a little maid, like her Nellie, as well as a cook, and be more comfortable than we have been for years—and, I think, at an economical rate. . . . Oh, we shall have real bona fide friends in Our dear Old Home." Sophia also enjoyed the company of Mrs. Lathrop, who had taken up residence in England while Frank pursued his study of art there. The Lathrops would take a house in Kensington, Sophia speculated, and Rose and Frank could visit galleries together.[55]

Rose was in dire need of money and had, to Sophia's mind, exhausted the usefulness of her art instructors in Dresden. Una's health was improving, though she could not truly be considered well. Nevertheless, Sophia believed that with caution she and Una could proceed to Dresden to fetch Rose. Sophia wanted to reach Dresden by June 18 so that she might see Julian before he returned to America. She acknowledged how difficult these months in Dresden must have been for Rose, yet thought that her daughter would come to appreciate the experience: "Have not you and Julian become dear friends?"[56]

54. Sophia Hawthorne to Rose Hawthorne, n.d., May 15, June 5, 1870, all in ASRIC.
55. Sophia Hawthorne to Rose Hawthorne, May 22, 1870, in Hawthorne and Lathrop Collections, MA 3400; Sophia Hawthorne to Rose Hawthorne, n.d., June 3, 1870, both in ASRIC.
56. Sophia Hawthorne to Rose Hawthorne, May 30, June 3, 11, 1870, all in ASRIC.

Sophia and Una arrived in Dresden on June 19. Julian left for America shortly thereafter because of the outbreak of war in Germany, which affected Sophia's departure with her daughters as well. "Mama, Una, and I rushed for our lives," Rose wrote, "leaving Dresden with delight, and plunging headlong into whatever dangers were brewing on our road."[57]

Arrival in England brought hopes of a place for the Hawthornes to settle—of sending for their furniture and "nicknacks" from America and making a home at last. Rose and Frank Lathrop began to take art lessons together at the Kensington art museum, and Julian, now safely in America, was planning his wedding to Minne. Julian saw a good deal of George Lathrop, and Rose had frequent reports of George through Frank and his mother. Mrs. Lathrop received "huge letters every week from her son . . . (who was such a fine fellow)," Rose observed. Indeed, England promised to provide that happiness and security that had for so long eluded the Hawthorne women. Rose wrote to her aunt Mary Mann: "I never believed we should be so peaceful again. But after all, the earth bears some gladness for us on its maternal bosom, even if one does begin to doubt the fact in one's teens."[58]

57. Rose Hawthorne to [Mattie L. Stearns?], August 10, 1870, in Berg Collection.
58. *Ibid.;* Rose Hawthorne to Mary Mann, August 26, 1870, in Berg Collection.

III / Rösl

WHEN Rose arrived in England she was nineteen, and she had matured beyond the emotional pendulum swings that had characterized her earlier adolescence. Her relationship with George, who affectionately referred to her as Rösl, seems to have been her first enduring and serious attraction to a young man. A few months ago, in Dresden, for the first time in her life, Rose had expressed a dissatisfaction born not of a realization of her failures—as was her earlier despondency over being moody, selfish, and un-self-controlled—but of a desire for greatness. "I have felt so unsatisfied with my idle life," she wrote one friend, "though I have really been busy about something all the time this year . . . I felt I was not using my best faculties, and developing at all." Art, Rose thought, might be the vehicle through which she "could have an excuse for being in this world. . . . [This would be] the ideal sensation of all others, and I trust to realize it by and by, if I draw anything to send a thrill of pleasure through anyone."[1]

Painting, the artistic medium that her mother had pursued and her father had approved, seemed the appropriate path to excellence and self-esteem. Yet the pursuit of art was not to be as easy as she and Sophia had anticipated. The art academy, it appeared, was a "place for young gentlemen rather than ladies." Moreover, Rose's skill paled in comparison with that of her companion, Frank Lathrop,

1. Rose Hawthorne to [Eliza?] Clapp, November 28, 1869, ASRIC.

whose considerable talent eventually afforded him a career and some notable achievements in the artistic world.[2] Nonetheless, the rhetoric of Rose's friend Mary Betts—"I am sometimes wild to go out among the suffering, and be a nurse and comforter"; and "Speak for the rights of women, their right to be honored as equals, reverenced as women"—did not, at this time in Rose's life, express her own aspirations.[3] Indeed, had Rose aspired to care for the suffering, the immediate future would have provided her with that opportunity.

Sophia had always been susceptible to bronchial problems, and nowhere was this truer than in England. She seemed to have forgotten her husband's conclusion that there was "no air fit for her to breathe" in that country. In her optimism about the cultural, financial, and social advantages that she assumed life in London would bring, Sophia failed to consider the reality of her own poor health, and by the winter of 1871, she was seriously ill.

While the Hawthorne women were still in the process of settling into a new home and establishing a little studio for Rose, Sophia became increasingly pale and tired. By mid-February she was bedridden, spitting blood and continually nauseated, her very symptoms augmenting the fatigue that would prevent her recovery. Unable to take in anything but milk diluted with water, and incapable of tolerating even the tolling of neighborhood church bells, Sophia depended on Una's constant care. "I think I must understand something of the agony of love with which a mother would rush to her child," Una recalled, "for our positions seemed reversed." Indeed, Una's care for her mother was like Sophia's unceasing care for Una when Una was near death in Rome. Perhaps that episode had forged a special bond between mother and daughter, for if Una's account of Sophia's last illness is accurate, Sophia wanted only her elder daughter's care. Rose was conspicuously absent during Sophia's illness, ac-

2. Rose Hawthorne to [Mattie L. Stearns?], August 10, 1870, in Henry W. and Albert A. Berg Collection, NYPL. After Frank Lathrop returned to New York to salvage his father's failing finances, he conducted painting classes at the Cooper Union Institute, and in 1878 he assisted John La Farge in the decoration of Trinity Church in Boston. During his artistic career, Frank Lathrop produced *The Light of the World,* on the reredos of Saint Bartholomew's Church in New York; a panel for the chapel at Bowdoin College; *Apollo,* over the proscenium of the old Metropolitan Opera House in New York; the Marquand Memorial Window, in the Princeton University chapel; and *Widows and Orphans,* for the Equitable Life Assurance Corporation in New York (see *Dictionary of American Biography,* VI, 14–15).

3. Mary Betts to Rose Hawthorne, August 21, 1867, May 21, 1868, both in ASRIC.

cording to Una. On one occasion the younger sister became "hysterical and frightened" when she entered Sophia's room. Rather than Rose, Mrs. Bennoch's maid, Ellen, was the person who gave Una brief moments of respite from nursing.[4]

As Sophia's suffering increased, hopes for her recovery vanished. During her last moments the attending physician told Una that chloroform would give her mother some relief, though it might hasten her death. "It was very hard for me to say yes," Una later wrote Julian, "but suddenly mamma said, 'Why do you wait? Can't you give me anything?' And I said, 'Yes, anything to give her a moment's ease.' So the chloroform was sent for." With both of her daughters present, Sophia died. Una's twenty-seventh birthday was the day before her mother's funeral. "I sat beside her a long time," Una wrote, "and her presence seemed to bless me, as she had always done upon my birthday." On March 4, 1871, Sophia was buried in Kensal Green. The simple inscription on her gravestone reads: Sophia, Wife of Nathaniel Hawthorne.[5]

By the time Julian received the news of his mother's death, he was employed as an engineer in New York, and had the additional responsibility of caring for his wife, Minne, who was pregnant. He therefore considered himself unable to make the voyage to England to bring his sisters back to America after Sophia's death. Julian delegated the duty to George Lathrop, whom he regarded as his "kindred spirit."[6] What ensued, however, caused a major rift between Rose and her brother and sister.

Shortly after George's arrival in England, in August, 1871, Rose and George were planning to marry. That announcement was greeted with apparent pleasure by Mrs. Lathrop, whose happiness over their betrothal nonetheless mingled with grief over the recent death of her friend Sophia. Although she at first hesitated to communicate with Rose in mourning, Mrs. Lathrop soon wrote, expressing her delight at speaking the "new word 'daughter' . . . am I really and truly to know the delight of so sweet a possession?" Rose's relatives, however, did not handle the conflicting emotions they were experi-

4. Sophia Hawthorne Account Book, 1871 (Henry W. and Albert A. Berg Collection, NYPL); J. Hawthorne, *Hawthorne and His Wife*, II, 361, 366.

5. J. Hawthorne, *Hawthorne and His Wife*, II, 367, 371.

6. Bassan, *Hawthorne's Son*, 56.

encing as gracefully, and they expressed clear disapproval of her marriage. Perhaps they believed that Rose and George, both barely twenty, were too young to marry or that their decision was made too hastily or that Rose had not observed a proper period of mourning. Aunt Lizzie Peabody minced no words, and her remarks, George informed her, "offered prolific causes of annoyance for Rose. . . . [There is] much in your letter to which we cannot agree. . . . The final decision as to the course of our affairs rests with us alone."[7]

Julian, who now saw himself as head of the family, may have resented the fact that his consent had not been sought. Although there had been evidence of a close relationship between George and Rose, Julian had apparently been unaware of the true nature of their feelings. He also may have believed that George was taking unfair advantage of his position on his mission to England. In any event, Julian now looked with disdain upon the man whom he had once treasured as a close friend, and referred to his sister's marriage as "an error, not to be repaired."[8]

Una, too, opposed the marriage. Some have speculated that she had assumed herself to be the subject of George's special attention and that the real source of the depression and melancholy she experienced at this time was her own unrequited love. There is no evidence, however, that Una, who was seven years George's senior, had any romantic interest in George or had misunderstood his affections as directed toward herself. Whatever her motives, Una did not attend Rose's wedding, which took place at Saint Luke's Anglican Church in Chelsea on September 11, 1871. Frank Lathrop was the only family member in attendance.

Within two days after the wedding, Una's mental state had become alarming, and Rose felt compelled to write to Henry Bright that her sister had had a "relapse into a violent state of insanity, which I who know her condition of mind so well, was sure would soon be the case. She has returned to the asylum." Elizabeth Palmer Peabody came to England in November to attend to Una, who was also cared for by the Bennochs while staying in their home. When Una eventually regained some degree of health, she began working with

7. Frances Lathrop to Rose Hawthorne, August 26, 1871, George Parsons Lathrop to Elizabeth Palmer Peabody, September 26, 1871, both in ASRIC.

8. Bassan, *Hawthorne's Son,* 57.

Robert Browning toward the publication of Nathaniel's book *Septimius Felton*.[9]

Several writers have addressed Una's ill health at the time of her sister's marriage and have interpreted her subsequent collapse as early evidence of George's presumed unfit character. Theodore Maynard, in *A Fire Was Lighted,* refers to a notice George published in the New York *Tribune* on June 25, 1879, correcting information that had appeared in print elsewhere. Maynard does not mention that George was writing to refute "A Rare Flight of the Imagination" printed in a Cincinnati newspaper and signed by "Gleaner," who had asserted, among other untruths about the Hawthorne family, that Nathaniel was a drunkard who had at one time jilted Sophia. The refutation, published in the personals column, reads: "George Parsons Lathrop writing in contradiction of some romantic flights of fancy lately published concerning the Hawthornes. 'I never was engaged to . . . Miss Una Hawthorne, though I had a high regard for her both on account of her character and as the sister of my wife.'" George concludes thus: "The assertion in the article about the origins of the difficulties which have occurred between Mr. Julian Hawthorne and myself are untrue. Finally, Miss Una Hawthorne did have an attack of insanity in London, having also had one ten years before."[10]

Why George felt compelled to expose these private details may be explained by the fact that the Hawthorne family had apparently been plagued by celebrity mongers, whose use of half-truth or untruth made sensational reading in the press. In this case, George must have sincerely believed that correcting the record justified further publicity of unsavory facts because, as will be seen later, he refused on occasions when he was affected more directly to use the press to correct misinformation.

9. Hull, "Una Hawthorne," 116–17.

10. Maynard, *A Fire Was Lighted,* 180; New York *Tribune,* June 25, 1879, p. 4. Maynard, in citing these portions of the notice, comments: "I can merely say that I find no evidence for anything that can be called insanity—unless Una's early infatuation with George is to bear that name. It is a great pity that after Una's unhappy life, George should have written things which were so patently unmanly and disingenuous." Maynard's characterization of these circumstances is adopted both by Vernon Loggins, in *The Hawthornes: The Story of Seven Generations of an American Family* (New York, 1951), 312, and by Bassan in *Hawthorne's Son,* 115. Maynard was apparently unaware of Una's attack of insanity in 1871 and of the nervous collapse approximately ten years earlier for which she was treated with "medical electricity." Hull's discovery of manuscript evidence in the form of a letter corroborates George's statement in the *Tribune* (see Hull, "Una Hawthorne," 116–17).

Raymona Hull's contention that the origin of Una's collapse in 1871 "was no doubt an emotional one—Una's realization that she was left completely alone" is probably accurate. Without father or mother, and with Julian settled in America, she may have felt abandoned by the sister with whom she hoped to make a home. Whatever the reasons for her relapse, Una's estrangement from Rose and George continued through the fall of 1871. Una did not communicate with her sister and brother-in-law directly, and news of her improvement came to them from Aunt Lizzie. This "happy account" of Una, George responded, caused "us almost as much pain as joy; for now that the unnatural constraint and horror are removed . . . we feel the loss, I of a sometime dear friend, Rose of her only sister. Undoubtedly it is best that the separation should continue for some years at least, and it is that makes us sad."[11]

By the end of 1871, Rose and George were planning to leave England. Having decided against the study of law, George was attempting to begin a career as a writer. He was by this time reconciled with Aunt Lizzie to the extent that he had already solicited her help in having a poem published.[12] At the end of December, he and Rose boarded the *Oceanic* to return to New York. The winter crossing was marked by storms and extraordinarily rough weather, rougher than the captain had seen in nine years. At one point the crew of the *Oceanic* was obliged to rescue some men from a wrecked vessel. Rose was constantly seasick and fearful. She had been saddened as a child by the drowning of her aunt Louisa Hawthorne and of Fanny Wrigley's father. She had even cautioned her own father not to "sail about too much, for fear that you will get drowned." No longer could she seek solace by nestling against a maternal bosom as she had during a journey in her youth, and no longer, so she thought, could she look to her brother and sister for support. For the young bride, this crossing from one continent to another was also a passage to another kind of life.

Rose's fears reached a hysterical peak late one night. She and George had retired early, and George lay fast alseep while Rose listened to each quivering sound that the ship made. Those noises alone would have been "enough to make one cling to George and scream

11. Hull, "Una Hawthorne," 104; George Parsons Lathrop to Elizabeth Palmer Peabody, November 4, 1871, in ASRIC.

12. George Parsons Lathrop to Elizabeth Palmer Peabody, October 29, 1871, in ASRIC.

idiotically," Rose later recalled. Suddenly she heard the clamoring of bells and the stampede of passengers to the deck. Screaming, she roused George, who attempted to calm her while bidding her to dress and leave the cabin. Then George stopped, "dropped his arms in sleepy disgust and exclaimed, 'New Year's Eve.'"[13]

After twenty days at sea, Rose and George arrived in New York. If there was a good side to the voyage, it was in restoring the perspective of sisterly affections. Una, having heard of the ship's arrival through a newspaper announcement, wrote to Aunt Lizzie that she was "most anxious to have a letter from [Rose], for I am afraid she must have suffered a great deal." Una was also concerned that Rose's situation, first living with her husband and his mother in New York and then moving with George to a little country house miles from the city, would be without "many comforts in the intensely cold weather. But," reflected Una, "we must hope for the best, which is the concluding formula of all my speculations about her." Rose wrote to Una within days of her arrival in New York, confiding to her sister the grim details of her sea voyage as well as her happiness in George's "ever-present love."[14] Thus the constraint between the sisters occasioned by Rose's marriage decreased, but there is no evidence that Rose communicated with Julian for some period of time.

The Lathrops' finances dictated that they then accept a friend's offer of a house outside Concord, New Hampshire, "a thorough farm house," Rose called it, "but with so many advantages and graces that we find it to be the very haven for which we have longed." Neither the cold nor the lack of comforts bothered Rose as Una had feared, for Rose and her husband enjoyed the pleasures of being newly wed, as well as such simple diversions as a sleigh ride, popcorn, and the use of a local gymnasium.[15]

Soon George was engaged in a variety of writing projects. To coincide with Una's publication of *Septimius Felton; or, The Elixir of Life,* forthcoming from J. R. Osgood and Company later that year, he began writing an article entitled "History of Hawthorne's Last Romance." Rose wrote to Una requesting "any of Papa's manu-

13. Rose Hawthorne Lathrop to Una Hawthorne, January 8, 1872, in Berg Collection.

14. Una Hawthorne to Elizabeth Palmer Peabody, January 14, 1872, in ASRIC; Rose Hawthorne Lathrop to Una Hawthorne, January 8, 1872, in Berg Collection.

15. Rose Hawthorne Lathrop to [Thomas Wentworth] Higginson, February 1, 1872, in American Collection, BPL; Rose Hawthorne Lathrop Account Book, March, 1872 (Henry W. and Albert A. Berg Collection, NYPL).

scripts" to provide George with the information he needed, and his essay appeared in the *Atlantic Monthly* in October, 1872. George also began publishing poetry, and he corresponded with James Russell Lowell and William Dean Howells, soliciting their opinions of his work, although on at least one occasion he did not accept Howells' advice.[16] In the summer of 1875, George published his first book of poems, *Rose and Roof-tree,* with Osgood and Company. By the end of that year, his literary reputation was sufficient for him to obtain a position as associate editor of the *Atlantic Monthly,* which was under the general editorship of Howells. Rose and George then took up residence in Cambridge.

Notwithstanding Rose's aspirations as an artist before her marriage, her interest in painting all but disappeared after her return to the United States. Perhaps lacking maternal influence and encouragement in that direction, Rose was freer to develop her writing, that mode of self-expression that had been so congenial in her youth but had been repressed by her father. She began to write poetry and fiction, although she did not place her works with publishers as easily as did her husband and her brother. Her earliest publication was a short story, "Browning the Meerschaum," published in *Harper's Bazar* in 1874, followed by a poem entitled "A Wooing Song," which appeared in *Galaxy* in December, 1875.[17]

In addition to writing for publication, Rose attempted to use her poetry to thaw her icy relationship with Julian, who had by now abandoned the pretense of a career as an engineer. Rose dated the following poem, which apparently accompanied tea with Julian on her twenty-third birthday, May 20, 1874.

> Dear brother, I have little wit
> To greet you on this day;
> But I beseech you pardon it,
> And please accept this tray.
>
> A spirit broods within the pot—
> A fairy in the bowl—

16. Rose Hawthorne Lathrop to Una Hawthorne, June 24, 1872, in Berg Collection; George Parsons Lathrop to James Russell Lowell, October 21, 1874, November 12, 1875, both in James Russell Lowell Collection, HL.

17. Rose Hawthorne Lathrop, "Browning the Meerschaum," *Harper's Bazar,* 1874 (Clipping in ASRIC); Rose Hawthorne Lathrop, "A Wooing Song," *Galaxy,* XX (1875–76), 799, rpr. in R. H. Lathrop, *Along the Shore* (Boston, 1888).

And in the jug a Hottentot,
With cows at his control.

They all conspire to gladden you,
As you will surely see,
For nought on earth can sadden you
When you've your "cup o' tea"!

And may the cream be ever thick
Upon your life's deep cup,
And Fortune bring her sugar-stick
For you to stir it up.[18]

Presumably, then, Rose was to some degree reconciled with Julian when, in 1874, he moved with his growing family back to England, where Una had become established doing settlement work in conjunction with Anglican nuns. In December of that year, Una returned to the United States, where she met and eventually became engaged to Albert Webster. Rose eagerly anticipated this first visit between the sisters since her marriage to George, but she asked Una not to speak of "past difficulties, abroad or here . . . [Mrs. Lathrop] has a sad persistency of speaking about things which had best be forgotten." What these "past difficulties" were Rose did not specify, but she told Una that George thought Mrs. Lathrop would have been "thus to any woman [he] would have married without a fortune."[19]

Indeed, until George was employed by the *Atlantic Monthly,* the young couple had no steady source of income. This may have been more difficult for the elder Mrs. Lathrop to accept than Rose, who was accustomed to the burden of limited finances. If the poem George composed for their second anniversary is any indication, the affection and romance present in the early years of their marriage more than compensated Rose for any lack of material comfort. The poem was entitled "A Lover to a Rose."

How old we grow! Two years have vanished since
We wedded. Yet that sleeping maid whose prince
Awoke her with a kiss began her love
With hundred years behind her. And hence I prove
That, should a century glide from us away
In the sweet trance of married years, this day,
When prince stirs beauty from her sleep at morn

18. Rose Hawthorne Lathrop, untitled poem, May 20, 1874 (MS in ASRIC).
19. Rose Hawthorne Lathrop to Una Hawthorne, April 18, 1874, in Berg Collection.

With reverenced lips, would bring new-born
Our love to life again, or still anew
Baptize it with fresh sunlight and sweet dew.[20]

George's position as an associate editor of the *Atlantic Monthly* coincided with another professional and financial opportunity; he was commissioned by the publishing house of Ticknor, Fields, and Osgood (previously Osgood and Company) to write a study of Nathaniel. George worked assiduously on the manuscript during the early months of 1876, feeling compelled to produce the work quickly and drawing frequently upon advances from Osgood. George used information Rose had at her disposal, as well as material he obtained from her cousin Richard Manning, but he was aware that Rose's other relatives did not approve of his writing about Nathaniel. Thus, what should have been a boon to Rose and George was the occasion for yet another rift between the couple and Rose's family, most particularly Julian.

George asked for a written consent from Richard Manning to use the material he had provided. "I have worried myself with inquiring what different people will think," George wrote to his cousin-in-law, "and have been so bruised by the outbreak from Julian, Una, and Elizabeth Hawthorne that I don't think anything can make me feel worse than I already have felt." So concerned was George about the Hawthornes' possible reaction to the book, which appeared on May 17, 1876, that he inserted the following lengthy disclaimer in the first chapter:

It will be seen, therefore, that my book makes no pretension to the character of a life. The wish of Hawthorne on this point would alone be enough to prevent that. If such a work is to be undertaken, it should be by another hand, in which the right to set aside this wish is much more certainly vested than in mine. But I have thought that an earnest sympathy with the subject might sanction the present essay. Sympathy, after all, is the talisman which may preserve even the formal biographer from giving that injury to his theme just spoken of. And if the insight which guides me has any worth, it will present whatever material has already been made public with a selection and shaping which all researchers might not have time to bestow.[21]

20. George Parsons Lathrop, "A Lover to a Rose" (MS in ASRIC).
21. George Parsons Lathrop to Richard Manning, May 3, 22, 1876, [May?] 3, 1876, all in Hawthorne-Manning Collection, EIL; G. P. Lathrop, *A Study of Hawthorne,* 17.

George's attempts to appease were of no avail. Julian's reaction to the book was harsh and public. Contending that George had no right to the materials he had used as sources, on July 8 Julian wrote a letter to the New York *Tribune* containing the following remarks:

> [We] used every means at our disposal to prevail upon Mr. Lathrop to surrender the papers of which he had thus accidentally got control. Mr. Lathrop at first maintained that he had an equal claim to them with myself; but subsequently he agreed to return them after having had opportunity to make himself familiar with their contents. . . . If the testimony of one who knew his father well, and has diligently studied his writings and meditated upon his mind and character, and whose opinion is substantiated by those of his own sister and of the sister of Nathaniel Hawthorne,—if such testimony carry any weight, then Mr. Lathrop's "Study" will not be taken at its own valuation. It was composed and published in violation of a trust and in the face of repeated warning and opposition; and after all it conveys no just or truthful representation of its subject.[22]

George, who was in Marblehead when Julian's denunciation appeared in the *Tribune,* wrote immediately to Osgood requesting that the "letter of protest" as well as all the ensuing newspaper comments be sent to him by express mail so that he could prepare a rejoinder. His statement was published in the *Tribune* on July 13. George told Osgood that he wished to confine his remarks to an explicit denial of wrongdoing; beyond that, he refused to continue a public discussion of the issue. Indeed, George's public remarks were the model of restraint, and his best defense came from the community. The author of one newspaper account chastised Julian thus: "The violent and personal letter which he has written to the New York press about this little book and its author proves very conclusively how unfit he himself is to attempt what Mr. Lathrop has pleasantly and modestly carried out."[23] In indicting George's work, Julian had cast only himself in a bad light while augmenting the credibility of *A Study of Hawthorne* by confirming that it was based on family archives.

This public support may have been some comfort to George, as certainly were the letters he received from Osgood, Horatio Bridge, and James Russell Lowell. George confided to Lowell that his letter

22. Bassan, *Hawthorne's Son,* 116–17.

23. George Parsons Lathrop to J. R. Osgood, July 11, 13, 1876, in J. R. Osgood Collection, HL; Bassan, *Hawthorne's Son,* 118.

was particularly welcome for its praise and because George at times felt himself to be

> without all comfort of human opinion. . . . You will not laugh at this if you have any idea of the false position in which I was placed at the time of my marriage, (partly through Julian's agency, too) in which I stood several years acutely suffering, and almost dead of the anguish that comes of being foully misconstrued without the power of setting oneself right except by persisting in breathing. . . . I strove a long time to prevent the breach which now has widened into publicity. Julian was my great admiration before my marriage, and when he utterly disappointed my conception of his character, it did not rouse hostility in me, but only weary sadness.[24]

The pain George suffered during this incident was shared by Rose, who had, after all, provided her husband with some of the family material he used in the book. She was solidly in her husband's camp, hurt by her brother's outburst and saddened that he was capable of such paltry behavior. She wrote to her aunts:

> Julian's shocking noise in the papers has been a great grief to me. His dishonesty has been a heavier blow than mere cruelty would have been. . . . He has only injured himself—so terribly that my heart aches for it—but George has come to know more forcibly the depth of his friends' trust and love, and the good estimation of the public has been gained instead of averted. It is a sad thing for us both to have so unfit an occurrence connected with Papa—and the wear of even so unjust an attack has been great upon George.[25]

Adding to Rose's concerns at this time was the fact that she was pregnant, and thus she had to experience another of life's passages without the comfort that her brother and sister might have afforded. George's mother, who talked about the dangers of pregnancy and the need for good medical attention (the birth of her own children had been assisted by her husband), told Rose that she had no real knowledge in these matters and therefore could not help Rose in "the moment of her great suffering."[26]

Rose's pregnancy, however, provided the occasion for a reconciliation with her aunt Elizabeth Hawthorne, who in September, 1876,

24. George Parsons Lathrop to James Russell Lowell, August 9, 1876, in Lowell Collection; George Parsons Lathrop to J. R. Osgood, July 31, 1876, in Osgood Collection; George Parsons Lathrop to Horatio Bridge, July 31, 1876, in Bridge-Maurice Papers, BCL.

25. Rose Hawthorne Lathrop to [Elizabeth Palmer Peabody? and Mary Mann?], July 18, 1876, in ASRIC.

26. Frances Lathrop to Rose Hawthorne Lathrop, August 26, 1876, *ibid.*

sent Rose a present for the expected baby. In her letter of thanks, Rose alluded to the "sad difference of opinion which has separated me from you for so long." Aunt Ebie's criticism of George "hung like chains about my hands," Rose continued, but her aunt's "scout letter has made me feel more than ever how much happiness is lost by family dissensions." Rose concluded the letter with a comment on her happiness about Una's engagement to Albert Webster and her "hope for a beautiful union between them."[27]

On November 10, 1876, Francis Hawthorne Lathrop was born. George announced happily to Richard Manning that both Rose and "the boy are doing finely." Within a few weeks, however, George wrote with different news. "Rose seemed to gain strength quite rapidly after the birth," he reported, "but she had so many discomforts to suffer that I gave almost all my time to her care from the first." Then George observed signs that were far more worrisome. The "symptoms of hallucination and mental distress began to appear, enough to make me very anxious, though I did not know the drift fully till after some days more; and finally the doctor pronounced insanity clearly developed. The manifestations became entirely unmanageable, although there were four of us devoting our entire energies to it. . . . Doctors Walcott and Wyman recommended that Rose be sent at once to the McLean Asylum, there being among other alarming features of the case, great danger of exhaustion from her refusal to take food."[28]

At the McLean Asylum for the Insane, the oldest psychiatric hospital in the country, Rose was attended by Dr. George Frederick Jelly, who had been appointed head of the asylum in 1871. Jelly, a Harvard medical school graduate and highly regarded psychiatrist, probably diagnosed Rose's condition as puerperal insanity—a condition whose symptoms are documented in medical records of the nineteenth century and conform in astonishing detail to George's description of Rose's illness.[29] Today Rose's condition would undoubtedly be diagnosed as postpartum psychosis.

27. Rose Hawthorne Lathrop to Elizabeth Hawthorne, September 30, 1876, *ibid.*

28. George Parsons Lathrop to Richard Manning, November 10, 1876, George Parsons Lathrop to Rebecca Manning, December 2, 1876, both in Hawthorne-Manning Collection.

29. Jelly went on to become chairman of the Massachusetts State Board of Insanity in 1898 according to Howard A. Kelly and Walter Burrage, eds., *The Dictionary of American Medical Biography* (New York, 1928), 659.

Puerperal insanity was most frequently reported among genteel women who did not nurse their babies and who had given birth between the ages of twenty-five and thirty. The textbook symptoms included depression; restlessness and sleeplessness; suspicion, especially of poisoning (hence the refusal of food); and hysterical or violent behavior, including excessive loquaciousness and even the use of obscene language. Immediate removal from the home was mandated to prevent the patient from harming herself or others. Additional possible treatments were warm baths, drugs such as digitalis to reduce agitation and opiates to induce sleep, and forced feeding. The McLean Asylum also used its own particular invention of "strong rooms" to subdue violent patients without the use of drugs or manacles. These bare stone rooms, constructed with a great deal of privacy for the patient, were well ventilated and could be heated from below to maintain a uniformly comfortable temperature. Potentially violent patients could thus be kept naked, without the clothing with which they might do themselves harm.[30]

Rose was receiving state-of-the-art treatment for her condition, which appeared to improve markedly upon her removal to the asylum. George was confident in Jelly's assurance that "insanity from this cause . . . almost invariably ends in a perfect cure, and we therefore hope that Rose's trouble will pass off in a few months at the most, and possibly in a few weeks, because it has been subjected to the best care before it has gone too far. She now takes abundant nourishment and is less violent than she was at home."[31]

However optimistic George was about Rose's recovery, her illness nonetheless grieved him. His mother and a woman who had been his nurse joined him in taking care of the infant, Francie. Yet the child's well-being was not nearly as important to George as was his wife's. He wrote Rose, "Not to be with you all the time has—do believe

30. John Charles Bucknell and Daniel Hack Tuke, *A Manual for Psychological Medicine: Containing the History and Nosology, Description, Statistics, Diagnosis, Pathology, and Treatment of Insanity* (Philadelphia, 1859), 235–39; George M. Burrows, *Commentaries on the Causes, Forms, Symptoms, and Treatment, Moral and Medical, of Insanity* (1828; rpr. New York, 1976), 362–408; M. B. Cantab and J. Thompson Dickson, "A Contribution to the Study of the So-Called Puerperal Insanity," *Journal of Mental Science*, XVI (October, 1870), 379–90; Morrill Wyman, *The Early History of the McLean Asylum for the Insane: A Criticism of the Report of the Massachusetts State Board of Health for 1877* (Cambridge, 1877), 1–15.

31. George Parsons Lathrop to Rebecca Manning, December 2, 1876, in Hawthorne-Manning Collection.

this—been as hard for me as your absence from the little boy to you; for you are more to me than my child, and, as I am not the mother but only a father, the baby's presence has only made me miss you more." George told Rose that he thought about her constantly. He visited her as often as he was allowed and offered her words of encouragement, assuring her that her return home would be "the happiest, most quieting thing in the world."[32]

Rose's recovery progressed according to the best prognosis, and she left the asylum during the early months of 1877 to resume her life as wife and, now, mother. The following poem, expressing the joy she found in motherhood, was probably composed to celebrate the occasion of Francie's first birthday.

> Pray have you heard the news?
> Sturdy lungs and thews
> There's a new baby!
> Ring the bells of crystal life,
> Wave boughs with blossoming tip;
> Think what he may be.
>
> Love cannot love enough,
> Winter is never rough
> All round such sweetness;
> One of a million more
> Lent to the glad heart's door
> In their completeness.
>
> Though in each ear 'tis told,
> Such news is never old
> Of a first birthday:
> Welcome thou ray of light,
> In joyous wishes dight,
> Sail down thy mirth-way.[33]

32. George Parsons Lathrop to Rose Hawthorne Lathrop, January 1, 1877, in ASRIC.
33. Rose Hawthorne Lathrop, "The Baby," in R. H. Lathrop, *Along the Shore,* 53–54.

IV / Mrs. George Parsons Lathrop

GEORGE withheld tragic news from Rose while she was recovering at the McLean Asylum. Albert Webster, Una's fiancé, had been traveling to Honolulu—a trip prescribed by Dr. Lathrop as a cure for the young man's tuberculosis—when he died on board ship on December 27, 1876. He was buried at sea.[1]

Albert Webster had been an aspiring writer in whom all the Lathrops seem to have taken an interest. Mrs. Lathrop had corresponded with him to the point of being, as she described herself to Rose, "exhausted by the Webster affair." George had made an effort to help Albert raise the money needed for his Pacific voyage. In October, 1875, George had written to Henry Wadsworth Longfellow, reminding him of his previous offer of monetary aid to the young man. Longfellow did apparently lend the young man some money because after Albert's death, George once again corresponded with Longfellow, this time offering to assume Albert's debt to him.[2]

The news of Albert's death reached Una in England. Her mental and physical condition had been delicate for years, and the grief she now experienced precipitated a decline from which she did not recover. At first, Una attempted to maintain her daily routines, but she grew progressively weaker, and soon her hair turned gray. Her

1. Thomas Wentworth Higginson, "Una Hawthorne," *Outlook,* LXXVII (1904), 524.

2. Frances Lathrop to Rose Hawthorne Lathrop, October 13, [1875?], November 1, 1876, both in ASRIC; George Parsons Lathrop to Henry Wadsworth Longfellow, October 11, 1875, February 2, 1877, both in Henry Wadsworth Longfellow Collection, HL.

stamina failing, she went to stay with the Anglican sisters in Clewer, where she died on September 10, 1877. Julian, who was still residing in England, saw to her burial in Kensal Green beside their mother.[3]

In addition to the death of her only sister, George's problems at the *Atlantic Monthly* augmented Rose's difficulties at this time. William Dean Howells had had differences of opinion with George during the latter's two-year tenure as associate editor. George thought that Howells had undervalued his contributions both as an editor and as a writer, and he particularly objected to Howells' insistence on changing parts of the manuscript of *Waverly Oaks,* which was about to be published. George wished to have his writing appear before the public anonymously if Howells could not accept it without editorial interference. These differences were exacerbated in July and August of 1877; at one point Howells observed that if George "never wrote another word in the *Atlantic Monthly* it would not affect its fortunes in any degree." Their disagreement culminated in George's resignation on September 1 of that year.[4]

Notwithstanding Howells' impression of George's literary merit, George was writing and publishing prolifically. Among his publications at this time were numerous poems in the *Galaxy* and several book-length works with Roberts Brothers: *Afterglow,* in 1877, and *Somebody Else* and *A Masque of Poets,* both in 1878. Rose was also writing and attempting to have her work published, though she did not meet with the same success as her husband in placing her works with the *Galaxy.* Her novel *Miss Dilletante,* which was rejected by Roberts Brothers, was eventually published in installments in the Boston *Courier* while George was its editor, a position he held for two years beginning late in 1877.[5]

But neither Rose's marginal success as a writer nor the vicissitudes of her husband's career nor the far greater misfortune of losing her sister through death and her brother through feuding was a setback to Rose's complete recovery from the emotional difficulties that followed Francie's birth. In fact, in spite of the problems facing the

3. Rose Hawthorne Lathrop to Elizabeth Hawthorne, n.d., in ASRIC.

4. George Parsons Lathrop to William Dean Howells, July 4, 1877, August 29, 1877, both in William Dean Howells Collection, HL.

5. Niles to Rose Hawthorne Lathrop, December 28, 1877, in ASRIC; Rose Hawthorne Lathrop to William Conant Church, January 12, 1878, in William Conant Church Papers, NYPL.

couple during these years, Rose and George appear to have enjoyed a period of great domestic happiness and marital stability. Rose communicated as much to a lifelong friend and correspondent, Mattie: "Nothing is so sunny, I think, as married happiness, though there is so much else that is beautiful and sweet in the world. I wish you could see our lovely boy;—I am so glad George lives all day at home, so he can see the boy in all moods and ways—if he had a business to take him to town, it would cause him to lose so much of the child's lovely life and character." George was equally happy with his life: "Rose and the boy-bud are well. They do tempt one to write poems; but I never feel I can quite do them justice, so I just go on loving them in prose." The following poem, however, demonstrates that George could be eloquent when expressing his love in verse.

I Loved You, Once—

And did you think my heart
  Could keep its love unchanging,
Fresh as the buds that start
  In spring, nor know estranging?
Listen! The buds depart:
  I loved you once, but now—
  I love you more than ever.

'Tis not the early love;
  With day and night it alters,
And onward still must move
  Like earth that never falters
For storm or star above.
  I loved you once; but now—
  I love you more than ever.

With gifts in those glad days
  How eagerly I sought you!
Youth, singing hope, and praise:
  These were the gifts I brought you.
In this world little stays:
  I loved you once but now—
  I love you more than ever.

A child with glorious eyes
  Here in our arms half sleeping—
So passion wakeful lies;
  Then grows to manhood, keeping
Its wistful, young surprise:
  I loved you once, but now—
  I love you more than ever.

When age's pinching air
  Strips summer's rich possession,
And leaves the branches bare,
  My secret in confession
Still thus with you I'll share:
  I loved you once, but now—
  I love you more than ever.[6]

George clearly anticipated a long, happy life with Rose and Francie. The child was, moreover, very much the center of attention in both his immediate and his extended families. He received fond messages from his grandmother, who, though she did not often visit, was typically effusive in her praise of him. Rose's aunt Mary Mann was attentive, as was her aunt Ebie, who looked forward to the young family's visits, but not at the risk of Francie's exposure "to perils of infectious diseases in closed cars. . . . You cannot be too careful of him," she advised Rose.[7]

Rose was particularly solicitous of Aunt Ebie, who was elderly, frail, and living on limited means and in whom Rose found "a magic resemblance" to her father. Rose corresponded with her cousin Richard Manning frequently about Aunt Ebie, arranging for him to invest money to provide a better income for her. Rose believed that caring for Ebie, particularly by freely advancing money despite her own circumscribed resources, was "transacting a matter for my father. . . . I consider the obligation sacred."[8]

When, in the spring of 1879, the Wayside became available, Rose may have viewed purchasing it from, in George's words, "alien hands" as another homage to the memory of her father. Rose and George extended themselves to their financial limits to borrow the money needed to acquire the Wayside, and since this diminished their ability to support Aunt Ebie through periodic advances of cash, they may have reasoned that they could improve her care by having her live with them in their new home. Rose attempted to enlist the Man-

6. Rose Hawthorne Lathrop to Mattie L. Stearns, June 25, 1878, in Henry W. and Albert A. Berg Collection, NYPL; George Parsons Lathrop to Richard Henry Stoddard, February 5, 1878, in Alfred Williams Anthony Collection, NYPL; George Parsons Lathrop, "I Loved You Once—," in G. P. Lathrop, *Dreams and Days* (New York, 1892), 43–44.

7. Mary Mann to Rose Hawthorne Lathrop, May 20, 1880, Frances Lathrop to Rose Hawthorne Lathrop, September 13, 1879, and Elizabeth Hawthorne to Rose Hawthorne Lathrop, July 29, 1878, all in ASRIC.

8. Rose Hawthorne Lathrop to Richard Manning, May 15, 1880, in Hawthorne-Manning Collection, EIL.

nings' help in persuading Ebie to move into the Wayside: "I wish you would use your influence to induce her to come to us, for I am sure I could make her comfortable." But Ebie preferred to find her own "home near the open lands."[9]

The Wayside had been Rose's home twice before and had been the only home in which she had ever lived for an extended period of time. She and George therefore anticipated its adding to the happiness they already experienced as a family. But the house had a strange effect upon Rose, and her thoughts there took on a foreboding, gloomy quality. She wrote to Lillian Aldrich of her apprehension in language much like that her father might have used: "Sitting here so much alone in this old house, The Wayside, as I have done of late, I see things between slumber and waking, a bright, queer time for insights, though they are always sad ones; and I wonder if all the saints about us avert anything except from themselves. Amelioration is sometimes quite another thing, and sometimes I detest it."[10]

A few months after Rose penned these thoughts, her life took another tragic turn. Francie became sick with diphtheria. On February 6, 1881, only four days after the first symptoms of the disease appeared, he was dead. That very day George removed Rose from the Wayside. "I shall not let her return," he told Aunt Lizzie. First the couple proceeded to Boston, then to New York, Rose's doctor believing that she "must come away from familiar scenes." Ebie wrote to George that he and Rose would be each other's best consolation but that he, being the father, not the mother, of Francie, could not feel the loss of the child as profoundly as did Rose. George was, however, deeply affected by Francie's death, as his elegy for his son demonstrates.

The Flown Soul
(Francis Hawthorne Lathrop)
February 6, 1881

Come not again! I dwell with you
Above the realm of frost and dew,
Of pain and fire, and growth to death.
I dwell with you where never breath

9. George Parsons Lathrop to Horatio Bridge, April 10, 1879, in Bridge-Maurice Papers, BCL; Rose Hawthorne Lathrop to Rebecca Manning, April 20, 1880, Rose Hawthorne Lathrop to Richard Manning, May 20, 1880, both in Hawthorne-Manning Collection.

10. Rose Hawthorne Lathrop to Lillian Aldrich, November 2, 1880, in Thomas Bailey Aldrich Collection, HL.

Is drawn, but fragrance vital flows
From life to life, even as a rose
Unseen pours sweetness through each vein
And from the air distills again.
You are my rose unseen; we live
Where each to other joy may give
In ways untold, by means unknown
And secret as the magnet-stone.

For which of us, indeed, is dead?
No more I lean to kiss your head—
The gold-red hair so thick upon it;
Joy feels no more the touch that won it
When o'er my brow your pearl-cool palm
Its tenderness so childish, calm,
Crept softly, once. Yet, see, my arm
Is strong, and still my blood runs warm.
I still can work, and think and weep,
But all this show of life I keep
Is but the shadow of your shine,
Flicker of your fire, husk of your vine;
Therefore, you are not dead, nor I
Who hear your laughter's minstrelsy.
Among the stars your feet are set;
Your little feet are dancing yet
Their rhythmic beat, as when on earth.
So swift, so slight are death and birth!

Come not again, dear child! If thou
By any chance couldst break that vow
Of silence at thy last hour made;
If to this grim life unafraid
Thou couldst return, and melt the frost
Wherein thy bright limbs' power was lost;
Still would I whisper—since so fair
This silent comradeship we share—
Yes, whisper 'mid the unbidden rain
Of tears: "Come not, come not again!"[11]

Beyond the initial grief, Francie's death affected George in unforeseen ways. There was a "gulf in Rose's life and mine," he observed, but the two were sustained in their sorrow by the warmth of friends who rallied about them. "I have done as much as I could," wrote

11. George Parsons Lathrop to Elizabeth Palmer Peabody, February 6, 1881, in ASRIC; Rose Hawthorne Lathrop to Emma Holland, February 20, 1881, in CFPL; Elizabeth Hawthorne to George Parsons Lathrop, February 10, 1881, in ASRIC; George Parsons Lathrop, "The Flown Soul," in G. P. Lathrop, *Dreams and Days,* 132–33.

Rose in response to a letter of condolence from Emma Holland, "with the aid of a circle of precious friends to keep my mind away from the enormous grief and the terrible but holy insights of this loss."[12]

Julian, whose enmity with Rose and George had prevented him from ever seeing his nephew, could no longer remain distant. "Without seeming to intrude upon you or your husband," he wrote Rose, after receiving the news of Francie's death, "I venture to write to you as if nothing stood between us." Julian recalled the daily childhood quarrels upon which he and his sister had never allowed the sun to set: "Is there any quarrel so just that it may not be made up before the last nightfall of us all? What are the years that they should have the power to change us so? . . . You and I are all that is left now; and it is strange that we should stand apart." Julian concluded this letter with an invitation to Rose and George to visit him in England, and they accepted.[13]

Little did George realize, when he and Rose set sail for England, that their child's death was the first in a series of sad separations. Ten years earlier Rose had traveled from England to America to begin a new life as wife and, then, mother. Now, with her child gone, her voyage from America to England was the beginning of another new life—a life apart from her husband.

Rose's reunion with Julian was a consolation. "It has been a great experience, indeed, to come back to him," she wrote; but the reality of her child's death continued to intrude. "I am as one that has seen and felt a sight, an impression that half kills forever. I am more with my child than here. I hope to have the strength to overcome this feeling sufficiently to do some good work."[14]

After a relatively brief visit, Rose and George left Julian and his family, she to travel to Paris and he to go to Spain to do preliminary work on *Spanish Vistas.* That work completed, George was already in negotiation with Osgood over a novel, *In the Distance,* when he and Rose were reunited in London by the day of their tenth anniver-

12. George Parsons Lathrop to Thomas Wentworth Higginson, February 20, 1881, in Thomas Wentworth Higginson Collection, HL; Rose Hawthorne Lathrop to Emma Holland, February 20, 1881, in CFPL.

13. Julian Hawthorne to Rose Hawthorne Lathrop, March 15, 1881, in ASRIC.

14. Rose Hawthorne Lathrop to Mattie L. Stearns, June 16, 1881, in Berg Collection.

sary, September 11, 1881. A month later they returned to the United States.[15]

The pattern of living apart from George that Rose had begun in Europe continued. The couple's separations initially may have been occasioned by the desire of each to pursue different professional opportunities. Rose went to Concord that fall to make sketches of the Wayside for publication in a periodical. She joined George at Christmas in Philadelphia, where he was working on the manuscript of *In the Distance,* which Osgood was to publish in 1882. That year George also published *An Echo of a Passion* with Houghton Mifflin, and in 1883 Harper and Brothers brought out *Spanish Vistas.*[16]

Notwithstanding Rose's newly achieved reconciliation with Julian, she soon became embroiled in another unpleasant and public incident with him. Julian had returned to the United States and was planning to bring out an edition of *Dr. Grimshawe's Secret* from an original manuscript of Nathaniel's that Julian claimed was in his possession—a manuscript Rose was sure did not exist. In 1872, Rose had solicited from Una their father's manuscripts to help George prepare his essay "History of Hawthorne's Last Romance." A manuscript of *Dr. Grimshawe's Secret* had not appeared then, nor had Julian ever told Rose about it. Rose's kindest surmise was that this manuscript represented an early draft of *Septimius Felton.* Her final conclusion, plausible, but erroneous, was that the story was a forgery and Julian the perpetrator of a hoax.[17]

After the announcement that this novel was about to be published, Rose demanded a public correction of what she thought was a serious error. In a letter in the New York *Tribune* on August 16, 1882, she asserted: "No such unprinted work has been in existence. . . . It cannot be truthfully published as anything but an experimental fragment."[18]

Julian's response to this attack was quite unlike the public posture he had assumed toward George some years earlier upon the publica-

15. Rose Hawthorne Lathrop to Nellie Hill, July 7, 1881, in ASRIC; Bassan, *Hawthorne's Son,* 119; George Parsons Lathrop to J. R. Osgood, September 11, 1881, in J. R. Osgood Collection, HL.

16. Rose Hawthorne Lathrop to Emma Holland, January 2, 1882, in CFPL; George Parsons Lathrop to J. R. Osgood, November 26, 1881, in Osgood Collection.

17. R. H. Lathrop, *Memories,* 443.

18. Bassan, *Hawthorne's Son,* 159.

tion of *A Study of Hawthorne*. Perhaps because he was dealing with his sister, rather than his brother-in-law, Julian felt the urge to be conciliatory, and perhaps because he held the proof, he saw no need to defend himself publicly. "Now my dear Sister, you know the reason why I have hitherto refrained from any defense or answer to the direct charge of forgery which has been again and again brought against me, always on the authority of your statements," he wrote Rose. "With the proof literally in my hands—ninety thousand words of this story in my father's handwriting—I sit here day after day and wait here for you to speak." In fact, so generous was Julian that when the novel came out in the Riverside Edition that year, he dedicated it "To Mr. and Mrs. George Parsons Lathrop, The Son-in-Law and Daughter of Nathaniel Hawthorne."[19]

That fifteen-volume edition of Hawthorne's works, which Houghton Mifflin published in 1882 to 1884, also included a biography of Nathaniel written by Julian and entitled *Nathaniel Hawthorne and His Wife*. Moreover, the edition contained in an appendix a "Biographical Sketch of Nathaniel Hawthorne," composed by George at Houghton's request. As he had when he wrote *A Study of Hawthorne,* George felt obliged to defend the propriety of his writing about Nathaniel. "I cannot think," he wrote, "that my sketch in the edition will interfere with Julian."[20] This time, however, George was worried about establishing his credibility, not before the public, but before Rose.

Soon after George agreed to write the "Biographical Sketch," Rose, who was living with her husband in a little apartment on West Ninth Street in New York City, learned that her aunt Elizabeth Hawthorne had died. Rose grieved over her aunt's death, not only because the two had been fond of each other, but also because Ebie had been especially connected with Nathaniel in Rose's memory. But Ebie's death provided Rose and her brother with some financial benefit through access to that portion of their father's estate that had hitherto gone to their aunt. For Rose, the prospect of even a small degree of financial independence had become particularly attractive.

Rose first wrote to Julian, asking him to administer Ebie's estate, but having no response from him, she made the same request of

19. *Ibid.;* Nathaniel Hawthorne, *Doctor Grimshawe's Secret* (Boston, 1882), Vol. XIII of [George Parsons Lathrop, ed.], *The Works of Nathaniel Hawthorne,* 15 vols.

20. George Parsons Lathrop to Elizabeth Palmer Peabody, n.d., in ASRIC.

Richard Manning. When Richard sent her the necessary papers made out in George's name, Rose returned them. Apparently feeling the need to justify her wish to have Richard handle her business affairs, she remarked, "You have been so kind to my aunt, and have the matter of her little property so clearly before your mind, that it seemed more courteous to request you to take the further responsibility."[21]

Despite this explanation of her motives, Rose evidently had other reasons for making these financial arrangements apart from George. She subsequently wrote to her cousin several times, with some urgency, asking when she would receive her portion of the legacy. She even asked for an advance in the form of a loan if some stocks could not be sold at an advantage. Richard's response to her entreaties would, Rose said, "simplify a question of some moment to me."[22]

Rose was apparently laying the financial groundwork necessary to leave George, as he abruptly discovered one morning. On April 11, 1883, George wrote to Thomas Bailey Aldrich that he was not disposed to work because his wife "by way of a little after breakfast surprise—announced that she had decided to go to Europe this summer. This has shaken me up somewhat."[23]

Rose also wrote Aldrich the same day to say that she was planning a trip with Emma Lazarus. Lazarus, Jeannette Gilder, Emma Holland, Lillian Aldrich, and Rose were all friends and socialized at the salon the Gilders held in their home in New York City. The Aldriches and the Hollands had been especially comforting to Rose when Francie died two years earlier. Now Rose's association with these people, who were so intimately connected with the writing and the publication of the foremost authors of the time, was important to her literary aspirations, even if she did hold them in varying degrees of awe.[24] Rose wrote of her friendship with Emma Lazarus: "[She]

21. Rose Hawthorne Lathrop to Richard Manning, January 23, 1883, in Hawthorne-Manning Collection.

22. Rose Hawthorne Lathrop to Richard Manning, January 5, 11, 14, 16, 23, February 12, 23, 1883, all *ibid.*

23. George Parsons Lathrop to Thomas Bailey Aldrich, April 11, 1883, in Aldrich Collection.

24. Jeannette Gilder was the sister and sometimes the assistant of R. W. Gilder, editor until his death in 1909 of the *Century,* which had succeeded *Scribner's Monthly* in 1881. Emma Holland was the wife of J. G. Holland, who had been the first editor of *Scribner's Monthly* from 1870 to 1881. Lillian Aldrich was married to Thomas Bailey Aldrich, who was editor of the *Atlantic Monthly* from 1881 to 1890.

and I sometimes walked and talked together (after meeting in the Gilders' salon). And she had such sweet delicacy of spirit that she never gave the least sign that she did not find a very secure footing for her mental exploration while accompanying a person who knew little Latin and less Greek. On the contrary, she assured me that I was a paragon for 'stirring her up with suggestions!'"[25]

Rose apparently did not take the proposed trip; she did, however, move into her own studio apartment on Broadway. George, later writing to Aunt Lizzie for help with his work on the "Biographical Sketch," said that he saw almost nothing of Rose and that he would not incur expenses for which she would also be held responsible. Should she make "a sudden decision to go away" on a trip, he remarked, "she will have her own money to go with." As another method of reducing expenses, George decided to rent the Wayside, at least for the summer.[26]

Rose presently moved to Cambridge, and throughout the period that George worked on and revised the "Biographical Sketch," she communicated her displeasure about his undertaking, along with other comments and corrections, through third parties. Writing to her cousin Richard that she did "not expect to return to Mr. Lathrop's care," Rose added, "Julian is writing a life of my father, and I dare say has asked you questions concerning him, which Mr. Lathrop may also ask, and I mention Mr. Lathrop's book that you may perhaps suggest to Mr. Lathrop, who, I believe intends to write a sketch of my father's life for Mr. Houghton's use . . . that a repetition or great similarity in information given by you to both Mr. Lathrop and Julian, would be to Julian's disadvantage; and certainly his book is the one of prior right and importance." Rose had apparently reviewed George's manuscript and was dismayed to note several errors of fact. She questioned Richard on the source of this misinformation, for she was particularly concerned that George, whom she acknowledged as "usually very careful," had speculated that Nathaniel was estranged from his own mother. Rose at first wanted to add errata, but then, knowing that "Mr. Houghton likes corrections to come

25. Heinrich E. Jacob, *The World of Emma Lazarus* (New York, 1949), 145.

26. George Parsons Lathrop to Elizabeth Palmer Peabody, n.d., April 20, 1883, both in ASRIC; George Parsons Lathrop to Thomas Bailey Aldrich, April 4, 1883, in Aldrich Collection.

from Mr. Lathrop," had asked Richard to send George a memorandum so that the plates could be altered. The deficiencies she discovered in Julian's biography were not nearly so troubling to her; she had thought her brother would call upon her recollections while writing the book, but when he did not, she kindly judged that his work "treats more of the spirit than of the letter."[27] Clearly, at this moment of her life, Rose was allied more closely with her brother than with her husband.

It was Julian, together with some other relatives, who persuaded Rose not to seek a legal separation from George at this time. "For the sake of much mutual happiness in the past, Mr. Lathrop and I can hold a more gentle relationship in separation," she wrote to Richard. By the fall and winter of 1883, while residing at 8 Chestnut Street in Cambridge, she appears to have had some misgivings about her status. Again she wrote to Richard, saying that she was "heavy hearted" and disliked seeing old friends because this contact made her more painfully aware of the alteration in her life. She asked Richard for help to "forget my loss and the absence of my husband. I am not sure what the future will develop for me in regard to him."[28]

Julian, who had by now established a home for himself and his ever-growing family in Sag Harbor, Long Island, did not share his sister's heavy heart over the absence of her husband. He seemed, in fact, rather pleased to have easy access to her sisterly affection: "For since I have been able to see that I might without danger love you as much as I wished to, I have felt a deficiency in the round of things which only you can fill; and I hope you will find it possible to fill it soon, and often, if not permanently."[29]

Spending Christmas of 1883 with Julian must have done much to assuage Rose's loneliness, and Julian's high praise for her literary works, which were being published regularly now, was another boost to her spirits. Julian, with uncharacteristic self-abasement, recounted a newspaper comment in reference to Rose's poetry that "Hawthorne's mantle, which had slipped from the shoulders of the son, was appearing on those of the daughter," and concluded, "You

27. Rose Hawthorne Lathrop to Richard Manning, April 28, October 12, November 14, and December 12, 1883, all in Hawthorne-Manning Collection.

28. Rose Hawthorne Lathrop to Richard Manning, May 7, October 10, 1883, both *ibid.*

29. Julian Hawthorne to Rose Hawthorne Lathrop, December 12, 1883, in ASRIC.

really have in you the entrails of Hawthorne's genius, if they are anywhere."[30]

Rose stayed with Julian until the spring of 1884, helping him with his family when Minne was ill and assisting them in their move from one house to another. Living with Julian may have also been a way for Rose to ease her financial burdens, for she had to request from Houghton advances on her portion of the proceeds from the sale of the Riverside Edition. George, meanwhile, motivated by economic necessity, had sold the Wayside, an action of no small significance to him or Rose. He sent Rose one thousand dollars from the proceeds of the sale, even though his lawyers informed him that this was not mandated by "her dower right."[31] Whatever monetary advantage Rose and George might have gained from disposing of this home could in no way have compensated for the loss of hopes that its sale must have symbolized.

In addition to writing at his normally busy pace—in 1884 he published *True and Other Stories* with I. K. Funk and Company and *Newport* with Charles Scribner's Sons—George undertook another task during this period. The lack of an international copyright law had for decades affected American writers adversely by allowing their works to be pirated abroad. At the same time the American market was flooded with pirated European texts; thus authors on both sides of the Atlantic suffered. Nathaniel Hawthorne himself, who had earned very little from the enormously successful sale of his books in England, was a prime victim of this inequity. In 1883 the Authors Club had united, among others, R. W. Gilder and Samuel Clemens, as well as Julian Hawthorne and George Parsons Lathrop, in pursuit of an international copyright law. For about a year George was secretary of the Executive Committee of the Copyright League, a position from which he resigned in May, 1885, although he continued to work for an international copyright law in other capacities. The following emphatic plea to Congress was signed by virtually every notable late nineteenth-century American writer, including Louisa May Alcott, William Dean Howells, Constance Fenimore Woolson, Thomas Wentworth Higginson, Edward Bellamy, and George

30. Julian Hawthorne to Rose Hawthorne Lathrop, December 26, 1883, *ibid.*

31. George Parsons Lathrop to Thomas Bailey Aldrich, January 28, February 15, 18, 22, 24, 1884, all in Aldrich Collection.

Washington Cable, in addition to George and his immediate circle: "The undersigned American citizens who earn their living in whole or in part by their pen, and who are put at a disadvantage in their own country by the publication of foreign books without payment to the author, so that American books are undersold in the American market, to the detriment of American literature, urge the passage by Congress of an International Copyright law which will protect the rights of authors, and will enable writers to ask from foreign nations the justice we shall then no longer deny on our own part."[32]

By the end of the summer of 1884, however, George had happier thoughts than international law to occupy his mind. He and Rose were once again living together, on East Fifty-fifth Street in New York City, and the couple and Julian had begun to feel at ease with each other. When Julian was on his way west for a lecture tour that fall, he made a point of paying Rose a visit, spending the night on her couch so that he might see "her ménage in New York City." As a couple once again, the Lathrops spent almost a year in what Rose called their "nice flat." She read, rested, and enjoyed conversations with friends—all of which she considered her consolation for being unable to earn much money from her literary efforts.[33]

In the fall of the following year, George did "hack work and tr[ied] to develop a steady income," he told Aldrich. The Lathrops' circumstances had improved sufficiently for them to move to an even more "charming apartment," one that George's artist-brother, Frank, had decorated handsomely for them. The two seemed to be settling into a comfortable pattern of writing, socializing with other writers, and enjoying the pleasures that New York offered. "Mrs. Lathrop and I like New York extremely, and are very happy here," George declared confidently.[34] Thus they lived until the summer of 1887.

32. George Parsons Lathrop to R. R. Bowker, May 27, 1885, in R. R. Bowker Papers, NYPL; Bassan, *Hawthorne's Son,* 165; *A Memorial of American Authors,* [*Autographs of American citizens . . . who . . . urge the passage by Congress of an International Copyright law.*], n.p., [1884?] (The copy I consulted is in the Main Reading Room, New York Public Library).

33. Julian Hawthorne to Rose Hawthorne Lathrop, October 18, 1884, in ASRIC; Rose Hawthorne Lathrop to Rebecca Manning, March 11, 1886, in Hawthorne-Manning Collection.

34. George Parsons Lathrop to Thomas Bailey Aldrich, October 28, 1885, in Aldrich Collection.

V / Rose Hawthorne Lathrop

WHAT prompted Mrs. George Parsons Lathrop one morning after breakfast to announce to her husband that she was leaving and what prompted her to return to him and live an "extremely" happy life in their "charming apartment" in New York remain uncertain. The answers to these questions are not to be found in her correspondence or in that of her friends and family. The only certainty that emerges from these letters is that she was the party who sought the separation, which her husband bore patiently and gently, as he had borne other crises in their lives.

Rose's preoccupations during this period, however, may be inferred from her imaginative writing, which she published under the name Rose Hawthorne Lathrop. Thus, readers would have immediately identified her with her father, her brother (who was enjoying a prolific literary career at this time), and her husband. Although one cannot assume an equivalence between aspects of her life and the themes, situations, and characters in her fiction and poetry, there is an apparent congruence between certain biographical facts and the content of Rose's publications between 1875 and 1892. Of particular interest is a collection of her poems entitled *Along the Shore,* which appeared in 1888 and received mixed reviews. Some praised it as a "little book of exquisite poems"; others condemned it for a "pessimistic spirit that permeates so much contemporaneous poetry."[1]

1. Reviews of Rose Hawthorne Lathrop's *Along the Shore,* in Boston *Pilot,* July 21, 1888, Chicago *Times,* June 23, 1888 (Clippings in ASRIC).

Rose's imaginative works may be generally classified according to genre and theme: fiction for or about children; fiction dealing with the relationships between the sexes; poetry about male-female relations; and poetry on the subjects of death and grief. Rose published a number of short stories that had a fairy-tale quality or that used children as the main characters. These narratives sound as if they might have originated in Rose's childhood imagination, for they contain events recognizable from her youth in England, in Rome, and at the Wayside. Some of these stories appeared in *St. Nicholas Magazine,* a periodical specifically for children; yet not all of these stories can actually be described as children's literature.

Several of Rose's stories explore the theme of initiation into some aspect of adulthood through the acquisition of knowledge and the concomitant loss of innocence or youth. "Princess Roundabout" is an allegory of initiation that takes place in a "kingdom of the far past." A petulant princess commands that "everything she saw or touched or played with should to some degree be shaped in a circle, or be so fat that it came almost to the same thing." But she must eventually comply with "Dame Experience . . . who is a wayfarer with a bag of straight lines on her arm, of which she makes you buy some, whether you wish or no (should you meet her on the road), and for no less than a few of the smooth round ones you carry on your cheek and chin." Even the smooth, youthful visage of a princess will become lined as a consequence of adult experience.[2]

Although not allegorical in structure, "Toy Mysteries" treats a similar notion of initiation. A little boy and his sister are playing with a toy dry-goods shop that, with the turn of a crank, moves the draper into the appearance of dispute with a customer. The conflict of the story is directly established through this authorial comment to the boy: "You allow your reverence for your mysterious toy's construction to be merged in a curiosity which makes you wish to open the wooden breast of your shopkeeper, and thus settle the question of *how* he clicks in that miraculous way." Much to his sister's dismay, the boy succumbs to his curiosity and takes the toy apart. Knowledge of the toy's mechanism, however, does not make him as happy as did awe of its mystery, for the story concludes with the boy in tears:

2. Rose Hawthorn [*sic*] Lathrop, "Princess Roundabout," *Independent,* 1875 (Clipping in ASRIC).

"Who knows how piteously the little rogue's throat ached with the lump of experience he felt there?"[3]

"Fun Beams" is another story set amidst the games that children play. Mr. and Mrs. Roseley prepare elaborate costumes to enliven Christmas festivities for their youngest child, four-year-old Dan, sometimes called "The Angel." Red-haired Marie, dressed elaborately as Titania, is reminiscent of Rose herself at the age of ten. Young Vernon, transformed into Saint Nicholas, is the dispenser of gifts selected with the same care Nathaniel had exercised in giving presents. Cara receives a French doll, as had Una during an idyllic Christmas in England. Dan is given a purse that bears the inscription Give This to the Poor. He precociously identifies the poor as "the sick-looking people on the street . . . [those who] were not invited to our great Christmas Eve." The story concludes with the family assembled in front of a roaring fire: "The old snow storm was still flickering down from the dark heavens . . . but it did not creep indoors at the Roseleys'. And it is doubtful whether it ever will."[4]

Other stories also have autobiographical overtones. "The Owl That Stared" is the story of five-year-old Trotty Derridown, who, exploring the treasures of her grandmother's attic, discovers a "good old negro dolly," much like one Rose had cherished at that age. Trotty also finds a talking owl, which announces: "I am the Bird of the Philosophers. I play ball with them. We throw questions and answers at each other." Through Rose's clever management of point of view, the reader realizes at the end of the story that this magical owl is really Trotty's older brother, Hal—a realization not shared by the five-year-old protagonist or, probably, by the children for whom the story was presumably written.[5]

"Lindie's Portrait" is another story that delves a child's mind and draws upon Rose's own experiences. Replicating Rose's childhood ordeal as Cephas Thompson's model, the protagonist is forced to sit still for what seems an interminable length of time while an artist paints her portrait. Again, the subtlety of the story must have ap-

3. Rose Hawthorne Lathrop, "Toy Mysteries," *Independent* (Clipping in ASRIC).

4. Rose Hawthorne Lathrop, "Fun Beams," *St. Nicholas Magazine,* XI (1884), 230–31. Another published story, "An Up Country Titania," July 12, 1879 (Clipping in ASRIC), existing only in fragment, obviously suggests Rose's experience as the belle of the masquerade she attended disguised as the queen of the fairies.

5. Rose Hawthorne Lathrop, "The Owl That Stared," *St. Nicholas Magazine,* IV (1876), 17–18.

pealed less to the children in Rose's audience than to their parents. The adults would have been amused by Lindie's misunderstanding of the painter's remark that he will have to arrange her ("Are you going to take me apart?" she asks) and by her mother's sage observation that "a child of her age is either all action, or all sleep, or else all ears."[6]

The childhood discomforts presented in these stories are caused by an immature understanding of the ways of the adult world. No real harm is possible in these sometimes-sentimentalized depictions of family relationships, in which young people are protected by wise, loving parents. Some elements in these works clearly suggest that Rose nostalgically used her own childhood memories to construct fiction. Her depictions of adult male-female relationships, however, are in no way as placid or idyllic as these narratives of childhood.

In "Browning the Meerschaum," Rose employs an awkward narrative technique to describe the perils of infatuation for a young man during his first social season. The narrator, Jack, quotes the lengthy monologue of his slightly older friend, Churchill, who wishes to impart what he has learned through unrequited love for the coquette Mystie Braddock. This story is thus again one of initiation—the painful loss of innocence and gain in knowledge—or, in the metaphor of the title, the browning, or breaking in, of a pipe made of meerschaum.[7]

This story also establishes a recurring situation in Rose's works about male-female relationships: A woman is pursued, often by more than one man, but her affections remain unattainable. This is essentially the plot of five of Rose's six published works of fiction that do not deal with children. Although some of these stories, which use a male narrator, portray the young woman as a flirt, others suggest complex though not always clear motivations for the woman's emotional inaccessibility to the man.

The title character of "Saagenfreed" is a simpering young man who becomes enamored of one woman after another. He declares his love to beautiful, blond Stenna Rowland, who is depicted as emotionally independent and morally superior to him. Saagenfreed even notices, to his chagrin, that she is taller than he. To test his fidelity,

6. Rose Hawthorne Lathrop, "Lindie's Portrait," *St. Nicholas Magazine,* XIV (1887), 512, 514.

7. R. H. Lathrop, "Browning the Meerschaum."

Stenna disguises herself as a darkly attractive Russian widow. When Saagenfreed, predictably, makes a fool of himself, he wonders, "Has she won the battle?" The story ends inconclusively with a number of reversals and Saagenfreed's hope that Stenna's sobs indicate she can forgive him. "Saagenfreed" was published in June, 1876, when Rose was pregnant with Francie and loyally defending George against Julian's public criticism of *A Study of Hawthorne*. Yet the story, with its military metaphors of domination and conquest, suggests none of the happiness in a relationship between a man and a woman that Rose and George were apparently experiencing at that time.[8]

"Prisoners!," published in two installments in 1883 while Rose and George were separated, develops more fully the theme of war between the sexes. This is Rose's longest, most complex, and most interesting work of fiction. Julian wrote Rose in praise of "Prisoners!," saying, "If you keep on writing you will certainly become the most memorable of the women novelists in this country."[9]

"Prisoners!" is the story of James Wentworth and his relationship with Clover Guerrinar, whose name would certainly have reminded readers of Clover Adams, the free-spirited photographer and wife of Henry Adams.[10] Wentworth woos Clover as part of his perverse plan to avenge his friend Stein, who died from unreciprocated love for her. The language describing Wentworth's initial impression of Clover establishes the tone, metaphors, and conflict of the story: "And as he was a natural actor, the hesitation and embarrassment which he felt, and which suited his role well enough, since he was trying to cut a limpish figure, were genuine, not due to stage fright. . . . 'You would make no mean adversary, Miss Guerrinar,' he said. 'I should almost be glad to have a conflict with you, mind to mind.' He thought with zest of the actual warfare which he was intending to wage with her. He gazed upon her admiringly, and even allowed himself to measure her height."[11]

8. Rose Hawthorne Lathrop, "Saagenfreed," *Appleton's Journal*, June 10, 1876, p. 745.

9. Julian Hawthorne to Rose Hawthorne Lathrop, October 16, 1883, in ASRIC.

10. Rose may have also had certain connotations in mind when she invented the name Clover Guerrinar. "Clover" evokes pastoral imagery and thus is an appropriate first name for a woman of "untrammeled impulse." "Guerrinar" suggests the French word *guerre*, or war, which reinforces the military metaphors so pervasive in Rose's works about male-female relationships.

11. Rose Hawthorne Lathrop, "Prisoners!," *Harper's New Monthly Magazine*, LXVII (1883), 509.

In language that suggests the contemplation of psychological rape, Wentworth fantasizes about the revenge he plans—inducing Clover to fall in love with him while he remains emotionally detached: "He beheld her yielding her love, as he confidently hoped that she soon would do, to him. Would his revenge be so sweet and eager when that fine creature gave him the key to her life, and he took it, knowing how he intended to assail her future? His heart leaped and fluttered as if in dread. He assured himself, however, with a savage smile, that his revenge would be supreme happiness in itself. He was entirely certain that he profoundly hated her."[12]

To achieve his goal, Wentworth assumes characteristics he believes Clover cannot resist. He appears to be weak, in need of her superior moral strength, and poor, for Stein had been rejected, he told Wentworth, among other reasons, because he was rich and she was not: "When strong girls like her get to thinking of absolute freedom, they seldom turn upon their steps. . . . I don't see what is to be done with these beautiful mutineers who grow so thickly now. They will cause trouble in the world."[13]

Wentworth has accurately assessed his adversary, for Clover desires a one-sided devotion, fearing that the loss of her own identity is the inevitable consequence of a mutual passion: "You adore me. I prefer that to the mutually intense love which absorbs or melts two creatures into one. We shall get along very well, I am sure." Thus a narrative built around dissimulation and disguise concludes with ironies and reversals. Wentworth has feigned the weaker part to ensnare Clover; she assumes that she "surrendered herself to him in a queenly mood; and, as it were, gave commands to society at large to crown him as her husband." After Clover and Wentworth's secret wedding, however, he discovers that "his revenge upon Clover seemed now to include himself," for though he had married her that she might be imprisoned in a loveless union, he recognizes that his true feelings for her imprison him.[14]

As a short story, "Prisoners!" is marred by improbability of situation and obscurity of motives, criticisms Julian leveled at the story notwithstanding his compliments. Faulty though its narrative struc-

12. *Ibid.*, 699.
13. *Ibid.*, 506.
14. *Ibid.*, 700, 701, 703.

ture may be, "Prisoners!" raises interesting but disturbing issues about men and women; the story suggests that neither sex is capable of engaging in a mutually satisfactory relationship. Wentworth needs to dominate, and Clover needs to remain free—a freedom she defines in terms close to Wentworth's own notion of domination.

That the conflicting needs of men and women was a recurring and fundamental preoccupation for Rose is demonstrated by the fact that even as late as 1892, she was still publishing short stories on the same theme. In "For a Lord" the British lord Floray is dismayed by the coquetry of Milly Minson. But her final words to a friend indicate that her fickleness stems from ideology rather than immaturity: "I tried to fall in love, Eva, and I couldn't. That is, love is different from what I supposed, and I don't like it. I'd ever so much rather come to call on you in the old humdrum way than receive calls from pocket volcanoes like Lord Floray."[15]

In "Troth," also published in 1892, Sally Spring is torn between obligations to her wealthy former guardian and present patron, Ned Seymour, and her feelings for his younger, impecunious stepbrother, Wayne Morris. The older man's affection and generosity have sustained Sally in her career as a concert violinist but have also imposed a financial obligation upon her. Her final decision to marry Seymour—illogical though it is in terms of plot and characterization—may be Sally's manner of discharging that debt; her feelings for Wayne, however, are without coercion. Thus the conflict in the story is not that of a typical romantic triangle but that of a financially limited woman's lack of freedom to become an artist and of the burdens she takes on by being in another's debt.[16]

Rose's only published story about men and women whose theme deviates from that of the pursued-but-unattained woman is "Huff and Tiff," published in *Harper's Weekly,* in 1882. In this tale, a young man has married an impoverished young woman against the wishes of his family. The couple experiences several so-called hardships; at one point Tiff, for example, fears she "might die before morning for want of an oyster patty." The couple's plight is artificially relieved at the end of the story through the intervention of Huff's sister—a conclusion as unconvincing as it is contradictory in tone. Despite its

15. Rose Hawthorne Lathrop, "For a Lord," *Harper's Bazar,* July 30, 1892, p. 615.

16. Rose Hawthorne Lathrop, "Troth," *Harper's New Monthly Magazine,* LXXXV (1892), 341–50.

flaws, the story is worth noting for its possible allusion to Rose's own situation as an unmoneyed bride.[17]

Rose's stories about children and male-female relationships raise interesting thematic issues at the expense of successful narrative structure. Her poetry, however, more satisfyingly unites technique and idea, a fact that Julian may have recognized when he advised Rose not to "forego your lyrical poetry" because of her success in placing stories for publication. "You can hardly do anything more valuable to literature than [poetry]," he wrote her, "though, of course, it is anything but remunerative to you."[18]

In Rose's poetry, as in her fiction, a recurrent theme is the relationships between men and women. In some poems Rose employs a conventional medieval setting to romanticize the idea of lost or unrequited love. In others she uses a male persona to lament or satirize the wiles of a coquette. But in contrast with her consistent depiction of a war between the sexes in fiction, her portrayal of male-female relations in poetry sometimes takes on a happily romantic tone. For example, "A Wooing Song," her first published poem, clearly reflects marital joy with none of the fear of loss of identity voiced by the heroine of "Prisoners!"

> O love, I come: thy last glance guideth me!
>   Drawn, too, by webs of shadow, like thine hair—
> For, Sweet, the mystery
>   Of thy dark hair the deepening dusk hath caught.
> In early moonlight gleamings, lo, I see
>   Thy white hands beckon to the garden where
> Dim day and silvery darkness are in wrought
>   As our two lives, where, joining soul with soul,
> The tints shall mingle in a fairer whole,
>   Oh, dost thou hear? I call, beloved, I call:
> My stout heart trembling, till thy words return;
>   Hope-lifted, I float faster with the fall
> Of fear, toward joy each fear alone can earn![19]

Two other poems, "Morning Song" and "Violin," both of which appear in *Along the Shore,* move from romance to eros. "Morning

17. Rose Hawthorne Lathrop, "Huff and Tiff," *Harper's Weekly,* September 2, 1882, p. 554.

18. Julian Hawthorne to Rose Hawthorne Lathrop, October 16, 1883, in ASRIC.

19. Rose Hawthorne Lathrop's "A Wooing Song" first appeared in *Galaxy,* XX (1875–76), 799, and was later reprinted in *Along the Shore,* 58. Subsequent citations of Rose's poetry published both in periodicals and in *Along the Shore* will refer to that collection only.

Song" is a brief lyric that describes the pleasures of awakening in the arms of a beloved.

> Turn thy face to me, my love,
> I come from out the morning;
> Give thy hand to me, my love,
> I'm dewy from the dawning.
>
> Touch my lips with thine, my love,
> I've tasted air at daybreak;
> Gaze into my eyes, my love,
> At the sky's waking they wake.

"Violin" uses the symbolism of a musical instrument to suggest yielding to sexual impulse.

> Touch gently, friend, and slow, the violin,
> So sweet and low,
> That my dreaming senses may be beckoned so
> Into a rest as deep as the long past "years ago!"
> So softly, then, begin;
>
> And ever gently touch the violin
> Until an impulse grows of a sudden, like wind
> On the brow of the earth,
> And the voice of your violin shows its wide-swung girth,
> With a crash of strings and a medley of rage and mirth;
> And my rested senses spring
> Like juice from a broken rind,
> And the joys that your melodies bring
> I know worth a life-time to win,
> As you waken to love and this hour your violin![20]

These poems, to some degree innovative in technique and daring in content for a nineteenth-century female writer, make statements strongly at odds with the themes of Rose's published stories and demonstrate that at least on an imaginative level Rose believed in fulfilling romantic and even sexual relationships between men and women. In all probability, however, these poems were grounded on more than imagination and issued from the real joys she experienced during some phases of her life with George.

More conventional are Rose's uses of a medieval backdrop in romantic ballads. "A Ballad of the Mist" recounts a rival suitor's killing of "Poor Hugh," the beloved of the Lady of the Merle. Archaic lan-

20. Rose Hawthorne Lathrop, "Morning Song," in R. H. Lathrop, *Along the Shore,* 60; Rose Hawthorne Lathrop, "Violin," *ibid.,* 21–22.

guage and stilted meter evoke a vague, remote setting but no pathos or interest. In "Hidden History," Rose adds interest to the quasi-medieval setting by locating an innovative situation there: a woman's death in the performance of a heroic deed. "Lost Battle" is a dirge about the futile but noble, solitary death of a soldier in a faraway, unspecified war. Again Rose employs a medieval background, this time for the purposes of nostalgia, in "Looking Backward." The narrator's trite lament, "O Chivalry, thy age was fair," characterizes that work. In "Unloved" and "The Fault-Demon," Rose renders the distant landscape with alliteration and repetition reminiscent of, if not patterned after, Poe. In "Unloved" Rose describes the woe of an unnamed maiden.

> Never, never, never more
> May her soul with joy be moved
> Silent, silent, silent,—for
> He was silent whom she loved.

In "The Fault-Demon," another "white-robed maiden" endures a stranger fate.

> And there came a wild black raven,
> So eager and so craven,
> And hid himself all silent in her fair gold hair.[21]

Imitative in style and form, conventional in content, these poems are period pieces, the exercises in literature typical of "accomplished" nineteenth-century women. Far more interesting because of their innovative forms and unconventional ideas is another group of poems. Set not in a remote past but in the contemporary beau monde, these poems depict male-female relationships as but one aspect of the overall frivolity and lack of vitality in society that are the targets of Rose's criticism. The following poem, entitled "At the Breakfast Table: Our Modern Amazon," makes extensive use of military metaphors to satirize the contemporary coquette:

> I'm trying on my armor, dear,
> With which my battles are won.

21. Rose Hawthorne Lathrop, "A Ballad of the Mist," in R. H. Lathrop, *Along the Shore,* 90–93; Rose Hawthorne Lathrop, "Hidden History," *ibid.,* 88–89; Rose Hawthorne Lathrop, "Lost Battle," *ibid.,* 84–85; Rose Hawthorne Lathrop, "Looking Backward," *ibid.,* 61–62; Rose Hawthorne Lathrop, "Unloved," *ibid.,* 63; Rose Hawthorne Lathrop, "The Fault-Demon," *New Century Magazine,* V (1883–84), 798.

I shall count some brilliant conquests before
  The summer sun has gone.

Here's a white dress and a lily-trimmed hat
  And a parasol like foam;
They'll make my eyes look darker yet,
  As I fetch my prisoner home.

You would not think this simple silk,
  As light as a sea-gull's wing,
Could bring down many a knightly heart
  In the lists of a "summering!"

Here's a fan—it is not smoke,
  But lace and ostrich feather;
It will be watched by eyes that ask
  My fancy's wind and weather.

And here's a yachting suit that says,
  Upon life's merry wave
I, like an admiral, shall win
  Engagements brisk and brave!

And at this shoe, all tipped with gold,
  A trembling slave shall stoop—
A vassal whom a rival queen
  Lost in some waltzing group.

In short, when autumn once more hangs
  The land with gorgeous hue,
I shall come riding back to town
  In triumph, wouldn't you?[22]

Using a female persona, in "At the Breakfast Table: Our Modern Amazon," Rose demonstrates a command of rhythm and meter and produces a spirited statement on the foibles of young ladies. Typically, however, she assumes a male voice to assail the emptiness of society life. In her first published poem using this technique, "The Lover's Fate," a male speaker bids the deceptive flirt named Pelluca (from the Spanish for wig) to

bind your hair
Within a golden net,
That the dark, clinging, sensate coils
I may forget.[23]

22. Rose Hawthorne Lathrop, "At the Breakfast Table: Our Modern Amazon," July 20, 1891 (Clipping in ASRIC).

23. Rose Hawthorne Lathrop, "The Lover's Fate," *Appleton's Journal*, XIX (January, 1878), p. 50.

In other poems Rose moves beyond satirical witticisms to introduce a more somber theme—that the lack of vitality in social activities indicates a lack of life. In "Just Bloomed," a male speaker addresses Marie:

> Let me but gaze upon your cheek,
> And catch the fervor of your eye,
> And note the dimple at your lip
> When I declare that I shall die
> Without your love!

Whether the clichéd expression "I shall die / Without your love" should be read as hyperbole or fact is uncertain, especially when one places this poem in the context of several others on the same theme.[24]

In "The Girls We Might Have Wed," a male persona addresses his "brothers":

> let us sing a dirge,—
> A dirge for myriad chances dead;
> In grief your mournful accents merge;
> Sing, sing, the girls we might have wed!

This poem is more than a lament over "the white hand of her we did not wed," for the simple ability to remember lost opportunities (the poem was originally published under the title "Fancy's Chances") assures the speaker that he is still alive. When memory fails,

> then may we know
> The heart is dead, the man is old.
> Life can no other charm bestow
> When girls we might have loved turn cold![25]

In "Used Up," the male speaker addresses a friend, James, while preparing for a ball. The narrator will dance with his fiancée, the "Fair doll of fashion" whose "heart [is] lost along with her fan." But the levity of the poem's tone is transformed in the penultimate stanza, in which losing one's heart must be taken both figuratively and literally.

> The heart which I lost—it is strange—
> I've been told it will yet be my death;
> And I think it quite likely I might

24. Rose Hawthorne Lathrop, "Just Bloomed," *Century,* XXXVIII (1889), 480.

25. Rose Hawthorne Lathrop, "The Girls We Might Have Wed," in R. H. Lathrop, *Along the Shore,* 68–69.

Waltz once too often tonight,
In spite of the music and Beth.
Death's a difficult move to arrange.[26]

"Youth's Suicide," another poem set in a ballroom, creates a grim travesty of that conventional scene. A young beau hands his lady a poisoned cup while the frivolous crowd continues its hilarity.

The mad world clustered, it seemed, around.
"Farewell!" she sighed, sinking; then from afar
Flowed the pealing laughter and wassail's sound
(For the dead the world will not stay!).

The disjunction between the young woman's death and the crowd's reaction is macabre and surreal.[27]

Well-executed and penetrating though these poems are, Rose's most skillful, subtle, and complex handling of the theme of the vacuity and lifelessness of social mores is entitled "Neither." This poem, published only in *Along the Shore,* utilizes a Prufrockian male persona who, in an interior monologue, questions his existence.

So ancient to myself I seem,
I might have crossed grave Styx's stream
A year ago;—
My word, 'tis so;
And now be wandering with my sires
In that rare world we wonder o'er,
Half disbelieve, and prize the more!

Yet spruce I am, and still can mix
My wits with all the sparkling tricks,
A youth and girl
At twenty's whirl
Play round each other's bosom fires,
On this brisk earth I once enjoyed:—
But now am otherwise employed!

Am I a thing without a name;
A sort of dummy in the game?
"Not young, not old?:"
A world is told
Of misery in that lengthened phrase;
Yet, gad, although my coat be smooth,
My forehead's wrinkled,—that's the truth!

26. Rose Hawthorne Lathrop, "Used Up," *ibid.,* 74.
27. Rose Hawthorne Lathrop, "Youth's Suicide," *ibid.,* 36.

I hardly know which road to go.
With youth? Perhaps. With age? Oh no!
    Well, then, with those
    Who share my woes,
  Doomed to mere fashionable ways,—
Fair matrons, cigarettes, and tea,
Sighs, mirrors, and society?

Is it folly still to twirl,
To smirk and promenade and querl
    About the town?
    I'll put this down:
  A man becomes downright blasé
Before he knows that he is either
That, or what am I, call it "Neither."

Oh, for a hint what we shall do,
We bucks whose comedy is through!
    Who'd be sedate?
    And yet I hate
  To pose persistently today
As one just trying flights, you know,
When I *did* try them long ago!

Suppose I hurry up the tide
Of age, and bravely drift beside
    Those hoary dogs
    Who lie like logs
  Around the clubs where life is hushed?
My blood runs cold! What? Say farewell
To this year's new bewildering belle!

Hold, man, the secret broad and huge,
With every well-known subterfuge!
    If bald and gray
    And thin, still say
  You're only thirty: don't be crushed;
But when your voice shakes o'er a pun,
Be off to China—your day's done![28]

This poem deserves careful analysis—first, because of its own poetic merit and, second, because it anticipates, indeed may have influenced, T. S. Eliot's "The Love Song of J. Alfred Prufrock."[29] Like

28. Rose Hawthorne Lathrop, "Neither," *ibid.*, 70–73.

29. Eliot would have had access to Rose's work while he was a student at Harvard, for the Harvard library had acquired *Along the Shore* through the James Russell Lowell bequest in 1891. A Unitarian interested in the tradition of Catholicism, Eliot praised Nathaniel Hawthorne in "The Hawthorne Aspect," *Little Review,* V (August, 1918), 48, as one of the few writers in

Prufrock, the speaker in "Neither" is a man approaching middle age whose self-deprecating monologue in the manner of Laforgue is about identity at a crossroad. Like Lazarus coming back from the dead, this speaker "might have crossed grave Styx's stream." He stands poised between two worlds, one of which "we . . . half disbelieve." The very uncertainty of his existence adumbrates his lack of identity ("Am I a thing without a name; / A sort of dummy in the game?") and lack of direction ("I hardly know which road to go"). Thus he is "Doomed to mere fashionable ways" in a society devoid of grander schemes for damnation. Issues of greater moment yield to trivial questions: "cigarettes, and tea, / Sighs, mirrors, and society?"

Representing the culmination of Rose's statements about the vacuity of society, this poem captures what has been described as the "chilling void" and "the barren chaos of American life" in late nineteenth-century New England.[30] With what would Rose have filled the void or ordered the chaos? If the themes that recur in her literary works are to be taken as an index of Rose's attitudes, then it appears that married life, though periodically satisfying, offered no constant or permanent happiness in her eyes. Neither did the round of social engagements, the entertaining, and the salon conversations provide anything ultimately greater than the subject matter for satirical poems.

Nor could Rose's literary career, though productive of some fine works, have given her lasting gratification. Much more successful than Rose at finding publishers for their works, George and Julian, rather than the public or editors, seem to have been her greatest fans. It was George who published her only novel, *Miss Dilletante,* in installments in the Boston *Courier* when it had been rejected elsewhere; and it was Julian who would soften the blow of R. W. Gilder's patronizing rejection of her poems. Gilder had addressed Rose as "My

---

whom "the New England genius had discovered itself." A Unitarian who by 1891 had converted to Roman Catholicism, Rose was frequently mentioned in the newspapers at the turn of the century, when she was beginning her work for the cancerous poor. Rose's name again appeared in the newspapers in 1912 and 1913, when she attempted to plead with President Wilson in behalf of her brother, another Harvard man. It is possible that Eliot's curiosity about Rose was sufficiently piqued for him to read her poetry at Harvard.

30. Lyndall Gordon, *Eliot's Early Years* (Oxford, 1977), 13, cites Henry Bamford Parkes's use of these phrases to describe Eliot's and Henry Adams' perceptions of American life and the sort of intellectual climate that necessitated Eliot's and Adams' flight to the "certainties of Dante and St. Thomas" (see Parkes, *The Pragmatic Test: Essays on the History of Ideas* [San Francisco, 1941], 37–38).

dear Provoking Poet" and then remarked cryptically, "I like this [poem]—or something in it—But—send it somewhere else." Julian consoled his sister, however, with the assurance that her poetry was very good, even if Gilder "says [it] is not quite good enough for that bloated magazine of his."[31]

Notwithstanding the support and encouragement of her husband and her brother, Rose's work seems to have been solicited only by the editors of children's magazines, such as Mary Mapes Dodge, at *St. Nicholas Magazine,* and the editor of the *Sunday School Times.* Typically, the work she sent to *Harper's,* the *Atlantic Monthly,* and the *Century* was unsolicited and rejected. Moreover, Rose's correspondence with the editors of those journals reveals her enormous insecurities as a writer. Although she quipped with Gilder that she hoped he would not "guillotine [her] two new verses," she obediently incorporated his suggested corrections, saying simply, "I will try to improve the lines."[32]

Rose's correspondence with Thomas Bailey Aldrich evinces similar anxiety. She was elated by anything that could be construed as praise: "I write so little that comes from the pen of the world, and not from the narrow individual life. If I write anything that sings again, I shall send it to you to test." But she was sensitive to any possible criticism and requested that Aldrich "be merciful if [my verses] are very poor."[33]

Such anxiety was to at least some extent the product of Rose's lack of confidence in, or even low opinion of, the worth of her work. Again she wrote to Aldrich: "Are these verses good or bad? . . . Your opinion will be of value to me even if I cannot turn it to money." Elsewhere Rose is self-effacingly apologetic to Aldrich for her inability to judge the value of a piece: "Will you forgive me, and believe that if I could know the real worth of what I write, I should not ask you to help me with your verdict?" Another time still she wrote to him, revealing that a need to please was at least a partial

31. R. W. Gilder to Rose Hawthorne Lathrop, March 1, 1882, Julian Hawthorne to Rose Hawthorne Lathrop, December 12, 1883, both in ASRIC.

32. Mary Mapes Dodge to Rose Hawthorne Lathrop, June 19, 1884, Patterson du Bois to Rose Hawthorne Lathrop, June 20, 1884, June 15, 1885, Editor, *Harper's New Monthly Magazine* [Henry Mills Alden], to Rose Hawthorne Lathrop, October 18, 1883, and R. W. Gilder to Rose Hawthorne Lathrop, January 7, 1884, all *ibid.;* Rose Hawthorne Lathrop to R. W. Gilder, March 1, [?], August 7, [?], both in Century Company Papers, NYPL.

33. Rose Hawthorne Lathrop to Thomas Bailey Aldrich, May 27, [?], August 22, [?], both in Thomas Bailey Aldrich Collection, HL.

motivation for her continued literary efforts: "Pardon me for sending you at once another attempt to please you, although you hold out no encouragement in your very kind note. . . . But it would be so nice to find something which you approved of among my thoughts and forms of thoughts."[34]

Rose's awareness that she bore her father's name augmented her aspirations, increasing as well her fears of failure. In a letter to Richard Henry Stoddard—who, with his wife, Elizabeth Drew Barstow Stoddard, reigned over late nineteenth-century literary taste from their New York salon—Rose said she was glad one of her poems had given them pleasure. "I wish," she remarked, "that I could feel that I did my relation to my father intellectual justice, but I do not expect to be a fine writer, though I mean to be. Now if you think there's anything conceited in that word underscored, most truly never was anyone less confident of the efficacy of all but hard labor than I am."[35]

Rose's life as wife and aspiring writer was fraught with disappointment, frustration, and self-doubt. Her life as a mother had provided no lasting happiness or fulfillment. Rose had borne the tragedy of Francie's death through the support of friends and family rather than an avowed religious ideology, demonstrating the secular nature of her and George's life at that time. Yet her reflections upon Francie's death and upon death as a fact of the human condition seem to have begun for her the evolution of a different focus and meaning.

Shortly after Francie died, Rose had written to Emma Holland about "the holy insights of this loss," and she exorcised her grief in the following poem:

Francie

I loved a child as we should love
Each other everywhere;
I cared more for his happiness
Than I dreaded my own despair.

An angel asked me to give him
My whole life's dearest cost;

34. Rose Hawthorne Lathrop to Thomas Bailey Aldrich, June 16, [?], October 10, [?], May 3, [?], all *ibid.*

35. Rose Hawthorne Lathrop to Richard Henry Stoddard, June 30, [?], in Alfred Williams Anthony Collection, NYPL.

And in adding mine to his treasures
I knew they could never be lost.

To his heart I gave the gold,
Though little my own had known;
To his eyes what tenderness
From youth in mine had grown!

I gave him all my buoyant
Hope for my future years;
I gave him whatever melody
My voice had steeped in tears.

Upon the shore of darkness
His drifted body lies.
He is dead, and I stand beside him,
With his beauty in my eyes.

I am like those withered petals
We see on a winter day,
That gladly gave their color
In the happy summer away.

I am glad I lavished my worthiest
To fashion his greater worth;
Since he will live in heaven,
I shall lie content in the earth.[36]

The altruism voiced in the first two lines—an expression of charity rather than maternal love—is a remarkable sentiment on the part of a mother who has lost her only child. It is as remarkable as the last two lines are bewildering: Is Rose saying that the child will experience eternal life though she will not? In any case, her consolation comes not from faith in an afterlife but from knowledge that she "lavished her worthiest" upon her child while he lived.

In "Power Against Power," a tribute to her father, Rose similarly ponders death outside of a specific religious context. She depicts Nathaniel as a wizard whose "magic pen" can do nothing to forestall the inevitable "Power": "The End approaches, and the man / Dreams of no spell for quelling Him." In "Closing Chords," death is not personified but rendered simply as the physical grave.

When I shall go
Into the narrow home that leaves
No room for wringing of the hands and hair,

36. Rose Hawthorne Lathrop, "Francie," in R. H. Lathrop, *Along the Shore,* 45.

And feel the pressing of the walls which bear
The heavy sod upon my heart that grieves,
(As the weird world rolls on)
Then shall I know
What is the power of destiny.[37]

In another, short poem, "The World Runs On," Rose makes a different statement about the meaning of death and its consequences for the living. She observes that mourning is difficult precisely because, as the poem title suggests, everyday life continues.

The sorrow is when we may not mourn,
  When the graves are sere for want of tears,
When no one measures our misery,
  And they tell us our grief is drowned with years!

The sorrow is when our laughter goes
  About the house while our sobs are still;
When never a word is said of woes
  That alight on our heart with a bird's wild thrill![38]

The speaker indicates that the passage of time does nothing to assuage a great grief, but she dissimulates (her "laughter goes / About the house while our sobs are still") and thus can continue with her life.

Although grief over personal loss is repressed in "The World Runs On," vicarious suffering admits expression of emotion in "For Others."

Weeping for another's woe,
Tears flow then that would not flow
When our sorrow was our own,
And the deadly, stiffening blow
Was upon our own heart given
In the moments that have flown!

Cringing at another's cry
In the hollow world of grief,
Stills the anguish of our pain
For the fate that made us die
To our hopes as sweet as vain;
And our tears can flow again!

37. Rose Hawthorne Lathrop, "Power Against Power," *ibid.*, 16–17; Rose Hawthorne Lathrop, "Closing Chords," *ibid.*, 48–50.

38. Rose Hawthorne Lathrop, "The World Runs On," *Harper's New Monthly Magazine*, LXXXI (1890), 845.

One storm blows the night this way,
But another brings the day.[39]

It is impossible to say how accurate an indicator of Rose's attitudes these poems are, but a review of her life and writing through 1892 reveals certain constants. The child Rosebud had become the girl Pessima. George's beloved Rösl had for a while been the adoring mother Mrs. Lathrop and the aspiring writer Rose Hawthorne Lathrop. But Rose was still a stranger to herself, and perhaps for that reason her writings are filled with characters disguising themselves or dissimulating their true feelings. Her uses of the past—both personal and historical—are the nostalgic and sentimental expressions of one longing for a better time. None of the personalities she had assumed, none of the roles she had played, none of the false starts she had made had thoroughly satisfied her. The following poem sums up the closing of one epoch and the opening of another:

The Roads That Meet

Art

One is so fair, I turn to go,
As others go, its beckoning length;
Such paths can never lead to woe,
I say in eager, early strength.
What is the goal?
Visions of heaven, wake;
But the wind's whispers round me roll:
"For you, mistake!"

Love

One leads beneath high oaks, and birds
Choose their joyous revelry;
The sunbeams glint in golden herds,
The river mirrors silently.
Under these trees
My heart would bound or break;
Tell me what goal, resonant breeze?
"For you, mistake!"

Charity

What is there left? The arid way,
The chilling height, whence all the world

39. Rose Hawthorne Lathrop, "For Others," in R. H. Lathrop, *Along the Shore,* 37.

Looks little, and each radiant day,
Like the soul's banner, flies unfurled.
May I stand here;
In this rare ether slake
My reverential lips, and fear
No last mistake?

Some spirits wander till they die,
With shattered thoughts and trembling hands;
What jarred their natures hopelessly
No living wight yet understands.
There is no goal,
Whatever end they make;
Though prayers each trusting step control,
They win mistake.

This is so true, we dare not learn
Its force until our hopes are old,
And, skyward, God's star-beacons burn
The brighter as our hearts grow cold.
If all we miss,
In the great plans that shake
The world, still God has need of this,—
Even our mistake.[40]

40. Rose Hawthorne Lathrop, "The Roads That Meet," *ibid.,* 100–102.

VI / Rose Hildegarde

New York was an exciting place to live during the 1880s. The cultural and social life epitomized by the Gilders' salon, the wealth and elegance displayed in shops, the technological advances signaled by such marvels as the Brooklyn Bridge, completed in 1883, and the erection of higher and higher buildings to accommodate expanding numbers of professional and financial offices—all these were clear evidence of a city that could rival Paris or London.

In 1886 the Statue of Liberty was placed in New York Harbor, providing the city with a symbol that was, in reality, somewhat ironic. Emma Lazarus' sonnet, inscribed on a bronze plaque on the statue's pedestal, lauded New York as the port of entry for "the wretched refuse" of oppression; yet these very refugees often found themselves suffocating in ghettos of poverty, crime, and disease in that same city to which they had come "yearning to breathe free." Although the immigrants increased New York's population and wealth through their work in the service industry and their labor in factories, they did so while working and living in deplorable conditions. The religious and cultural diversity they brought to the city often made their experience one of rejection and discrimination.

Had Rose been oblivious of these two sides of life in New York, Emma Lazarus' death from cancer in 1887, at the the age of thirty-eight, would have caused her to understand one particular facet of the inequitable treatment of the rich and the poor. Rose was deeply affected by her friend's untimely and painful death. Lazarus had, however, been supported both emotionally and financially until her death by her affluent family. Rose discovered that New York's poor with cancer were warehoused on Blackwell's Island, where they were subjected to horrible conditions. Without proper medical attention or any form of consolation, patients suffered—external cancers sometimes causing flesh to rot and to emit a putrid odor—and died.

Because cancer was thought to be contagious, it was perhaps the most dreaded disease of the late nineteenth century, and even families with means, unable to cope with their terror of the disease, sometimes expelled their own members to fend for themselves until death. In fact, the late nineteenth-century body of knowledge about cancer illustrates that presumed advances in science often justified more barbaric, rather than more enlightened, practices. The development of bacteriology and the discovery that tuberculosis was caused by the tubercule bacillus made plausible and reinforced the assumption that cancer was similarly caused by microorganisms. Thus fear of contagion was not prompted solely by hysteria or ignorance. Michael Boris Shimkin, in his history of cancer, records that between 1886 and 1907 medical literature was "replete with reports claiming or implying the identification and isolation of every variety of microorganism as the cause of cancer. In the early [18]90's, it appeared to have been a question, not so much as to the infectious origin of cancer, but as to which of the many parasites was the real causative agent."[1]

Thus it was that in New York City, the locus of so much scientific, technological, and cultural advancement, there existed as well the inhumane treatment of the poor and sick. Because of George's own ill health, however, he and Rose decided to leave that city at the very moment she began to understand this issue, which would radically alter her life. In 1887, George resigned his position as literary editor of the New York *Star,* and the Lathrops moved to New London, Connecticut. Perhaps Rose's poem "The Greater World," published in *Scribner's Magazine* in 1889, reflects the simple pleasures they experienced once they had abandoned city life.

> When you forget the beauty of the scene
> Where you draw breath and sleep,

1. Michael Boris Shimkin, *Contrary to Nature* (Washington, D.C., 1977), 175–76.

Leave city walls for gleams of sky that lean
To hills where forests creep.

The heights, the fields, the wide-winged air
Make the embracing day;
Not city streets. That little life of care
Steals our great joys away.

Live with the spaces, wake with the bird and cloud,
Spread sentient with the elm;
Our home is nature, even to the proud
Arcs of the sunset's realm.

Then say the scene God made is glorious!
Breathe deep and smile again.
The glow of noble dusks, victorious,
Disperse regrets and pain.[2]

Rose continued writing and publishing from her new location, but as had been her earlier fate, correspondence from editors included many letters of rejection, some telling her abruptly, some politely, that there was no market for her material, and others remarking that her work was "too difficult for our use" or too obscure. Even letters of acceptance were not always flattering or gracious. When the *Century* agreed to publish "Just Bloomed" in 1889, "the Power," as R. W. Gilder was dubbed, told Rose to omit the last stanza: "We don't care for that stanza much anyhow."[3]

An examination of Rose's manuscript material suggests why some of her short stories were being rejected at this time. Although she continued to write about unrequited love, romantic triangles, and dissimulating coquettes in "Love Kate," "Love Against Love," and "What a Man Will Do," Rose also began to explore themes of social justice in her short fiction. She did so extensively but awkwardly, through implausible and sometimes inconsistent narrative structures. Like "Troth," published in *Harper's New Monthly Magazine* in 1892, two of Rose's unpublished short stories, "An Earl's Cousin" and "The Silent Girl," explore the issue of obligation between benefactors and those in need.

In "An Earl's Cousin," Rose uses a remote setting to tell the story

2. Rose Hawthorne Lathrop, "The Greater World," *Scribner's Magazine,* V (1889), 536.

3. R. W. Gilder to Rose Hawthorne Lathrop, January 24, February 26, March 3, 30, May 3, 1889, all in ASRIC.

of a young gypsy girl, Bertina, who is adopted at the age of three by an earl. To make his beneficence more acceptable he pretends that she is his cousin, and he reveals his dissimulation only when she is old enough to marry him. Bertina is infuriated, and at this point fiction appears to be merely a pretext for debating complex questions of identity, authority, and justice. "Is it—is it to *you* that I owe everything? . . . You have made me most unwillingly your debtor, and . . . I hate you for it," Bertina declares. Elsewhere she muses: "I am wholly dependent upon a young nobleman, who has been obliged to furnish me even with a name. . . . I cannot bear this involuntary sense of obligation;—it turns my heart to stone."[4]

In "The Silent Girl," Rose appears to draw upon her adolescent experience as an impoverished student in a boarding school for wealthy young girls in telling the story of two orphans, one rich and one poor. Celeste Forrester, who comes to the school equipped with good clothing and a hefty allowance, is prevailed upon to accept as her roommate Emily Sandys, whose covetous glances and acerbic remarks present the antithesis of a clichéd, sentimentalized portrait of poverty. Although Celeste shares her possessions with Emily, the latter realizes that "it is not possible to receive idly frequent benefactions without succumbing to an unworthy greed." Emily eventually tricks Celeste out of one thousand dollars, shrewdly calculating that Celeste's generosity will prevent her from revealing her roommate's guilt. But Emily has not counted on the presence of her own conscience, which keeps her awake while Celeste sleeps, and the narrator remarks that the innocent have a defense against the guilty "because [the] very unshielded trust [of the innocent], and their unsordid arguments, can reach so far, and illuminate so unmistakenly, when the other soul opens a single crevice to the light." Of her own volition Emily returns the money to Celeste, who is in turn the recipient of her roommate's aid when Emily helps Celeste overcome her shyness with the other students. Neither girl is, then, in the other's debt, and their friendship can develop freely and without coercion.[5]

Although Rose was not attracting much public attention with her literary efforts, George and Julian continued to be her staunch sup-

4. Rose Hawthorne Lathrop, "An Earl's Cousin" (MS *ibid.*).
5. Rose Hawthorne Lathrop, "The Silent Girl" (MS *ibid.*).

porters and fans. George's career was still flourishing and he was in a position to be aggressive and confident in negotiations over his works with Gilder and the staff of the *Century.* George asked for and received $150 for "The Casket of Opals" in 1888, and $100 for "Marthy Virginia's Hand" in 1890, in contrast with Rose, who that same year sent a piece to the editor of the *Independent* remarking, "If you like this incident use it for the juvenile section . . . for $15.00."[6]

The content of George's works at this point had shifted, as had Rose's, away from romance to issues of national or ethical concern. In 1888 he had published *Gettysburg, a Battle Ode* with Scribner's. The ode had received good reviews and this note of praise from his mother: "The complete absence of national self-glorification in the poem is remarkable—one sees that George holds war to be like the surgeon's knife thrust into the bosom of one we love, only to save the life of that best beloved."[7]

George also succeeded in having several novels published: *Gold of Pleasure* with Lippincott in 1891; *The Letter of Credit* with Collier in 1890; and *Would You Kill Him* with Harper and Brothers also in 1890. *Would You Kill Him,* which was drawn from a contemporary New York crime case, was praised by a reviewer as one of George's best works of fiction, for it tackled the question of capital punishment: "Mr. Lathrop shows that there are punishments for murder which punish more than execution by hanging or electricity; and that it is but a low state of civilization and culture which cuts off the individual, no matter how degraded he may be, from all chance of expiation and atonement."[8]

Notwithstanding the critical acclaim and marketability of George's writing, Rose and George endured their greatest financial difficulties at this time. Mrs. Lathrop wrote to Rose expressing her "hop[e] that George's harvest of fame will turn to fortune." She said that she admired Rose's fortitude amidst limited finances and that she wished she could be of more help in caring for George. She encouraged Rose to prevent him from becoming despondent and undernourished. "I

6. George Parsons Lathrop to R. W. Gilder, September 18, 28, 1887, in Century Company Papers, NYPL; Rose Hawthorne Lathrop to Mr. Ward, January 10, 1890, in ASRIC.

7. Frances Lathrop to Rose Hawthorne Lathrop, July 2, 1888, in ASRIC.

8. Review of George Parsons Lathrop's *Would You Kill Him,* in *Harper's New Monthly Magazine,* LXXX (January, 1890), 328, Sup. 2.

hope it isn't actual poverty but a lack of luxuries [that you feel]," wrote Mrs. Lathrop.[9]

The changes that had taken place in Rose and George's life—their abandonment of New York gaiety for the more constricted financial and social circles in New London, their metamorphoses from writers of romance to fledgling analysts of social injustice—did not suggest the deeper upheavals they were experiencing. Thus, when the news of their conversion to Roman Catholicism under the direction of Father Alfred Young at the Church of Saint Paul the Apostle, in New York City, on March 19, 1891, was carried in no fewer than fifty-six newspapers nationwide, the public's reaction was uniformly one of surprise, if not shock.

The Catholic church in nineteenth-century America was populated with immigrants; Catholicism was, by and large, the faith of the servant class. The Hawthornes themselves had had a devoutly Catholic maid during Rose's adolescence at the Wayside. When finances permitted, Rose employed an Irish servant in New London, Nellie Sullivan, who was also Catholic. But Rose and George, a conspicuous and an established New England couple, "both highly esteemed in the literary world, having entrée into the most exclusive and high-class magazines," were exceptions to the general rule. The Catholic presses announced the Lathrops' conversion with pride. One such press, however, the *Catholic Messenger,* anticipated the reaction of "bigots [who will] question their conversion as in every age, when intellectuals come to the Church." Some reports of the Lathrops' conversion strove to remind the public about the constitutional freedom of religious choice. The *Reporter* in Fond du Lac, Wisconsin, asked, "Don't people have a right to change religion?" and the Philadelphia *Standard* queried, "Why is it necessary in the nineteenth-century era of religious freedom to explain one's conversion?"[10]

Nevertheless, most of the secular papers were overtly hostile to the Lathrops' conversion, sometimes using it as an occasion for *ad homi-*

9. Frances Lathrop to Rose Hawthorne Lathrop, July 2, 1888, January 9, 20, 1890, all in ASRIC.

10. Sophia Hawthorne to Rose Hawthorne, April 30, 1868, in Hawthorne and Lathrop Collections, MA 3400, PML; Nellie Sullivan to Rose Hawthorne Lathrop, September 16, 1891, November 29, 1892, both in ASRIC; *Catholic Messenger,* April 4, 1891, Fond du Lac *Reporter,* March 30, 1891, Philadelphia *Standard,* April 11, 1891 (Clippings in ASRIC).

nem attacks upon George. The Boston *Traveler* condescendingly remarked that the announcement of the couple's conversion "will not surprise so many people as Mr. Lathrop fancies. It is just like him." The Boston *Beacon* stated, "Considerable publicity ha[s] been given to the fact that an author of limited importance has joined a certain church." This report continues with the erroneous information that this was George's third or fourth change in religion. Similar distortions of fact were printed in other newspapers. The *News* in Tacoma, Washington, printing as its headline "Turned Catholic / George Parsons Lathrop and Wife," reported that the news of the Lathrops' conversion was originally disbelieved because of their "agnostic tendencies."[11]

So virulent were these attacks, specifically upon George, that he published an apologia in the April 30 New York *Independent,* a newspaper that had roundly condemned his actions. George denied the contention that he and Rose had been unbelievers: Rose had been a Unitarian, and he, an Episcopalian; thus, he explained, "Christianity was not belated study." George defended his conversion, insisting upon "reason as an essential groundwork of belief." Protestantism, he wrote, was "pre-eminently a matter of the heart and sundry vague 'leadings' of the spirit; and that between reason and belief there is a gap which can be crossed only by using a sort of leaping-pole of unquestioning, unreasoning belief." Catholicism, said George, allowed for a union of head and heart. Responding to objections that he was now surrendering his intellect to the arbitrary control of the pope, George retorted that "unreasoning obedience is absurd"; Catholics, he asserted, are obligated to obey the pope only when he speaks *ex cathedra.* Nonetheless, George found papal authority a comforting "provider of unity." He maintained that Protestants "magnify personal judgment into a sort of fetish."[12]

Clearly George was drawn to Catholicism by what he perceived to be a reasoning and an ordering principle. He derived intellectual satisfaction from the notion of a consistent papal authority, as did Orestes Brownson, the New Englander whose voyage through Uni-

11. Boston *Traveler,* March 28, 1891, Boston *Beacon,* April 4, 1891, Tacoma *News,* April 1, 1891 (Clippings in ASRIC).

12. New York *Independent,* April 30, 1891 (Clipping in ASRIC).

tarianism and transcendentalism and support for the Brook Farm experiment culminated in what has been called "a flight to the patriarchal structure of Catholicism." Using an essentially masculine approach to explain and justify his conversion, George did not, however, persuade his detractors. They retorted that though he had spoken "much about reason he gave no reason" but seemed "to be grasping air."[13]

Rose was not similarly compelled to justify her conversion for the public record. Given the temper of the times, the motives for her conversion seem, at least on the surface, less logical than George's were for him, less consistent with the person she appeared to be. One would have assumed that Unitarianism—with its historical associations with the *Dial* and the Brook Farm experiment; with its tradition of support for benevolent and reform causes, including the movement for the enfranchisement of women; with its membership encompassing some of the most important women's rights activists of the nineteenth century—would have been more compatible than Catholicism with the clearly feminist attitudes she had expressed in her poetry and fiction.[14]

For an understanding of Rose's conversion, then, one must look beyond the conditions of religious denominations and women in nineteenth-century America to the junction between Rose's personal experience and the feminization of American religion. *Feminization* in this context does not refer to the fact that women constituted the majority in American Protestant churches during the nineteenth century, though this was, of course, true; nor does it refer to the increasing access to positions of governance women were experiencing in some denominations. Rather, in late nineteenth-century America, religion was feminized by the incorporation into belief and practice qualities conventionally associated with or characterized by the feminine—the aesthetic, sentient, emotionally satisfying aspects of worship. This feminization of religion was an antidote to the cerebral, excessively rational, unemotional, and masculine approach to religion epitomized by Unitarianism.

13. Barbara Welter, *Dimity Convictions: The American Woman in the Nineteenth Century* (Athens, Ohio, 1979), 86; New York *Independent,* April 30, 1891 (Clipping in ASRIC).

14. George Willis Cook, *Unitarianism in America* (Boston, 1902), 155, 322–69.

When Rose reflected in her memoirs upon her parents' writings about Catholicism as they encountered it during their sojourn in Italy, she was particularly attracted by the elements that could be considered feminine. Rose was drawn to their description of a religion that added solace, comfort, solemnity, and pageantry to the human condition. Nathaniel himself had written: "The popish religion certainly does apply itself most closely and comfortably to human occasions." Indeed, one reviewer of *The Marble Faun* had remarked that "Mr. Hawthorne seems to have been greatly attracted by Catholicism." Sophia and Nathaniel had attempted to dismiss lightly the public's reaction to Nathaniel's "tantalizing vagueness and conscienceless Catholicity." Nonetheless, Sophia had more than once been made uneasy by the attraction she and her husband felt toward a religion they had previously held in contempt, and she had felt compelled to assure her sister Elizabeth that there was no "danger of Rose being anything else but a Unitarian."[15]

The world of art and the great masters, Rose thought, had provided Nathaniel and Sophia with their most immediate access to Catholicism: "In art, Catholicity was utterly bowed to by my relatives and their friends, because without it this great art could not have been." Rose further concluded that her parents believed Catholicism "capable of being wholly perfect. Glorious scenes were constantly soothing this sense of human sorrow, scenes such as cannot be found in regions outside the Church." Rose recalled her mother's description of the Church of Santo Spirito in Florence upon entering it for a moment's respite from the heat. There she happened upon the funeral service for a child. The glow of candles and the altar cloths created a "splendid picture. . . . [T]he organ burst forth in a kind of tender rapture, rolling pearly waves of harmony," wrote Sophia. Rose, possibly comparing this description to Francie's funeral, interpreted her mother's reaction thus: "The pettiness of a brief burial service in a private parlor or in a meagre meeting-house would not have touched [Sophia's] heart so profoundly, because it would not have recalled heaven so impressively in all its grandeur and tender-

15. J. Hawthorne, *Hawthorne and His Wife,* II, 178, 252; R. H. Lathrop, *Memories,* 411; Sophia Hawthorne to Elizabeth Palmer Peabody, n.d., in Hawthorne and Lathrop Collections, MA 3400.

ness. She evidently perceived here the sweet and even cheering veracity of a devotion that is glad to remember all the possibilities of reverent observance, each motion and aspect of which have a reference to God and to religious history."[16]

In addition to interpreting her parents' experience of Catholicism, Rose recalled her own childhood religious encounters in Rome. She thought the processions that came through the city were "child's play," but, she wrote, in the cathedrals "the monks and boys impressed me differently. Who does not feel, without a word to reveal the fact, the wondrous virtue of Catholic religious observance in the churches? The holiness of these regions sent through me waves of peace." Whether these are accurate representations of impressions acquired some thirty-five years earlier is not as important as the meaning these experiences assumed when Rose reflected upon Catholicism. This religion was not for her something that she could, even if she so desired, explain or defend rationally. Rather, through symbol, aesthetic experience, and feeling, Catholicism gave Rose an ineffable peace "without a word to reveal the fact."[17]

If Rose's conversion seems illogical given her former life and beliefs, it may well have been, for a logical faith was not what she sought. Unlike George, who attempted to explain his conversion in intellectual terms, a method that suggests an apotheosis of Unitarian rationality, Rose seems to have perceived Catholicism as the antithesis of Unitarianism, and to have delighted in the difference between the two. She filled the "chilling void" with a church she perceived to be overflowing with tradition and history. Rose's conversion can be compared to that of Sophia Ripley, another New Englander from a prominent Unitarian family historically associated with the Brook Farm experiment. As Barbara Welter maintains, Catholicism brought into religious belief and practice "the love and warmth so characteristic of women and so necessary to them," uniting Ripley "for the first time with humanity, and that chill intellectual pride which New Englanders wore like Eleanor[e]'s mantle at last melted away."[18] It is interesting that Welter's analysis of Ripley's

16. R. H. Lathrop, *Memories,* 369, 389, 390.
17. *Ibid.,* 377.
18. Welter, *Dimity Convictions,* 101.

conversion alludes to a short story by Nathaniel Hawthorne. In "Lady Eleanore's Mantle," the title character, proud and beautiful, scorns her connection with common humanity. The lavishly embroidered mantle that she wears, symbolizing both wealth and haughtiness, is in reality the carrier of an infectious disease. This disease, which becomes an epidemic in colonial New England, disfigures and eventually kills Eleanore.

Precisely the warmth and humanity perceived to be part of Catholicism was what Julian could affirm when he wrote to his sister about her conversion, for, though the press and public reacted harshly, some of the Lathrops' friends and relatives responded with tolerance, if not complete sympathy. "The Catholic Church," Julian wrote, "offers more substantial assistance than any other to the leading of a worthy life; and the grandeur of its ritual, and its venerable history, win the mind and soothe the heart." Perhaps Julian had been mollified by Rose's gesture in selecting Hildegard as her patron saint and Hildegarde as her confirmation name when she and George were confirmed by Archbishop Michael Augustine Corrigan on March 21. Hildegarde was the name of Julian's oldest daughter, now a young woman, who had always enjoyed a special bond of closeness with her aunt. After her conversion, Rose sometimes referred to herself as "Rose Hildegarde."[19]

Hildegarde Hawthorne, too, wrote Rose and George that despite their religious differences, she hoped that "our Father will make you happy." Rose's lifelong friends Mattie and Nellie expressed similar sentiments, emphasizing their oneness with Rose as Christians and their consolation in the Lathrops' apparent happiness. George's aunt Amelia voiced her hope that conversion would give Rose "the rest which her soul craves." Not all of the couple's relatives, however, were so optimistic, for Mrs. Lathrop asserted, "Your catholicity appears to my mind totally disintegrating in its influence." And Rose's

19. Julian Hawthorne to Rose Hawthorne Lathrop, March 27, 1891, in ASRIC. In the Catholic tradition, a confirmand takes the name of a saint whose life represents a model the person being confirmed wishes to emulate. Rose may have chosen her name in honor of Saint Hildegard, the twelfth-century visionary, poet, and theologian. Hildegard's life, as described by Barbara Newman, in *Sister of Wisdom: St. Hildegard's Theology of the Feminine* (Berkeley, 1987), would have been an inspiration to a newly converted Catholic woman who was also a feminist.

cousin Mary Peabody expressed her opinions on the matter just as indelicately: "One is apt to think of the lower class of Romanticism in thinking of the Catholics."[20]

Julian had predicted that religion would supply a powerful stimulus to the imagination, and thus he wrote to Rose on her fortieth birthday that he expected "great things" in the realm of literary production both from her and from George as a consequence of their conversion. But that did not occur. George's poor health did not allow him to write with his previous energy, although he did publish a collection of poems, *Dreams and Days,* with Scribner's in 1892, affectionately dedicating the volume to Rose. Nor did conversion act to improve the quality of Rose's imaginative productions if the pile of rejections that she continued to amass from *Harper's,* the *Century,* and other periodicals is any indication. William Dean Howells returned one manuscript without any excuse or apology, stating simply, "I think it is all the more annoying when editors make excuses in returning manuscripts."[21]

These rejections must have been less distressing to Rose now than they were earlier in her life, for her perspective on writing was undergoing a metamorphosis. In March, 1892, Rose acknowledged that "much of my labor has been on long stories that have not yet either been finished, or else have not succeeded. But I am working very hard to dignify my efforts by the name of a profession." Nevertheless, by October of that year, her enthusiasm for writing fiction and poetry had begun to dissipate. "I write a few stories and verses for money solely," she wrote Mattie, "having no time to make more heroic attempts in literature, and am getting old enough of course to begin to lose that fine agony for artistic effort which has made many an hour exquisite pain for me, and yet a sweet pain after all, as pain goes!" Those poems she did continue to write and succeeded in publishing, now frequently in Catholic periodicals, became vehicles for discussing issues of social justice, Christian duty, and the plight of

20. Hildegarde Hawthorne to Rose and George Lathrop, May 7, 1892, Amelia Smith Shotwell to Rose Hawthorne Lathrop, April 8, 1891, Frances Lathrop to Rose Hawthorne Lathrop, March 15, 1892, and Mary C. Peabody to Rose Hawthorne Lathrop, April 13, 1891, all in ASRIC.

21. Julian Hawthorne to Rose Hawthorne Lathrop, May 20, 1891, William Dean Howells to Rose Hawthorne Lathrop, April 30, 1892, both *ibid.*

Rose as a child, painted in 1858 by Cephas Thompson in Rome. Rose drew upon her experience of posing for this portrait in her short story "Lindie's Portrait."

George Parsons Lathrop, in his late twenties or early thirties. George became a successful writer and editor after his marriage to Rose.

Francis "Francie" Hawthorne Lathrop, Rose and George's only child, in what Rose called a "characteristic" pose. The child died at the age of four.

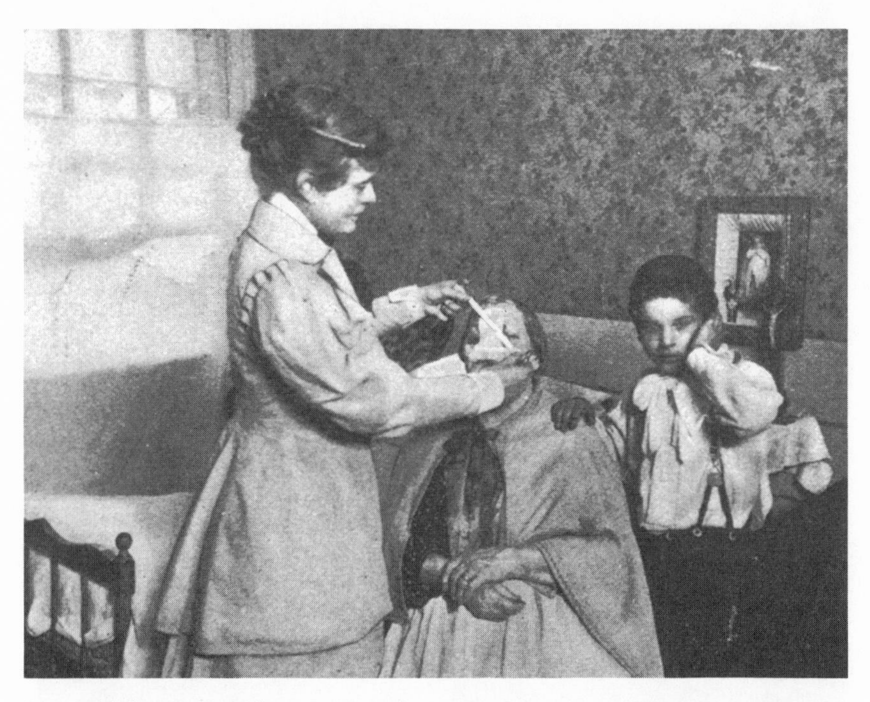

Rose with her first resident cancer patient, Mrs. Watson, and Mrs. Watson's grandson, Willie. The boy became a source of conflict between the women when he moved in with them.

668 Water Street, the second site of Rose's home for cancer patients.

Alice Huber. This young artist from Kentucky began her work with Rose by volunteering one afternoon a week at the Water Street home, but within three months, she had resolved to make nursing the cancerous poor her life's work.

Saint Rose's Free Home for Incurable Cancer, named after Saint Rose of Lima, at 426 Cherry Street. This building, the third location for the home, was bought with donations.

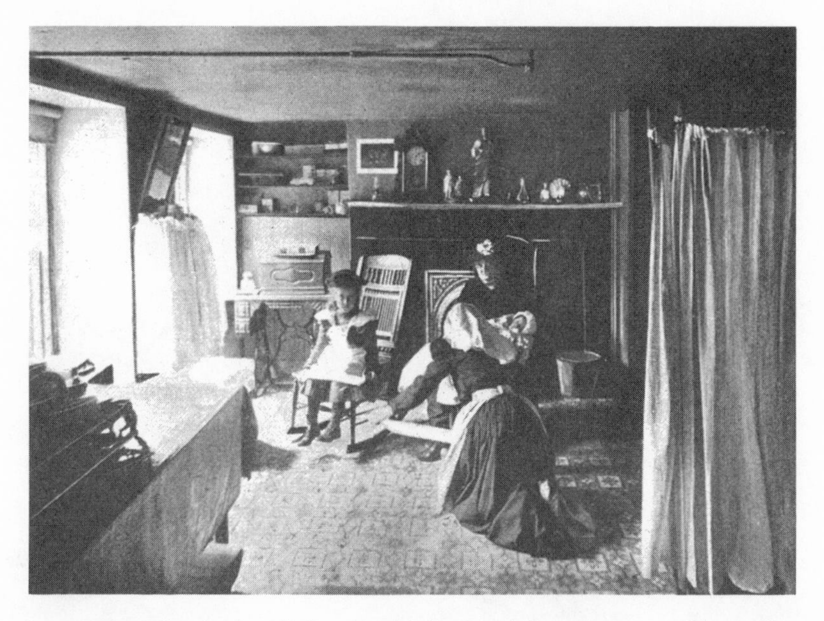

Patients and worker in the relief room of Saint Rose's Free Home, on Cherry Street, where outpatients were received and salve and medicine dispensed. This picture was probably taken before September, 1899, when Rose and her co-workers became Dominican tertiaries and dressed in white gowns.

A patient in the Saint Vincent de Paul Room of Saint Rose's Free Home, on Cherry Street. Vincent de Paul was the founder of the Sisters of Charity, who work among the poor and infirm.

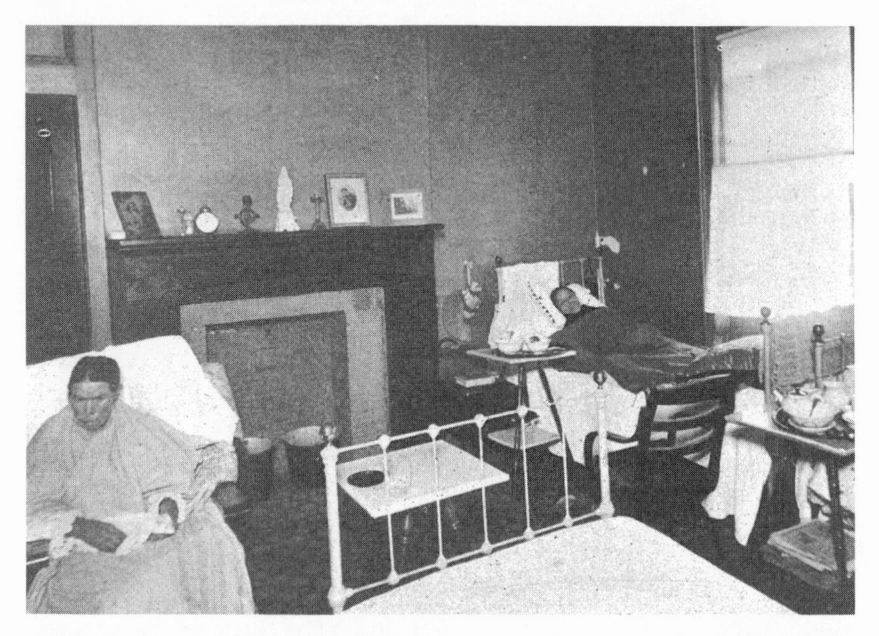

Patients in the upper back room of Saint Rose's Free Home, on Cherry Street. When mass was celebrated in the upper oratory, the doors of that room were opened to allow patients in adjacent rooms to hear it.

Rosary Hill Home. The Servants of Relief for Incurable Cancer had some alterations made to the original structure, purchased from Father I. M. Cothonay in 1901.

Alice Huber, in the habit of the Servants of Relief. After the construction of Rosary Hill Home, Alice, who had taken the religious name Mother Mary Rose, was head of Saint Rose's Free Home in New York City.

Saint Joseph's Home. This transitional fireproof structure was opened as an annex in 1924 and housed patients from Rosary Hill Home until that structure was rebuilt on the original site.

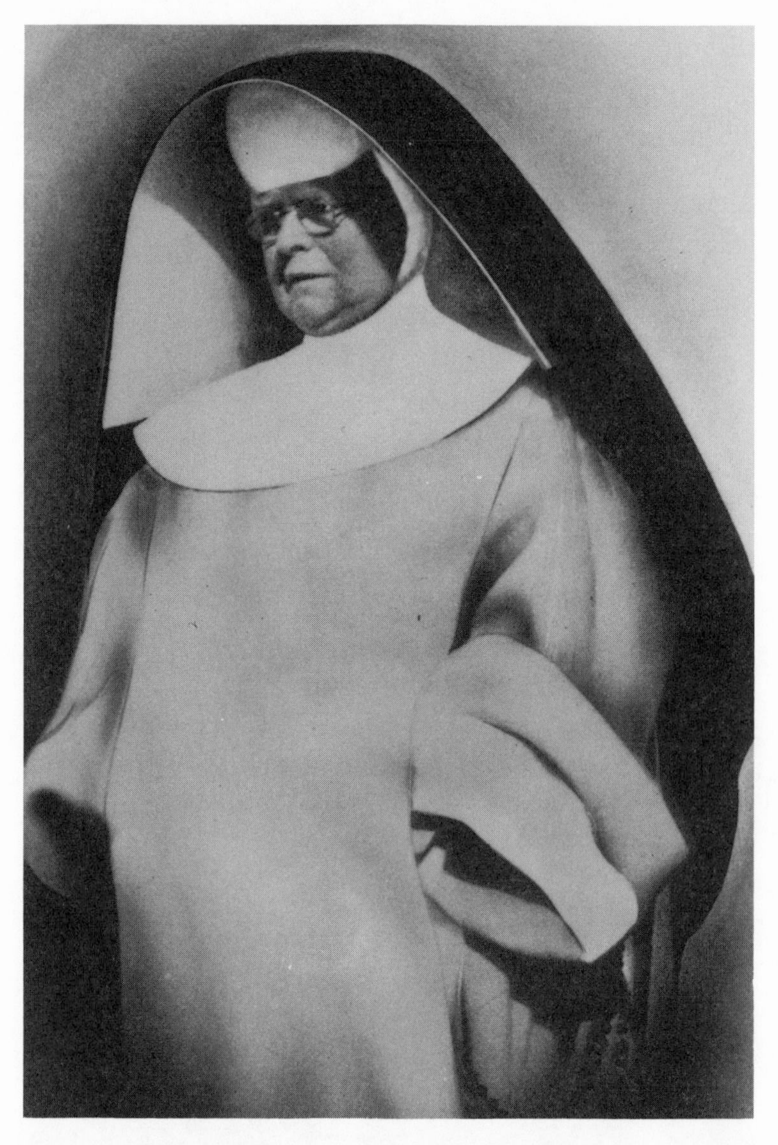

Mother Mary Alphonsa. Having taken a religious name and having been vested with the full Dominican habit, Rose spent the rest of her life caring for cancer patients and serving as mother superior of the Servants of Relief.

the poor and sick. "The Choice," which appeared in the *Catholic World* in October, 1892, is such a poem.

> O lover! filled with glorious joy
> Of heart's success,
> If in your loving be the base alloy
> Of selfishness;
> If for the adored you would not bravely pay
> Service of tears,
> And prove your stalwart fealty day by day—
> Turn not this way!
>
> Lover of Life! if you would ever know
> Life's meaning deep;
> Or how the maimed and fevered thousands go,
> As funerals creep,
> Across the hospital's sad threshold borne;
> If too much pain
> Comes with the life lived round us day by day—
> Turn not this way!
>
> Image of God! if you would serve Christ's love
> But as you will,
> And like the worms with aimless longings move
> In darkness still;
> If too much heart's blood flows when you would pray
> Before the Cross
> When saints their daily tribute duly lay—
> Turn *you* away![22]

Rose sent a copy of this poem to her mother-in-law, and although Mrs. Lathrop praised it, she told Rose emphatically: "You feel that [the] choice for a moral life can be made only within one true church. I do not." In spite of their continuing disagreement over religion, however, Mrs. Lathrop was particularly solicitous and supportive of Rose during this period. Mrs. Lathrop was worried about her son and daughter-in-law's lack of finances. She was distressed, too, by George's poor health and the burden this placed upon Rose. George had been debilitated since his departure from New York by what Rose described as "gastric trouble of the most severe nature." Until

22. Rose Hawthorne Lathrop to Bessie Hunt, March 10, [1892?], in Sophia Smith Collection, NL; Rose Hawthorne Lathrop to Mattie L. Stearns, October 9, 1892, in Henry W. and Albert A. Berg Collection, NYPL; Rose Hawthorne Lathrop, "The Choice," *Catholic World,* LVI (October, 1892), 17.

1892 he was under doctor's orders not to work, which reduced the Lathrops to poverty and forced Rose to assume all household duties. Mrs. Lathrop undoubtedly wished that her daughter-in-law might have what Rose herself desired, the "freedom from so much anxiety" caused both by her confinement to the house in caring constantly for George and by her efforts to save pennies by doing all the mending and other housework. Even Rose and George's friends knew that the couple was in financial difficulty. Helena De Kay Gilder wrote Rose and took the "tremendous liberty" of sending her some money. Mrs. Gilder told Rose that she had heard from her husband, Richard, that the Lathrops were in a "tight place."[23]

In 1892 Rose and George's prospects began to brighten. Mrs. Lathrop wrote to Rose that she was delighted by the occasions when her daughter-in-law could spend "time in literary work rather than society, amateur painting, housework, embroidery, and all that eats up one's days so remorselessly." George's health had begun to rally, and he required less of Rose's attention. In October, Rose and George moved to a new house that, Rose wrote to Rebecca Manning, "we feel will be our permanent home, a pretty little place on a hill, with a view." The period of "bitter money anxiety" now over, "all seems hopeful and easy. We are quite well and happy, and thankful beyond words." Rose was even more expansive about her happiness when she wrote to her sister-in-law, Minne, shortly after Christmas: "George is often well and never very ill now and I cannot thank heaven as I ought for my present life."[24]

Both Rose and George continued to diversify their interests at this time and undertook a variety of projects and challenges. Rose wrote a provocative article entitled "Woman," which was published in the *American Lady* and became the subject of lively discussion between Rose and her mother-in-law. Although both Rose and George gave lectures and had, according to Mrs. Lathrop, "praise from admiring

23. Frances Lathrop to Rose Hawthorne Lathrop, November 11, 1892, February 7, 1892, both in ASRIC; Rose Hawthorne Lathrop to Rebecca Manning, December 4, [1892?], in Hawthorne-Manning Collection, EIL; Rose Hawthorne Lathrop to Mattie L. Stearns, October 9, 1892, in Berg Collection; Helena De Kay Gilder to Rose Hawthorne Lathrop, April 28, 1892, in ASRIC.

24. Frances Lathrop to Rose Hawthorne Lathrop, October 9, 1892, in ASRIC; Rose Hawthorne Lathrop to Rebecca Manning, June 2, [1893?], in Hawthorne-Manning Collection; Rose Hawthorne Lathrop to Minne Hawthorne, January 5, 1893, in Berg Collection.

crowds in New London enough to turn your heads," adulation did not produce income, and the couple began to look for the fruition of larger, and possibly more lucrative, projects.[25]

Rose had become acquainted with Mina Edison, the second wife of the famous inventor Thomas Alva Edison. Through this relationship George had attempted a series of biographical essays on Edison. When Edison disapproved of this idea, George suggested a collaborative science fiction venture, to which the inventor consented. In 1890, with Edison's full agreement, George negotiated a contract and obtained advances from *McClure's Magazine*. Edison, however, proved to be impossible to work with; he failed to respond to George's correspondence and neglected to read the drafts George sent him. By August, 1891, George found himself in an extremely awkward situation: "McClure has made me certain payments on the work which I am not in a position to refund," he wrote Edison, "and I ought not to be left liable to refund them through delay on your part. . . . I have never been placed in such a position before and shall take exceedingly good care never to be led into a similar predicament again." Although Edison never fulfilled his obligations concerning this project, he apparently arranged for George to write the brochure that General Electric used at the Chicago world's fair of 1893, thereby offsetting some of George's financial losses on this project.[26]

Undaunted by this failure, George turned his energies to an effort for the benefit of young people. In conjunction with the Missionary Society of Saint Paul the Apostle (the Paulist priests) he established the Catholic Summer School of America in New London during the summer of 1892. Rose helped as George's secretary while he attempted to fulfill his literary obligations, for this work with the summer school produced no income. It did, however, bring Rose and George into daily contact for the first time in their lives with priests and nuns, people Rose perceived to be "those devoted more completely and definitely to God." Rose was fascinated by the encounter: "To know these priests and nuns at all intimately is to know that their daily energy, their daily renunciation of natural impulses for comfort and ease and freedom from moral severity possess a power and virtue

25. Frances Lathrop to Rose Hawthorne Lathrop, September 1, 25, 1892, both in ASRIC.
26. Robert Conot, *A Streak of Luck* (New York, 1979), 340–42.

beyond our lay energy, our lay asceticism. I feel that I pass close to spirits that purify and give strength."[27]

Late in 1892 Rose and George began another large project, one that fostered their reflection upon the means of creating a perfected human society. They traveled to Washington, D.C., where they examined the archives of the convent of the Visitation of the Blessed Mary to collect material for a history of that order in America. Published by Houghton Mifflin in 1894, *A Story of Courage: Annals of the Georgetown Convent of the Visitation of the Blessed Mary* bears the names of George and Rose as coauthors. In fact, the work was written in the early months of 1893 by Rose alone, with her husband assisting in a limited editorial capacity. George was sometimes in poor health, and Rose spent January through April of that year working on *A Story of Courage* while attending to his needs, running errands for him, and praying for his recovery and relief from pain.[28]

A Story of Courage met the type of mixed and partisan reception accorded the news of the Lathrops' conversion. The *American Catholic Quarterly Review* explicitly identified the content of this with the conversion of its authors, assuming "that they like the Visitation sisters have had to deal with hostility." The Boston *Courier* was fairly objective in its assessment of the work, citing the authors' position that religious bodies "are the only organizations that have solved the problem of community life on a great scale." Another review, however, stated that the book was "disfigured by proofs of sectarian narrowness and traces of old bigotry and new zeal imperfectly mellowed." Still another review began by remarking harshly that "all Protestantism never has made and never can make a nun," though some denominations produce "types of termagant women, who believe in saving the world by sewer gas and temperance pledges," but concluded that "the convent, like Dante . . . is the sacred heart of Christendom."[29]

27. Rose Hawthorne Lathrop to Mattie L. Stearns, October 9, 1892, in Berg Collection.

28. See, for example, Rose Hawthorne Lathrop Diary, January 9, 13, 14, 19, February 1, 3, 1893 (ASRIC).

29. Reviews of George Parsons Lathrop and Rose Hawthorne Lathrop's *A Story of Courage: Annals of the Georgetown Convent of the Visitation of the Blessed Mary,* in *American Catholic Quarterly Review,* n.d., 215, Boston *Courier,* n.d., New York *Globe,* January 7, 1895, p. 47, and *Critic,* May 25, 1895, p. 378 (clippings in ASRIC).

As a history, the work is flawed by inconsistency and inaccuracy, but the narrative biographies of some of the early members of the community, several of whom were relatives of prominent Americans, nonetheless make interesting reading. Many of the women described in the book became nuns in midlife, some leaving their families behind to do so. Jane Frances de Chantel, the cofounder of the order, which began in France, was one such woman, and her life makes particularly entertaining and provocative reading.

Born in Savoy, France, in the sixteenth century, de Chantel was a wealthy widow with children when she was drawn to extend her benevolence and consolation to the poor and dying. Believing "the poor are not merely suffering human beings; they are our Lord himself concealed under rags," she decided to leave her family to devote herself exclusively to this task. Rose drew a portrait of de Chantel as a woman who

> was considered by everyone in her family and acquaintanceship almost—inhuman for daring to propose to leave her four children and her father and her father-in-law to take some care of themselves. But the result proved her wisdom. Her service for her children, her care for them, and her inspiration given to them, were helps such as few children received from their mother. She not only had the capacity to be a nun, but a consummate woman of business as well. . . . She was as strong-willed and full of the fire of executive ability as a man, but was also in possession of a woman's lavish mercy and sensitive recognition of her dependence upon divine power. Here were two opposing forces in the noble soul of Jane de Chantel.[30]

Rose evidently held a high opinion of this woman for whom altruism was a more potent force than maternal feeling—the former sentiment akin to the one Rose herself had expressed in her poem about her child's death: "I loved a child as we should love / Each other everywhere." Rose also praised de Chantel's exercise of will and her ability to function in a traditionally male sphere as the executor of her own estate and the conventual holdings. For women living in cultures that expected marriage and child rearing to be the inevitable course of events, Catholicism presented historical models of women who were sanctioned to function outside the domestic sphere. These

30. George Parsons Lathrop and Rose Hawthorne Lathrop, *A Story of Courage: Annals of the Georgetown Convent of the Visitation of the Blessed Mary* (Boston, 1894), 134, 140.

models were as necessary in the nineteenth century as they had been in the sixteenth, and thus for Rose, and doubtless many other women, the Catholic church offered ways of life that were not incompatible with their feminist views.[31]

Rose clearly admired the positive influence upon society exercised by women like de Chantel, and she recalled the remarks of French philosopher and critic Hippolyte Taine on the benefits nuns had provided to society by "choosing to devote themselves to dangerous, revoltant, and . . . ungrateful services." The Visitation convent in America, Rose stated, was a "historic monument of great value. . . . [I]t appears, to us in our modern day, as the work of women, who have demonstrated through it their power in practical, executive management as well as in the exercise of holy influences."[32]

Thus Rose praised and was drawn to the tangible good works as well as the intangible "holy influences" of the nuns' way of life. Recalling previous secular experiments in forming "community associations"—she was without doubt thinking of the Brook Farm experiment, with which her father, her aunt, and some of her acquaintances had been associated with varying degrees of enthusiasm—Rose declared that religious women "have solved the question of community life on a great scale." She wrote, "The science of humane love of our kind—usually 'in the world' exemplified only in a mother's love—is a part" of a greater, more perfect love. "In the world we are apt to think this 'brotherly' love among the human family is the most spiritual thing possible, the *summum bonum,* the complete circle of everything not material and selfish. To the nun, this mother's love, brother's love, love of friend, is the mere A B C, or beginning of the language of spiritual works; the instrument of the poetry of higher action, which must be brought into play, towards all human creatures alike."[33]

Rose ended *A Story of Courage* along much the same line of

31. Sister Elizabeth Kolmer, in "Catholic Women Religious and Women's History: A Survey of Literature," in *Women in American Religion,* ed. Janet Wilson James (Philadelphia, 1980), 138, speculates that, because Catholic women had for centuries the option of careers and non-domestic ways of life afforded through sisterhoods, Catholic women did not share their Protestant sisters' need to identify themselves with the women's rights movement in the nineteenth century.

32. G. P. Lathrop and R. H. Lathrop, *A Story of Courage,* iv.

33. *Ibid.,* v, 135.

thought: "The private family, essential though it is, and beautiful as it is when imbued with holiness and sacramentally blessed is only a type of the whole human family, and hence is less important than that." In her study of the Visitation sisters, Rose perceived a mode of living that embodied thoughts and feelings inchoate in her for more than a decade. "Nothing is so sunny, I think, as married happiness," she had written to Mattie at the height of her domestic joy as wife to George and mother to Francie. Yet even in the midst of this happiness she had avowed, "There is so much else that is beautiful and sweet in the world," and conventual life presented itself to her as just that. Combining benevolent works for society with a communal existence that Rose regarded as almost utopian, life in a religious community made family and married life pale by comparison.[34]

While Rose's life was beginning to change, her brother had undertaken a move. At the end of 1892, Minne Hawthorne had asked Rose and George to use their influence with R. W. Gilder to have him, in turn, intercede with President Grover Cleveland to appoint Julian as consul to Jamaica. Although Julian failed in his attempts to become consul, he was able to move his family to Jamaica into a home that they called the Gardens.[35]

Rose had, by this point in her life, all but abandoned poetry and fiction. Lecturing and writing articles and essays were becoming Rose's true métier and one that the public rewarded. The Catholic Columbian Congress was being held in Chicago in conjunction with the World's Columbian Exposition, and Rose traveled there to deliver an impassioned speech for women's rights: "Oh, woman, the hour has struck when you are to arise and defend your rights, your abilities for competition with men in intellectual and professional endurance, the hour when you are to prove that purity and generosity are for the nation as well as the home."[36] Evidently Rose experienced no incompatibility between her recently acquired religion, her enthusiasm for religious communities, and her decidedly feminist sentiments.

34. *Ibid.*, 373.

35. Minne Hawthorne to Rose Hawthorne Lathrop, December 30, 1892, in ASRIC; Bassan, *Hawthorne's Son,* 197.

36. James J. Hennesey, *American Catholics: A History of the Roman Catholic Community in the United States* (New York, 1981), 191.

In March, 1894, Rose's article "My Father's Literary Methods" was published in the *Ladies' Home Journal.* The topic was one that the magazine had chosen for her. Accompanied by lovely photographs Rose had provided and sketches she had made of the Wayside, this article makes pleasant reading, though it reveals as much about Rose's values as it does about her father's literary habits. Nathaniel's method, Rose avowed, "was to love and pity mankind more than he scorned them." Elsewhere she stated that "he did not waste time. . . . Men of success detest inactivity," and that "he did not write anything wholly for the pleasure of creative writing, but had moral motives."[37]

The article, the first Rose had written about either of her parents, was immensely popular and prompted invitations to make speeches and give public readings, which she did, perhaps to the point of exhaustion. In June, 1894, Rose began corresponding with Bessie Hunt, a childhood friend, about one such invitation. Rose found "alluring indeed" the prospect to "air my views and absorb nice little sums of money. . . . I will ask the remuneration I have hitherto; $25.00 and my expenses for each reading." She offered to read from her own poetry, to present one of two essays, "The Art Above Art" or "Resolution," or to give "sketches of Emerson, Thoreau and Alcott." Final arrangements were delayed, however, owing to what Rose described to Bessie as a "break down . . . in the nature, I suppose, of nervous prostration; I have felt it coming on for months, and have had a good deal of trouble with my heart, which culminated in a pretty alarming state."[38]

Rose eventually proceeded with these lecture plans, possibly because of the encouragement of her mother-in-law, husband, brother, and friends, who persuaded her that she "should find it so interesting." Undoubtedly a more cogent reason for undertaking these lectures was that she perceived them to be "useful," for "to do something that is of use to good ends," she wrote Bessie, "is my longing." Therefore, during the summer of 1894, she had half a dozen such engagements booked in a variety of places, and Rose, as

37. Rose Hawthorne Lathrop, "My Father's Literary Methods," *Ladies' Home Journal,* XI (March, 1894), 371.

38. Rose Hawthorne Lathrop to Bessie Hunt, June 10, August 20, October 4, [1894?], all in Sophia Smith Collection.

well as George, was pleased, particularly by the income these talks generated.[39]

Rose sought to capitalize further on the popularity of her article on Nathaniel. In the spring of 1894, she began corresponding with Gilder about what she called "the Lenox material," a number of theretofore-unpublished letters of her mother's that recounted Sophia's early life with Nathaniel. George helped both as an editor—he suggested condensing some letters—and as an advocate for Rose with Gilder. "The Hawthornes in Lenox: Told in Letters by Nathaniel and Mrs. Hawthorne" was published in the *Century* at the end of 1894.[40]

Rose immediately began planning to incorporate other unpublished letters in a series of reminiscences. She wrote to Gilder about a projected work of 25,000 to 30,000 words and sent him an outline of "Memories of Hawthorne," her recollections from "the girlish standpoint." Rose pointed out to Gilder that this would be the last work on her father from the family material, containing some of his unpublished letters. She defended the propriety of presenting her parents' life so intimately, stating that the letters represented "a good idea of the general atmosphere, and so on, of my father's early English impressions." Although Rose originally asked for one thousand dollars from Gilder, she changed her request to five hundred dollars for a shorter work. The *Century,* however, did not publish the work.[41]

During 1894 George also corresponded with Gilder about a large and ambitious project, an operatic version of *The Scarlet Letter.* George was writing the libretto, and he wanted it published separately and in advance of the opening of the opera, which Walter Damrosch was to produce and score. Rose wrote to Bessie of the pleasure she and George had experienced listening to Damrosch play the music for the opera on the piano, "singing the words as well as he could. The fervor of this young man and the beauty of his music, to

39. Rose Hawthorne Lathrop to Bessie Hunt, June 10, August 20, [1894?], both *ibid.;* Rose Hawthorne Lathrop to Rebecca Manning, June 23, 1894, in Hawthorne-Manning Collection.

40. Rose Hawthorne Lathrop to R. W. Gilder, July 15, [1894?], in Century Company Papers. "The Hawthornes in Lenox: Told in Letters by Nathaniel and Mrs. Hawthorne," *Century,* XLIX (November, 1894–April, 1895), 86–98.

41. Rose Hawthorne Lathrop to R. W. Gilder, March 12, 13, May 3, 13, June 11, July 2, [1894?], all in Century Company Papers.

say nothing of the noble words, made the experience an enchanting one."[42]

On January 5, 1895, Rose and George attended a "pleasant event" at Carnegie Hall in New York City—the first act of the opera. Emma Eames took the part of Hester, accompanied by a chorus of five hundred voices. "I am in ecstasies over the whole thing," Rose wrote to Bessie, "as I wholly enjoy the new guise of the great book. . . . [M]y father says in his Note-books that the novel could be made into an opera, but not into a play. The music gives the atmosphere rendered by the description part of the novel, which would be lost in drama alone."[43]

The Lathrops stayed with the sculptor Augustus Saint-Gaudens and his wife in New York, one of many reasons this trip was a personal and professional triumph for both Rose and George. Rose was obviously thrilled with the conception and execution of her father's masterpiece as an opera, the realization of which was largely due to her husband's inspiration and effort. As a couple, Rose and George seemed to be enjoying "New York social delights" with their "friends, people artistic and otherwise."[44]

While in New York Rose continued to write to Bessie about arrangements for a talk she was planning to give in Boston in several days. When she returned to New London, she proceeded with these preparations, alluding briefly to a trip she was planning to Jamaica. "It has been about decided," she stated, "that I start on a visit to my brother and family in the West Indies on February 9th." In a later letter, explaining to Bessie the constraints upon her schedule, Rose mentioned the "arranging of my house and little affairs for my absence in Jamaica." Only a hint of the radical nature of this voyage came in a letter dated January 26, 1895, when once again explaining her inability to assume further engagements to lecture, Rose remarked, "I have so much to attend to . . . getting my odds and ends in order in case I am stopped by fire or water from ever returning to my little home."[45]

42. Rose Hawthorne Lathrop to Bessie Hunt, December 15, [1894?], in Sophia Smith Collection.

43. *Ibid.*

44. *Ibid.;* Rose Hawthorne Lathrop to Bessie Hunt, January 7, [1895?], in Sophia Smith Collection.

45. Rose Hawthorne Lathrop to Bessie Hunt, January 13, 19, 26, [1895?], in Sophia Smith Collection.

Rose sailed for Jamaica as scheduled, and upon her arrival she recorded her impressions of the beauty of that tropical island with the detail of any tourist traveling merely for pleasure. The purpose of this trip, however, was not sight-seeing. Rose was placing a lasting wedge between herself and her husband of more than twenty-three years. In a lengthy letter to her friend Charlotte Holloway, Rose described the circumstances surrounding her departure from George. This leave-taking had undoubtedly been traumatic for both of them with its "taint of ugly talk and degrading quarrelsomeness . . . [and] the wordy and one-sided violence that fills my days and home more and more." Rose believed that because she was a devoted Catholic, she had a "duty towards usefulness," and, although Rose was sensitive to George's distress, her resolution was firm: "It was not without years of prayer and thought and patience and weighing wise counsel, that I have taken the step I have in leaving my husband's care forever. His pain now in the separation is very sad. I doubt that it is greater than the long pain I have suffered and ever much suffer. When he learns to offer this pain to Christ and make it purify him, he will ennoble it and become helpful to others who have not as much courage."[46]

In this letter, Rose made clear that her decision to leave George was tied to her desire to lead a religious life. Convent life, she believed, would be perfectly "suited for one of my temperament and associations and talents (such as they are)." Therefore, she concluded, "This idea and longing have been so constantly with me for three years, so constantly the object of my prayers, that I have no doubt they are the greatest love of my heart . . . [the] beauty of a home is dross compared to the beauty of the shabbiest altar. . . . I would have suffered anything to prevent scandal, because my husband and I are Catholic converts, but I could not prevent it. . . . I hope my husband will grow to lead a holy life."[47]

On Palm Sunday of that year, George sent Rose a blessed palm with the words "To Rose with love from George" written upon it. Perhaps George wanted to symbolize that he believed her religious fervor to be compatible with their married life. But Rose was reso-

46. Rose Hawthorne Lathrop to Charlotte Holloway, April 22, 1895, in Berg Collection.
47. *Ibid.*

lute and sought to prevent further unwanted approaches from her husband. Thus, when she planned her departure from Jamaica in May, she wrote to Houghton, with whom she had corresponded about a position for her nephew Henry Hawthorne, that she was proceeding to Canada. She said that she wished to reside with the Grey Nuns of Montreal "without publicity or interference."[48]

Rose voyaged upon the *Alena,* which docked briefly at Cape Hatteras. There she wrote to Mattie in detail about her plans. The convent of the Grey Nuns was a residence where women could go on retreat, and rooms could be rented inexpensively. Rose envisioned that a sojourn there would prepare her to adopt the life of a nun, for the boarders at this convent could

> take part in care of the sick, in the hospital attached to the convent, or visit the poor, or do *anything* they choose in their own lines of work. My hope has been to learn *nursing,* and the way has at last been opened and granted to me. After I have learned this blessed art to some extent, and also become familiar with devotional exercises, and the care of souls of the sick and dying . . . I can *intelligently* teach the poor who are ignorant of God the wonders of his love, or fulfill the devout exercises they long for in their distress, [and I wish] to work in New York. . . . I feel very weak and stupid at the entrance to my work, but I know that this is usually the way, for Mr. Satan knows where to attack better than any general.[49]

Rose arrived at the convent on June 7, 1895, and contrary to her wishes, George discovered her whereabouts. In his concern for Rose's well-being, he wrote to the superior of the convent, Mother Deschamps, requesting that she convey a note to Rose and that the nun write him weekly about his wife. Mother Deschamps responded to George's letter, saying that she had given Rose his note and had "advised [Rose] to correspond frequently with [him]. For my part," she continued, "I shall let you know should anything extraordinary occur in reference to her, but must decline your invitation to write each week."[50] Thus George began to realize that his wife's absence from his life was not to be temporary.

Rose left the Grey Nuns at the end of August and took up resi-

48. Rose Hawthorne Lathrop to H. O. Houghton, May 14, 1895, in H. O. Houghton Collection, HL. The inscribed palm leaf is located in the Berg Collection.

49. Rose Hawthorne Lathrop to Mattie L. Stearns, May 26, 1895, in Berg Collection.

50. Mother Deschamps to George Parsons Lathrop, June 18, 1895, AGNM.

dence with the Sisters of Charity of Saint Vincent de Paul of Halifax in Wellesley, Massachusetts, where she made another retreat. The success of her articles on Nathaniel and Sophia continued to bring her invitations to make public appearances. "Some Memories of Hawthorne" appeared in the *Atlantic Monthly* in four installments from February through May, 1896, and then was republished as a book with some revision in 1897 by Houghton Mifflin under the title *Memories of Hawthorne.* Again her articles about her family were well received. Fellow author Elizabeth Stuart Phelps Ward wrote her, "This is just to tell you how moved I am by portions of your papers about your father." Rose enjoyed the praise: "I am so happy in the nice things that were said . . . by people whose taste I value. . . . It seems I have quite hit the literary circles."[51] Ironically, Rose was finally receiving acclaim in the literary world just as she had decided to leave it.

Rose had worked on this series during a period of unhappiness, as she wrote to Rebecca, "and, therefore, ill-health." She had received the sanction of the Catholic church for her separation from George by February, 1896. Although Rose never wavered in her resolution to leave him, she was not insensitive to the sadness this decision brought him, and she wrote to Richard Manning of her "greatest admiration for Mr. Lathrop's powers, and hope for his complete sanctification." Rose continued to be supportive of George's accomplishments. She was enthusiastic about the opening of *The Scarlet Letter* at Carnegie Hall and sent tickets to H. O. Houghton, whom she informed of George's other successes as a lecturer. Houghton was probably the "friend" who accompanied Rose to the gala opening of the opera, "concealing me up in the balcony, and taking care of me lest I meet anyone who might annoy me."[52]

51. Rose Hawthorne Lathrop to Charlotte Holloway, October 9, [?], in Berg Collection; Robert King to Rose Hawthorne Lathrop, December 31, 1895, in Hawthorne and Lathrop Collections, MA 3400; Rose Hawthorne Lathrop, "Some Memories of Hawthorne," *Atlantic Monthly,* LXXVII (1896), 173–86, 373–87, 492–507, 649–60; Elizabeth Stuart Phelps Ward to Rose Hawthorne Lathrop, April 30, 1896, in Hawthorne and Lathrop Collections, MA 3400; Rose Hawthorne Lathrop to Mattie L. Stearns, February 15, 1896, in Berg Collection.

52. Rose Hawthorne Lathrop to Rebecca Manning, January 31, 1896, Rose Hawthorne Lathrop to Richard Manning, February 7, 1896, both in Hawthorne-Manning Collection; Rose Hawthorne Lathrop to H. O. Houghton, December 17, 1895, in Houghton Collection; Rose Hawthorne Lathrop to Mattie L. Stearns, February 15, 1896, in Berg Collection.

Houghton, who was in poor health, was Rose's frequent companion during the spring of 1896. Rose, too, was often ill. Undoubtedly the strain of her separation from George was affecting her, for he refused to accept that their marriage was over. Although she attempted to prevent George from corresponding with her, he did manage to locate her while she was residing with a friend at 125th Street in New York City. He wrote that, at the very least, he wished to be able to send Rose her things from Overdale, as they called the home they had built in New London.[53]

On one occasion George arranged for the two of them to discuss their problems with Father William Pardow, a Jesuit, whom they both knew from the Catholic Summer School and who appears to have functioned as a counselor for them at this time. "I have kept the path open," George wrote to Rose, "for a truly Christian and dignified restoration of harmony." Everyone, George insisted, "has difficulties in a marriage as in every relation, but we were extraordinarily happy a great part of the time." When Rose denied this, he reminded her of "scores of letters and dedications of poems as proof." George must have become concerned that her behavior was symptomatic of a recurrence of the psychiatric disorder she had suffered many years earlier. "It seems to me," he wrote Rose, "that the best hope for your health, peace, and usefulness in this world lies in your putting yourself under thorough and special medical care for the restoration of your nervous system." This suggestion infuriated Rose, and she retorted that George "would prefer to have me in a mental asylum than working for charity."[54]

George wrote again, expressing regret that his words had given Rose pain. But he insisted that she could not truthfully say she no longer loved him or had never loved him. "As you have been the one person most beloved in my life," he declared, "I cannot help thinking of you always. I might as well forget my own existence." But George could say and do nothing to halt the direction of his wife's life. On May 21, 1896, one day after her forty-fifth birthday, Rose Hildegarde

53. Rose Hawthorne Lathrop to Mrs. Lorenz Reich, April 9, 1896, George Parsons Lathrop to Rose Hawthorne Lathrop, April 20, 1896, both in Hawthorne and Lathrop Collections, MA 3400.

54. George Parsons Lathrop to Rose Hawthorne Lathrop, April 10, 20, 27, 1896, all *ibid.* After the close of the April 27, 1896, letter from George, Rose had added her comments.

Hawthorne Lathrop was installed at the New York Memorial Hospital, learning how to care for the dying.[55]

55. George Parsons Lathrop to Rose Hawthorne Lathrop, May 2, 1896, *ibid.;* Rose Hawthorne Lathrop to Mattie L. Stearns, May 21, 1896, in Berg Collection. New York Memorial Hospital was also known as New York Cancer Hospital, although according to Charles Rosenberg, in *The Care of Strangers: The Rise of the American Hospital System* (New York, 1987), 306, general hospitals in New York City refused cancer patients even as late as 1909. Rosenberg cites Thomas Addis Emmet's remarks in *Incidents in My Life* (New York, 1911), 196, that "Memorial Hospital" was the euphemistic title employed by private institutions to avoid the dreaded name "Cancer Hospital."

VII / Sister Mary Alphonsa

When Rose made the decision to dedicate the remainder of her life to caring for the dying, she was not insane, nor was she manifesting symptoms of deteriorating mental health. Nonetheless, her decision to leave George and all that was known and familiar in order to live in poverty with society's outcasts during their last painful moments certainly was not motivated by reason or logic. Rose herself was conscious that what she set out to do was contrary to what some would call good sense. In one of the many essays she wrote after she had turned her pen away from imaginative writing, Rose described the following situation:

> I once heard it told of a young doctor in New London, Connecticut, that several acquaintances of his had accidentally learned of his nursing a poor old woman who was dying of cancer in her meager home, which of course she did not wish to leave for the County-home. His secret was somehow discovered, and our admiration was profound. But we did not dream of emulating him; we kept a firm hold upon our horse-sense. That is a crippling thing after all. There is an ignorance that "blows somebody good," by not knowing in attempting charity work, the manners of liveried civic organized work for the sick and poor.[1]

In June, 1896, an article by Rose entitled "Hawthorne as Worker" was published in the *Cambridge Magazine*. This article, like "Some Memories of Hawthorne," refracts new images not so much of her father as of the person Rose was becoming. In "Hawthorne as

1. Rose Hawthorne Lathrop, "A Knock at the Door" (MS in ASRIC).

Worker," Rose employs an associative method, focusing upon, in her recollections of her father, those qualities that were beginning to dominate her own moral horizons. Thus she describes the theme of Nathaniel's "The Artist of the Beautiful" as "Ideal Fidelity." In this short story, her father drew the character of Owen Warland, who persisted in his solitary attempts to infuse motion into a mechanical butterfly. Having attained his goal, Warland was not himself crushed by the destruction of the butterfly. Hence Rose writes, "We appear even to ourselves, at times, foolish to be so true to our ideal impulses, our weary, persistent labor. . . . We wonder if, after all, our vision is a mere illusion of to-day's material reality, a mechanism of screws and glass; but we know at heart that our faith in honor, our vision of the Beautiful, is the one reality that never breaks or vanishes; and the more miraculously we can give it semblance in this world, the happier for us." Rose concludes this article with the following reflection on the end of her father's life: "Faithful but weary, uncomplaining but destitute of strength, as one is penniless who has given all his substance for the poor, in obedience to the simple direction of Christ when He was asked the whole truth—white-haired, pale, a laborer spent, Hawthorne ended his vigilant life at the close of sixty years of honesty and kindness, keenest perception, and exquisite hope."[2]

Both in this article and in *Memories of Hawthorne,* Rose associates with her father those qualities that she held in high esteem. Nathaniel eschewed all unproductive activity and trivial conversation, she writes. He demonstrated sympathy for all humanity, particularly for those whose poverty was both spiritual and material, as can be seen in his efforts while consul in England in behalf of shipwrecked sailors, his use of his own funds to bury indigents, and his care for destitute travelers. Two separate incidents, however, emerge as particularly significant in her recollections.

On one occasion Nathaniel saved a vase from crashing to the floor. Rose's account of this incident contains as well her analysis of its meaning.

> I remember his standing once by the fire, leaning upon the mantelpiece, when a vase on the shelf toppled over in some way. It was a cheap, lodging-

2. Rose Hawthorne Lathrop, "Hawthorne as Worker," *Cambridge Magazine,* II (June, 1896), 72–73, 79.

house article, and yet my father tried to save it from falling to the floor as earnestly as he did anything which he set out to do. His hand almost seized the vase, but it rebounded; and three times he half caught it. The fourth time he rescued it as it was near the floor, having become flushed and sparkling with the effort of will and deftness. For years that moment came back to me, because his determination had been so valiantly intense, and I was led to carry out determinations of all sorts from witnessing his self-respect and his success in so small a matter. People of power *care* all the time.[3]

This incident struck Rose as important because it demonstrated her father's refusal to abandon to its foregone fate even something that had no apparent value.

Rose was similarly fascinated with Nathaniel's gesture toward a child in an English almshouse. Apparently craving affection, a leprous orphan had approached Nathaniel, who sufficiently overcame his revulsion at the child's diseased appearance to embrace him. Although Nathaniel had recounted this incident in *Our Old Home,* he had not identified himself as the "gentleman" who showed kindness to the child. Sophia, however, revealed the gentleman's identity in a letter to Annie Fields after her husband's death and commented upon the nature of Nathaniel's deed: "Was that not divine! Was it not Christianity in one action—what a bequest to his children—what a new revelation of Christ to the world was that!" This event had occurred when Rose was a child of four and a half with her mother and her sister in Lisbon. Rose had no firsthand knowledge of the incident, but she became aware of Nathaniel's magnanimity by reading his work. Rose's father had ignored the possibility of contagion as he would have in hugging his own children, and thus his embrace of the diseased child acquired for Rose the status of legend and—as Sophia had correctly foretold—legacy. So profoundly did this incident affect Rose and attach itself to her desire to work for the terminally ill that twenty-six years after the original publication of *Memories of Hawthorne,* when the Riverside Press published a new edition of the volume, she made the following remarks in the preface to that edition:

The perfect charity, the instant and practical sympathy of my father for suffering human beings, make the reprinting of my book for the sustenance of victims of a terrible disease very appropriate. The patients of the Servants of Relief for Incurable Cancer, as we call ourselves, are of the class to which belonged the child whom my father found in an English hospital which he

3. R. H. Lathrop, *Memories,* 301–302.

visited and of whom he wrote in *Our Old Home*. His words in regard to this little child, whose flesh reeked with parental desecration, made a deep impression upon me when I read them as a girl; and I was glad to have the latter years of my life devoted to a field of diseased poverty.[4]

Rose had been motivated, in part, by the desire to finance her charity work when she sought the publication of both editions of *Memories of Hawthorne*. During the fall of 1896, she labored on the proofs of the book while she was living in a cramped tenement residence and nursing the terminally ill. Thus her work on the book must have been a particularly arduous task. Nonetheless, she refused help with the index for *Memories of Hawthorne* when she was informed that she could save fifteen dollars by preparing it herself, and she requested a one-hundred-dollar advance in January, 1897, to discharge some debts. But she would "at all costs" to herself correct a "blemish" in the text, for, as she told Houghton, "I hope I have done this work in honor of my father and mother without offending their judgment."[5]

Some reviewers of *Memories of Hawthorne,* however, maintained that Rose had exceeded the boundaries of good taste in publishing her parents' letters to each other and revealing what were considered to be intimate details of their lives. A reviewer for the *Nation,* for example, cited the "indelicacy of revealing Sophia and Nathaniel Hawthorne's love affair." Another reviewer, for the Hartford *Courant,* asserted that the book would appear to some readers a "distasteful thing" and questioned whether "Sophia herself could ever have been reconciled to this display of her adoring love." The reviewer for the *Spectator* felt sure that Nathaniel "would have objected to personal revelations." This sentiment was echoed in the *Critic:* "[It is] curious that Nathaniel Hawthorne should be known so intimately after his death since he was so shy."[6]

Critics also faulted the style of the book, due in large measure to

4. Nathaniel Hawthorne, *Our Old Home,* ed. William Charvat, Roy Harvey Pearce, Claude M. Simpson, and Matthew T. Bruccoli (Columbus, Ohio, 1970), 300–301, Vol. V of William Charvat, Roy Harvey Pearce, and Claude M. Simpson, eds., *The Centenary Edition of the Works of Nathaniel Hawthorne,* 22 vols. projected; Rose Hawthorne Lathrop, *Memories of Hawthorne* (New ed.; Boston, 1923), vi.

5. Rose Hawthorne Lathrop to H. O. Houghton, January 18, 20, February 26, 28, 1897, all in H. O. Houghton Collection, HL.

6. Reviews of Rose Hawthorne Lathrop's *Memories of Hawthorne,* in *Nation,* May 27, 1897, pp. 403–404, Hartford *Courant,* August 10, 1897 (clippings in ASRIC), *Spectator,* May 22, 1897, pp. 735–36, *Critic,* June 5, 1897, p. 389.

the tone created by abundant quotations from Sophia's correspondence. "Mrs. Lathrop's literary methods are inherited entirely from her mother's side," continued the reviewer for the *Nation,* and the reviewer for the *Athenaeum* pointed out that the "perpetual fragrance of incense is apt to stifle."[7]

Putting aside matters of propriety and style, the reviewer for the *Nation* complained simply that there was "still no good biography of Hawthorne." Although the reviewer for the *Dial* conceded that the book was "exceedingly interesting regarding [Nathaniel's] personal life," he concluded that "we don't learn a lot about him as a man of letters." Nonetheless, some of those same reviewers who found flaws could commend the book "to all who love the Hawthornes, and to all who love the best things in literature and life."[8]

Rose seems to have been oblivious of the negative reviews of *Memories of Hawthorne,* writing to Houghton soon after its publication that the "notices have been charming." Apparently what pleased Rose most was the income that the book generated, for she was happily surprised by the immediate revenue from its sale. "My work should often fall to the ground, if I did not have these sums from you," she wrote Houghton; but she attributed the ultimate cause of the bounty to the subject of her book and to "the care that still mercifully comes to me from my father, so long dead to sight."[9]

As grateful as Rose was for the funds derived from the sale of this book, her attitude toward money, or more precisely toward her perennial lack of it, had undergone a metamorphosis. In the past, Rose had often been worried about her unstable finances; but when Rose began her work with the cancerous poor, the lack of a predictable financial base was of no concern to her for she sought poverty as a deliberate and desirable way of life.

In September, 1896, after her summer of training at the New York Cancer Hospital, Rose had searched for rooms to rent in the poorest section of the Lower East Side of Manhattan. Her goal was to establish a facility for nursing the cancerous poor. In this area "with murderous characters about," she had lost her bag. This event did not

7. Reviews of R. H. Lathrop's *Memories of Hawthorne,* in *Nation,* May 27, 1897, p. 404, *Athenaeum,* July 31, 1897, pp. 153–54.

8. Reviews of R. H. Lathrop's *Memories of Hawthorne,* in *Nation,* May 27, 1897, p. 403, *Dial,* August 16, 1897, p. 96. Favorable reviews can also be found in *Literary World,* April 17, 1897, pp. 119–20, and *Outlook,* April 10, 1897, pp. 992–93.

9. Rose Hawthorne Lathrop to H. O. Houghton, May 3, 1897, in Houghton Collection.

make her despondent; rather, she saw it as emblematic, producing, as she wrote to Mattie, the "feeling strangely that here was another step forward towards the absolute poverty which is growing so dear to me." Her firm intention was "to be of the poor as well as among them," and she soon found a suitable apartment in a tenement at 1 Scammel Street. The landlady was remarkably supportive of the project, and the New York City board of health confirmed that no ordinance existed that would prohibit her undertaking the nursing of the terminally ill in these rooms.[10]

Shortly after Rose took up residence on Scammel Street, the New York *Times* ran this notice:

> The daughter of Nathaniel Hawthorne, Mrs. Rose Hawthorne Lathrop, wife of George Parsons Lathrop, the editor and author, has taken up her abode in the tenement house district on the east side of the city. . . .
>
> Mrs. Lathrop has chosen this abiding place in order to carry out her long cherished idea of devoting herself to the nursing of the very poor and lowly who are afflicted with cancer. . . .
>
> The house at 1 Scammel Street is a typical four-story tenement. The hall and stairway are begrimed, the balusters are sticky and unclean, the ceilings are cracked and smoked, and great patches of plaster have fallen off.[11]

The announcement concludes by noting that the rooms Rose occupied, so clean and cheerful, created a conspicuous contrast with their surroundings. When Rose first moved to Scammel Street, she was fully aware that the street was poor and dirty, and she was determined to "make [her] floor a model of neatness." Within ten short days she was able to write Mattie about the successful transformation: "I wish you could see the dirty dark holes I have made with water, paint and muslin, etc. two sweet little rooms."[12]

Life in the Manhattan slum exposed Rose to greater ugliness than dirt and darkness. Domestic violence could be as near as the apartment upstairs, and anti-Semitism caused a good deal of friction among the immigrant poor. Yet even upon these realities Rose seemed able to effect transformations. The woman who lived on the floor above,

10. Rose Hawthorne Lathrop to Mattie L. Stearns, September 14, 1896, in Henry W. and Albert A. Berg Collection, NYPL; Rose Hildegarde [Rose Hawthorne Lathrop], "Items in My Experience of Association with the Poor, as a Servant of Relief," September, 1896 (MS in ASRIC).

11. New York *Times,* October 1, 1896, p. 9.

12. Rose Hawthorne Lathrop to Mattie L. Stearns, September 14, 24, 1896, both in Berg Collection.

and who fought regularly with her husband, showed a gentler side of her personality when she would invite Rose to tea; and Rose reconciled her neighbors to a Jewish woman who resided beneath her on the first floor. Indeed, the first person treated in Rose's dispensary was a Jewish boy who wished to have his leg bandaged.[13]

Rose's life quickly settled into a daily pattern of receiving the sick at eight in the morning, then visiting the housebound sick until one, and then again receiving patients in her modest dispensary. At half past five in the evening she would return to her patients' homes to dress their wounds. All of these activities were interspersed with prayer.

Because of limited space, Rose initially invited only female patients to live with her. The first woman patient to reside with Rose was Mrs. Watson, whom she had met during her internship at the New York Cancer Hospital. Mrs. Watson, Rose recorded, was a person of "peculiar aspect," an accumulation of conflicting images, simultaneously grotesque and picturesque. She was, as Rose described her, "a piece of courage never to be forgotten." Her "crinkled hair was nut-brown, and arranged with a twist, in the style of a hundred years ago, above pretty white ears. . . . Her wrists were piquant and her fingers childlike. Her lips were cherry red, and her chin would have needed no alteration by an artist in dolls." Yet a portion of her face was habitually concealed behind "two neat white bars of adhesive plaster" through which her eyes peered "as if through a prison." Mrs. Watson had a grossly deforming cancer of the face that "was so terrible when wholly exposed" that, Rose remembered, she "trembled as with an ague when first put to the 'dressing' of it."[14]

Nonetheless, Mrs. Watson was the darling of Rose's ward because of her dignity, humor, and generosity. She also inspired admiration because of her devotion to her grandson, Willie, who had been placed in the Catholic protectory. She would venture out on monthly visits to him, bedecked in the "best clothes of the dead, once occupants of the surrounding beds. . . . Over everything else, as a last touch of perfection . . . a huge black lace veil (in reality a shoulder scarf) thus hideously enlarging a huge bonnet, secured on the score of intrinsic value, not of appropriateness or fit. One corner of the

13. Rose Hildegarde, "Items," October, 1896.
14. Mother M. Alphonsa [Rose Hawthorne Lathrop], *Christ's Poor,* I (September, 1901), 13.

heavily arabesqued veil covered her face, and she stood finished in so convulsing a state of spectral suggestiveness—gleams of white plaster glimmering here and there—that a child might have been haunted by her for life."[15]

When she visited her grandson, Mrs. Watson would bring him morsels of food that she had gathered from visitors to the patients in private rooms or by any other method her ingenuity might devise. Although she would leave for these visits in good humor, she would invariably return dejected by the sad condition in which Willie lived at the protectory, and by the more wretched life his widowed mother led in her tenement dwelling.

One day Mrs. Watson disappeared from the hospital, and Rose did not see her again until the woman appeared at the Scammel Street rooms. Mrs. Watson had responded to the announcements in the New York papers, alerting those in need to Rose's whereabouts. Rose was overjoyed to begin her work with Mrs. Watson as her first terminally ill resident patient. "My heart leaped with joy," Rose wrote, "to think that my life of usefulness had begun in earnest, as I stepped forth from the tumble-down tenement to bring my first patient to my hearthstone." In later years, however, Rose came to realize that this initial enthusiasm had been tinctured with naïveté, for Mrs. Watson was to teach Rose much about her new life—its difficulties, its limitations, its humiliations. "It is fortunate," Rose wrote, "that I knew so little as to what I was attempting, or how unreal joy is when come to the heart of human concerns. But life was still wonderfully simple to me, and I expected to make my old friend happy till her death, and then,—foolish arrogance,—I did not mean to let her die."[16]

The Scammel Street residence, with its brightly painted, yellow floor and its scanty furnishings, provided this unlikely pair a home that possessed nothing in the way of comfort, and little in the way of necessities. "We cooked our tea and coffee as gypsies do," Rose recalled, "over open flame, bricks on either side." Rose had warned Mrs. Watson that sometimes they might not have "fire enough on the hearth for cold days, or enough bread or milk for food." But Mrs. Watson was not put off and replied "that she would gladly

15. *Ibid.*, 14.
16. *Ibid.*, 15.

starve and freeze" with Rose, whom she regarded with motherly affection and even referred to as "daughter." Rose, in turn, regarded Mrs. Watson as a welcome companion who performed innumerable services for her, such as scrubbing the floor while Rose attended to errands. Mrs. Watson even reversed their patient-nurse roles during the fall of 1896, when she saw Rose through a bout of pneumonia. "It seemed strange to me," remarked Rose, "considering all this, that many persons who came, marvelled that I could endure the sight of such a terrible disfigurement, and call its possessor by loving titles, whatever was the heart she had. I was complacently satisfied; I neither doubted her worthiness of love, nor suspected my unworthiness of hers, as came about in sadder phases of time."[17]

Rose's relationship with Mrs. Watson slipped into its "sadder phases" when the woman's grandson moved in with them. They had relocated, in 1897, to a larger rented space at 668 Water Street, where they were able to accommodate six live-in patients at a time. Rose had invited Willie to visit his grandmother, and through Mrs. Watson's efforts, the visit evolved into a stay of indefinite length. Handsome though the boy was, Rose immediately perceived that "he was a flourishing slip from criminal roots," an opinion not shared by his grandmother. Although Willie set fires on the roof, hurled bricks down at passersby, and uttered all manner of profanity, Mrs. Watson persisted in believing that he was, if not "a little angel," at least "good-hearted." His presence became more intolerable to Rose when she discovered that "food was hidden away in dark corners for the cherubic, overfed pet, and his pranks and thefts were shielded and denied." Rose realized a humbling truth: It was not in her power both to save this boy from the course of his predispositions and to care for her dying patients. Her resources—emotional, material, and physical—were not sufficient. Rose faced a dilemma: "Should I let Willie be the death of us by keeping him, or should I be the death of Mrs. Watson by sending him back to the institution from which I had called him in foolish confidence?"[18]

Rose sent Willie back to the Catholic protectory, an action that irrevocably changed Mrs. Watson's perception of her. "She asked why I was no longer a saint," Rose recorded, "for I had dashed her dearest

17. *Ibid.* (October, 1901), 15–17.
18. *Ibid.* (November, 1901), 14–16.

illusion to pieces." As Mrs. Watson's health declined, she lost her sight and then her reason, and began accusing Rose of neglecting and starving her. The woman who had once been Rose's companion now became her trial. Nursing the dying with tender care was always to be a difficult task, but Rose now found it doubly so with Mrs. Watson. "I never ceased to 'dress' her face," Rose recalled, "and slept near enough to aid her at all times. . . . But I resented . . . her half insane complaints when we did our best."[19]

Mrs. Watson lingered on until May 3, 1898. In caring for her until her death, Rose had learned that even her own most altruistic actions could be alloyed with hostility. It was a valuable, humbling lesson for Rose to learn so early in her work.

> As I sat by her simple black coffin, in our shanty room, before taking her to our lot for burial, I had no thought for anything but the fact that I was a poor friend to the poor, a heartless judge of a kinder heart than my own, and a darker failure in a better light than the woman who had often prayed for me, and never injured me in the least. Had I not injured her?
>
> All one can conclude is, that God may have special constitutional clauses of mercy for those who try to reach heaven by Alpine climbing, and fall into a crevasse.[20]

Thus Rose came to realize that she would not be sustained in this difficult labor by the adoring gratitude of those for whom she cared. But her supports—financial, spiritual, and emotional—did come, and from a variety of sources. Rose continued to finance her work through donations from friends and acquaintances as well as strangers. Bessie Hunt helped by soliciting aid—as, for example, from the bishop of Manchester—and she also sponsored a lecture program for the benefit of Rose's work.[21]

Substantial donations came in response to Rose's constant appeals to the public through the press. In one lengthy letter to the editor of the *Sun,* Rose asserted that "destitute incurables should be cared for free of charge and until the end of their lives." Rose concluded this letter thus: "I have been obliged to find more airy and somewhat larger quarters, where I expect to remain during the summer, at 668

19. *Ibid.,* 16–17.

20. *Ibid.,* 17.

21. Alice Freeman Palmer to Bessie Hunt, February 7, [1898?], Dennis Bradley [bishop of Manchester] to Bessie Hunt, January 22, [1897?], and Rose Hawthorne Lathrop to Bessie Hunt, February 3, [1897?], all in Sophia Smith Collection, NL.

Water Street, Corlears square. I beg that any donations of money, clothing, or medicines may be sent to the above address." So cramped had her quarters on Scammel Street become that she had been forced to refuse certain donations, such as the offering of "weekly papers and magazines."[22]

What undoubtedly motivated the outpouring of public giving was Rose's own obvious generosity, springing from her deep and certain faith that God had called her to this work. "I see and know and thank God . . . now that I have come to the center of the world's hardest problem," Rose wrote to Bessie. So unrelenting were her efforts that Rose began to conceive of herself as a "machine for expressing love, with no particular personal life," propelled as she was by "the divine human tenderness . . . for all brothers and sisters who are sometimes treated as strangers from a darker star."[23]

As her work grew and flourished, Rose began to experience the emotional support derived from uniting with other dedicated women. Only a year after Rose moved to the lower East Side, she was joined by a young woman with whom she formed a deeply affectionate, supportive relationship and whose love and commitment would be of utmost importance to Rose for the rest of her life.

On December 15, 1897, Alice Huber came to Water Street with a letter of introduction from her spiritual adviser, Father Fidelis. Alice, twenty-six at the time, was a devout Catholic and an artist who had come to New York from Kentucky to further her career. Beyond her wish to be a successful artist, Alice was looking for spiritual perfection, and Father Fidelis had suggested Alice's participation in charitable work for the poor and sick as a means to it.[24]

Alice's initial reaction to the Water Street tenement and Rose's dying charges was one of revulsion. "Everything about the place and the

22. *Sun*, n.d. (Clipping *ibid.*); Rose Hawthorne Lathrop to Mr. Frost, January 4, 1897, in Norcross Papers, MHS.

23. Rose Hawthorne Lathrop to Bessie Hunt, January 5, [1897?], in Sophia Smith Collection.

24. Father Fidelis, born James Kent Stone, was particularly interested in Rose's work and may have felt sympathetic toward her position because of the similar paths his life and Rose's life had taken. According to Sister M. Joseph, in *Out of Many Hearts: Mother Alphonsa Lathrop and Her Work* (Hawthorne, N.Y., 1965), 53–54, Stone had been married, the father of three daughters, and the president of Hobart College. After his wife died, he converted to Catholicism, abandoned his career, and became a Passionist priest after he found a California couple to adopt his children.

neighborhood," she later wrote in her memoirs, "the untidy woman in the kitchen, the patients upstairs (who were certainly the most hideous we have ever had), seemed perfectly repulsive to me. I certainly did not want to stay. . . . I knew nothing whatever about taking care of sick people and felt great disgust to be near ordinary persons with sores, much less cancers." But as she departed she looked at Rose, "the only bright being in all that mass of ugliness and misery," and felt compelled to volunteer her services one afternoon a week.[25]

Alice returned the following week and recorded, "I loathed everything about the place, and still forced myself to dress a frightful sore that makes me sick to think of, even to this day." Rose had had other companions in her work, but none had been as compatible or as well loved as Alice soon became, and Rose was overjoyed by Alice's offer of help: "I marvel that you can look forward eagerly to coming to me to share my labors and misfortunes, which are all dear to me now." Alice quickly felt "attached" to this work in spite of her revulsion and volunteered her assistance twice a week. Then, by March, 1898, she wrote, "I resolved to leave the world and devote my life" to caring for cancer patients.[26]

Within a few months of beginning her work, Rose had become aware of its potential for growth, and she wished to attract other women to it. In April, 1897, she had written to Mattie: "I learn more of truth each month. That I am needed here, and many more women, is evident enough, in this one line of work." As much as she sought assistance, however, she was very selective about those whom she allowed to help, and even more particular about those whom she would consider lifelong companions. A trained nurse, for example, who offered her assistance exhibited "bad qualities greater than good," and Rose immediately requested that she leave. A woman from Boston joined Rose briefly but could not endure "the smells and sights . . . and has shown her queer streaks" and was therefore dismissed.[27]

25. Sister M. Rose Huber [Alice Huber], "Memoirs," 2 (MS in ASRIC).

26. *Ibid.;* Rose Hawthorne Lathrop to Alice Huber, February 26, 1898, in ASRIC.

27. Rose Hawthorne Lathrop to Mattie L. Stearns, April 18, 1897, in Berg Collection; Rose Hawthorne Lathrop to Alice Huber, July 1, 7, 1898, both in ASRIC; Rose Hildegarde, "Items," January 24, 1898.

There is little question why so few women persevered in this exceedingly difficult work. Rose expected herself and her companions to provide constant care for women who were dying of a dreadful disease—a task that was to be performed in the poorest and most adverse circumstances. "We were very poor at the time," Alice recalled. "Boxes served as chairs. We had a few of the latter but not sufficient to go around." Rose demanded that all involved in this work share completely the way of life of the patients, even to the point of using the same tableware. On one occasion Alice indulged her fastidiousness and sequestered a glass for her personal use; but when Rose discovered the hidden glass, she made Alice return it for general use.[28]

Rose's insistence on shared tableware was probably prompted not only by her belief that the workers should live in poverty along with the patients but also by her conviction that cancer was not a contagious disease, a position that was not commonly held. Rose was determined that in caring for the dying she would demonstrate that belief. In Rose's early writings publicizing her efforts, she always included among her objectives: "to prove that cancer is not dangerous to nurse, with the precautions used by any neat method, or even when accidents of contact unfortunately occur. This is one of the chief uses of the charity, since the dread of cancer is so great that much inhumanity is shown in the neglect to undertake proper 'dressings' of wounds and the desire to be rid of a member of the family who is afflicted with the malady."[29]

Difficult though Rose's life was during this period, she soon realized that she would succeed in founding a charity to console those dying of cancer. As the work grew, so grew her conviction that God was blessing and guiding her, and she recorded this ever-expanding religious consciousness in language reminiscent of writings of the great mystics. She recorded in her memoirs that during the night of March 23, 1898, she awoke to a vision of the crucified Christ speaking these words to her: "I love you, and you love me—then what is the trouble?" Immediately, Rose felt a "great peace overflowed me. I began to love Him only, as I have prayed to do for three years. . . . Jesus loves me, and everything is simplified and exalted." The next day, external events affirmed her internal conviction, as Alice Huber

28. Huber, "Memoirs," 3.

29. "The Objects of the Work" was published in every issue of *Christ's Poor.*

moved into the Water Street rooms to commit her life to working with Rose. A few months before, Rose had written, "I am so happy in . . . my Kentuckian assistant—she is like a sister to me."[30]

Rose's success and peace of mind contrasted notably, however, with the dissolution of George's career and the deterioration of his health. In October, 1896, the New York *Times* had published an article containing a statement, conveyed through an unnamed friend of the Lathrops, "to contradict rumors that there has been a separation growing out of incompatibility of temper and conflicting ambition." The friend asserts that George was in agreement with Rose's goal of helping the cancerous poor, but that "he would put limitations to the excess of his wife's self-sacrifice in that direction, desiring her to remain near him so that her well-being might not be injured."[31]

For the public record, then, George let it be known that he wished to maintain his marriage to Rose and the appearance of harmony. There is, however, no evidence that Rose saw George at any time during this period, though her journal records continued prayers for her husband as well as prayers to overcome impatience and anger. "I desire with all my heart," she recorded, "to have no feeling of resentment or unloving displeasure toward *anyone*."[32]

In July, 1897, George had written to Aldrich asking for two hundred dollars to tide him over during the summer until he could resume work on an article about Augustin Daly's theater. "The two years and a half of agony involved in my wife's desertion," he confided to his old friend, "the breaking up of my house, and the almost countless expenses connected with this and with the attempt to serve her kindly and to do helpful things for her when I could, notwithstanding her desertion, have brought me for the time being into considerable financial distress."[33]

Although George had published *Yaddo: An Autumn Masque* in 1897, his literary powers now seemed to fail him, and the work on the theater article, which should have been finished in October, dragged on. He corresponded, from a variety of addresses, with Gilder about its

30. Rose Hildegarde, "Items," March 23, 1898, Mother M. Rose Huber, "Memoirs," 2, both in ASRIC.

31. New York *Times,* October 31, 1896, p. 7.

32. Rose Hildegarde, "Items," February 4, 6, 1898, in ASRIC.

33. George Parsons Lathrop to Thomas Bailey Aldrich, July 7, 1897, in Thomas Bailey Aldrich Collection, HL.

publication in the *Century*. His last note to Gilder, now addressing this old friend formally as "Dear Sir," was scribbled in pencil on wrinkled stationery that George had apparently found in a telegraph office: "Pardon me for delay in returning proof of 'Inner Life of a Great Theatre,' herewith enclosed. I have been carrying it around in my coat pockets which have become mail bags, and intended to deliver it promptly, but forgot to do so. Therefore it is somewhat the worse for wear; but it is correct otherwise."[34] For a man usually so meticulous about his correspondence, the poor condition of this letter was an ominous sign.

On April 19, 1898, George died at Roosevelt Hospital in New York City. The state death certificate cites chronic nephritis, a recurring kidney ailment, as the chief cause of death. George's mother was with him when he died, but Rose, who had been called to his bedside only when it became obvious that he was dying, did not arrive in time.

Rose certainly had known of her husband's history of poor health. In 1888 the couple had left New York when George was under doctor's orders to find less stressful work, and until 1893 his ill health had adversely affected his literary career and the couple's finances. In 1891 Frank Lathrop had written to Rose expressing his fear that "something in the air" made recovery from "such attacks" as his brother endured "long and tedious." At Christmas of that same year, Frank had advised Rose not to leave George for any length of time or to accept dinner invitations even from Rose and George's neighbors, the Chappells, because of George's poor health. Rose herself had characterized George's illness in a letter to Rebecca Manning as "gastric trouble of the most severe nature," a description that coincides with the general symptoms of kidney disorders.[35]

Despite Rose's knowledge of her husband's ailments, she was apparently unaware of how much his health had deteriorated, and his death came as a great shock. On April 21 Rose wrote: "My beloved husband died on April 19th about half an hour before I reached him. . . . As I stood beside his body, soon after his death, the beauty

34. George Parsons Lathrop to R. W. Gilder, November 3, 7, 1897, March 15, April 1, 1898, all in Century Company Papers, NYPL.

35. Frank Lathrop to Rose Hawthorne Lathrop, April 16, December 24, 1891, both in ASRIC.

and nobility and the exquisite gentleness of his life and the eloquence which breathed from his unbreathing being of one who had died in the Lord, spoke plainly to me of his virtues, and the welcome our Lord had given him into His rest. My own soul was trembling in the dark uncertainty of all worthiness."[36]

Rose was truly grief stricken. George, whom she had married when they were both barely twenty, had been her husband, her companion, her lover, the father of her child, the critic and supporter of her literary aspirations, and the person with whom she had adopted the religion that had become so dear to her. Although Rose had made a definitive break with George, she had apparently harbored the hope that he would eventually join her work for the cancerous poor. She wrote to Bessie, "I had so fully believed that my husband would soon join me in my labors, in the ways in which a man can do so much, that I was stunned by his sudden death, and inconsolable that here on earth we could never again be in thorough sympathy." Rose conveyed similar feelings to Mattie, "I was crushed by George's death not having dreamed that I could ever bear his death at all, if it came before he had accepted my work as a wise measure and helped in it, and raised our lives to a high, united service of God."[37]

Both George's physical symptoms and Rose's generous appraisal of him are important factors in a final evaluation of this man's character, for he has been depicted by various biographers of the Hawthornes as unstable, alcoholic, and abusive to Rose. Randall Stewart's and Theodore Maynard's works, both published in 1948, describe the Lathrops' marriage as unhappy because of George's faulty character. Vernon Loggins' book, published three years later, reiterates the notion that the marriage was unhappy for Rose, and Loggins makes several explicit though unsubstantiated claims that George was an alcoholic. The view that George was "ill" and that Rose had separated from him because their life together "had become so unbearable, and even dangerous" is found again in Sister Mary Joseph's 1965 publication. Maurice Bassan, in his 1970 biography of Julian, cites Theodore Maynard as his source in accounting for Julian's continual displeasure with his brother-in-law. Bassan speculates that "perhaps rumors had

36. Rose Hildegarde, "Items," April 21, 1898.

37. Rose Hawthorne Lathrop to Bessie Hunt, October 25, [1898?], in Sophia Smith Collection; Rose Hawthorne Lathrop to Mattie L. Stearns, May 29, 1898, in Berg Collection.

[reached Julian] . . . about Lathrop's alcoholism, which, in the late 1880's, was rapidly to ruin [George's] once promising career." And as recently as 1980, James Mellow has cited Sister Joseph's book as the source of his conclusion that George was a man of "unstable character" with "pronounced alcoholic tendencies, which ruined a brilliant career as an editor and a journalist."[38]

Although it is clear how the depictions of George as an unstable drunkard were passed from one printed source to another, there is no evidence to be found in letters, journals, or any other record left by the Hawthornes or the Lathrops that supports these characterizations. Although family members may indeed have been reticent about alcoholism and thus omitted any mention of it from their writing, the accumulation of manuscript evidence does not confirm the judgment that George was in any way abusive to Rose or that he was an alcoholic. He was, rather, a man burdened with "gastric" disorders for the last ten years of a life described by Rose as one of "beauty and nobility and exquisite gentleness." Although George had shared almost every aspect of Rose's life for twenty-five years, he did not share her desire to work in poverty among the cancerous poor, and, as her husband, he resisted her abandoning their marriage to pursue her dream.

Rose came to believe that what George could not accept in life he had sanctioned after death, for two days after he died, she recorded in her journal, "Yesterday, early, his soul came, I am sure to console me, in his loveliest way of forgiveness." Rose elaborated upon this experience in her correspondence. She wrote Mattie, "He seemed to come to me and say, in his most enchanting mood of boyish tenderness, that of course he loved me, and of course we never could have any real misunderstanding of each other." Later she wrote to Bessie that she felt as if George was present, "with every bright and lovely trait of his. . . . Now I feel sure that he is in accord with me, and praying for the success of this charity." Believing George to be thus at peace and eternally reconciled with her, on May 1 she was able to

38. Randall Stewart, *Nathaniel Hawthorne: A Biography* (New Haven, 1948), 240; Maynard, *A Fire Was Lighted,* 172–73; Vernon Loggins, *The Hawthornes: The Story of Seven Generations of an American Family* (New York, 1951), 315, 316, 323; Sister M. Joseph, *Out of Many Hearts,* 9, 14; Bassan, *Hawthorne's Son,* 118; James Mellow, *Nathaniel Hawthorne in His Times* (Boston, 1980), 568.

write that "for the first time since George's death, [she] felt courage, and [was] very cheerful, *in Christ*."[39]

Thus three events of remarkable significance in Rose's life had occurred within a month's time. Rose had experienced a mystical affirmation of her life and work; Alice Huber had moved in with her; and now George's death had made her a widow, free from any impediment to pursue completely her religious aspirations. What followed during the next three years brought about—not without difficulty, however—the fruition of those aspirations with almost miraculous speed.

With Rose in the lead, she and Alice took the steps necessary to function under the auspices of traditional Roman Catholic religious practice. On April 15 they had obtained a rule with which to regulate their daily activities and religious devotion. This they had received from their spiritual director, Father Clement M. Thuente, of the parish of Saint Vincent Ferrer. On May 19, "on the monthly date of my husband's death," as Rose was aware, she announced her intention to take a radical step—to cut her hair and wear an outfit resembling a nun's habit. "I begged her not to do so," Alice recalled in her memoirs, but Rose "persisted in her design and cut off her beautiful hair and put on a linen cap something like that worn by the Sisters of Charity, a linen dress, and a white neckerchief." A few days later Alice adopted this manner of dress but refrained from cutting her hair for some time.[40]

Because they resembled Catholic nuns in appearance, the women were advised by Father Thuente and other friends, Father Charles Parks and Father Joseph McMahon, to obtain sanction for their attire and implied way of life from the archbishop of the diocese of New York, Michael Augustine Corrigan. Thus Rose wrote to Corrigan asking if she and her "life-helper, Miss Huber" might call upon him to show him their garb. "We tried to design something almost ugly in its rough severity," she explained to him.[41]

Corrigan initially refused to see the women, but Rose wrote to

39. Rose Hildegarde, "Items," April 21, May 1, 1898; Rose Hawthorne Lathrop to Bessie Hunt, October 25, [1898?], in Sophia Smith Collection; Rose Hawthorne Lathrop to Mattie L. Stearns, May 29, 1898, in Berg Collection.

40. Rose Hildegarde, "Items," April 15, May 25, 1898; Sister M. Rose, "Memoirs," 3.

41. Rose Hawthorne Lathrop to Archbishop Michael Augustine Corrigan, May 25, 1898, in AANY.

him again, stating that "as my hair is cropped very close I am obliged to wear a hood." Although Corrigan consented to this second petition, he was harsh with Rose when the interview occurred. Alice recorded that "at first the Archbishop was cross and spoke sharply to Mrs. Lathrop; her eyes filled with tears." Difficult though the interview was, Rose did obtain Corrigan's consent for them to wear their simple outfits, but only in private.[42]

Corrigan seems to have withheld both official, ecclesiastical support and personal enthusiasm for Rose's efforts for several years. At best he believed that Rose's work could better function as an arm of some other, established charity. He suggested, therefore, that she and Alice associate with another woman, Mrs. Starr, who, he thought, was engaged in similar charity work; but, as Alice recorded, Mrs. Starr told them emphatically: "It would never do. We have not the same idea at all. Your object is to keep people in the slums, and mine is to take them out."[43]

The reasons for Corrigan's hesitation to endorse Rose's work are not documented explicitly. Perhaps he believed that divine assistance was all that these women needed or should expect, for he said, "If it is not God's work it will go to pieces, and if it is God's work it will succeed." Perhaps, as his suggestion that Rose and Alice affiliate with an already established group implies, he did not wish to encourage small, independent charitable enterprises, which were possibly less effective than large, combined efforts. Perhaps he was skeptical about the perseverance of this recent convert to Catholicism who had taken so radical a step in midlife. Whatever Corrigan's reasons, his behavior was consistent with the posture of resistance often assumed by the Catholic hierarchy toward the establishment of female religious orders, many of which prevailed in spite of, rather than because of, the efforts of the male clergy. Even after Rose's work had been established for several years, Corrigan's response to someone who made inquiries about Rose carefully disassociated her from diocesan endorsement: "With regard to Mrs. Lathrop, the Diocese is in no way responsible for her work. She desired to form some sort of religious community for the work, but I told her that was too serious to be even thought of. I gave her a letter, in which I wrote that these

42. Rose Hawthorne Lathrop to Archbishop Michael Augustine Corrigan, May 28, 1898, in AANY; Sister M. Rose, "Memoirs," 4.

43. Huber, "Memoirs," 4.

women were good people engaged in what I believed to be a worthy charity. But the work is not under Ecclesiastical supervision."[44]

Thus, wearing their simple dress and following a routine of prayer and nursing, Rose, Alice, and Mrs. Cochrane, the only other helper at this time who met Rose's demanding standards, lived on Water Street with an ever-increasing number of women dying from cancer. Rose and Alice shared a small room that opened into a larger one filled with patients. They slept in a bunk bed, with Rose taking the lower berth. Their house was, in Rose's words, "ineradicably soiled by former occupants" and made even more distasteful during the summer of 1898 by the extreme heat, an infestation of insects, and a leaking roof. Adding to these discomforts was, according to Alice, "the odor from the patients (who were all in the last stages of the disease)." The three women's lives were so difficult that Alice admitted later, "We nearly collapsed." Indeed, on August 7, Mrs. Cochrane died. Still, Rose and Alice persevered.[45]

Summer turned to autumn, and in mid-October another helper, Cecelia Higley, joined Rose and Alice. By winter, the house on Water Street proved to be as ill suited to the cold weather as it had been to the hot. Alice recalled those months of difficulty in her memoirs.

> The winter proved to be as cold as the summer had been warm. I must say that Mrs. Lathrop and I nearly froze. The patients were in bed so were comfortable enough. The kitchen, which also served as a dining room, was so cold that we had to put on wraps to eat our meals, and the food would become icy cold before we could eat it. However, the winter passed as the summer did—patients died and others took their place—crowds of poor came to us. We did what we could to relieve them.[46]

The women's manner of relieving their dying charges was as much spiritual as it was physical. Although they did not attend to Catholic women only, a religious, or more particularly Catholic, perspective was at the center of their care. At Christmas, Alice, who enjoyed a

44. *Ibid.;* Archbishop Michael Augustine Corrigan to Dear Sir, April 27, 1899, in AANY. Kolmer, in "Catholic Women Religious," 130, cites the excessive demands of bishops, poverty to the point of starvation, and the hostility of neighbors as the "trials" typically endured by founders of female religious orders, despite the fact that they provided the society at large with indispensable services.

45. Rose Hawthorne Lathrop, "Sketch of Aims and Work of St. Rose's Free Home for Incurable Cancer," 2 (MS in ASRIC); Huber, "Memoirs," 4.

46. Huber, "Memoirs," 5.

somewhat better relationship with Archbishop Corrigan than Rose, petitioned him and received permission to have mass celebrated in the Water Street rooms. When the event occurred, on January 3, 1899, it represented a spiritual as well as an ecclesiastical milestone. Alice believed that this "bitter cold winter morning [had been] sanctified by the first great event of our then struggling lives." Soon after, acting upon the advice of Father Thuente, Rose began the process of affiliating her small band of women with the Third Order of Saint Dominic. Thus they would be recognized by the Catholic church as a group of laywomen living in a community under the rule of an established religious order.[47]

The poor condition of the Water Street rooms, combined with the number of patients who came to Rose, Alice, and Cecelia, were indications that the women needed a larger, permanent location that could be owned rather than rented. In the spring of 1899, Rose began looking for a suitable building, which she soon found at 426 Cherry Street. She intended to finance this home, as she had the other residences, through charitable contributions. Several faithful benefactors had begun contributing to the property on Cherry Street. Frances A. Moulton had donated one thousand dollars for the purpose of "securing any permanent home," and J. Warren Greene and several other men had given to this cause as well.[48]

Rose was determined to obtain a broad base of support through direct appeals to the public in the newspapers. It was her intent to appeal not to the rich alone "but to the vast number of people who make up the human family." In previous fund-raising efforts, however, the use of the press to draw attention to her work had drawn her criticisms and problems as well as contributions. On one occasion, imposters using the name of Rose's charity had begged money door to door, and Rose had to publish a notice stating that she authorized no such method of solicitation and that any donations for her work should be sent directly to the Reverend M. J. Lavelle at Saint Patrick's Cathedral.[49]

On another occasion, the public pleas for Rose's work had been criticized because she was caring for the dying in a home, not a hospital. A home, Rose had retorted, was precisely the environment she

47. *Ibid.*, 6.
48. *Ibid.;* R. H. Lathrop, "Sketch," 3.
49. New York *Times*, November 13, 1897, p. 6, December 10, 1897, p. 12.

desired, for a "corps of Doctors shall not be needed" to care for those who were without hope of recovery. Nor would Rose abide the hospitals, in which the terminally ill and indigent were the subjects of experimental surgery, for "no one," she had stated emphatically, "shall be taught or required to watch experiments."[50]

Such clear condemnation of current medical practice with regard to the dying did not pave the road for Rose's acceptance by the established medical community. When she sought, through New York's state board of charities, to incorporate in order to acquire property as a group rather than as an individual, her request was rejected. The commissioner of the board, Dr. Stephen Smith, gave as his reasons that hospitals with attending physicians could work with the dying better and that "contributions as a source of income were too precarious." When a reporter from the *Times* sought a response to these statements, he spoke to one of Rose's co-workers, probably Alice, who pointed out that hospitals had, as a point of fact, not cared for the dying at all, leaving them rather to the indignities of Blackwell's Island. This spokeswoman for Rose's work conversed with the reporter at the home on Cherry Street, testimony in itself that precarious though their financial base was, the women were extremely successful at raising needed funds.[51]

Indeed, Rose's "strong appeals" through the press, as Alice called them, proved highly effective. In April, 1899, the women were able to make their first payment of $9,500 on their Cherry Street home, and on May 1, they moved into Saint Rose's Free Home for Incurable Cancer, named after Rose of Lima—at that time the only female saint of the Americas. The very next day, new patients were added to their charge.[52]

Saint Rose's Free Home was far more comfortable and spacious than the Scammel Street and Water Street residences, allowing for the care of as many as twenty women at a time. "There is a homelikeness about all arrangements and rules that [is] very agreeable," Rose recorded. "In summer, the little yard, filled with plants, is a pleasant airing-place for the sick who are able to move about. . . . All who have seen the simple comforts of the sunny Home (for women who were on the verge of being sent to the City Hospital, or who have

50. *Ibid.*, July 13, 1897, p. 10.
51. *Ibid.*, May 25, 1899, p. 14.
52. Huber, "Memoirs," 5.

begged their friends to take them in) have been delighted with the methods of arrangement and management."[53]

Rose, however, was not so enamored of her new home that she became inured to the wretchedness of life in the slums or the hardship of her daily routine. In a letter signed "your own devoted Rose Hildegarde," she cautioned her niece not to consider visiting "this rubbish hole" during the summer. And even a year later, when Rose received "The Casket of Opals" as a gift, she refrained from thanking the donor immediately, for, as she eventually wrote him, the "clasp of death was upon my hand. . . . I do not dare to read [the poems] lest my life be given to memory, instead of the revolting daily work."[54]

Rose wrote to Mattie in June, 1899, proud that Saint Rose's Free Home was more than half paid. Within a year's time only $2,000 remained on that debt; in Rose's words, the contributions the charity had received were "a fortunate record of support for one year." Rose also took pride in the fact that this home would be called the "mother house" for herself and her two "companions committed for life . . . trusting that we are to have others by and by."[55]

Many women had expressed interest in joining Rose in her work. She documented that during her first three-and-one-half years approximately 150 women had either written her or called upon her to offer their assistance. Of this number, only 3 were, at this time, committed for life, all others "going away for various reasons:—the summons of their relatives, failing health or courage, unfitness, or unwillingness to adopt the religious rule." To attract women of "fine calibre, promising determination and usefulness," Rose once more took to her pen. An example of her persuasive writing can be seen in her article "A Cheerful View of a Hard Problem," which was published in the *Catholic World* in February, 1899, while she was still living on Water Street and actively raising funds for Saint Rose's Free Home.[56]

To solicit the aid of those interested in sharing her work, Rose in

53. Rose Hawthorne Lathrop to Mattie L. Stearns, June 4, 1899, in Berg Collection; Rose Hawthorne Lathrop, "Sketch," 3.

54. Rose Hawthorne Lathrop to Hildegarde Hawthorne, August 11, [?], in Berg Collection; Rose Hawthorne Lathrop to Thomas B. Mosher, July 8, [1900?], in HL.

55. Rose Hawthorne Lathrop to Mattie L. Stearns, June 4, 1899, in Berg Collection.

56. Rose Hawthorne Lathrop, "Sketch," 4; Rose Hawthorne Lathrop, "A Cheerful View of a Hard Problem," *Catholic World,* LXVIII (February, 1899), 659–69.

this article attempted the paradoxical task of making a repellent work appealing.

The subject about which I write, and which I would gladly make interesting to the general public, is one that can hardly be made agreeable; but nevertheless I can testify that such a life as I lead with a few companions in a poor district, among the sick, has many agreeable points. As it is my earnest desire to get women to join me who have a natural talent for nursing, and a natural inclination to nurse those who need it most, I think it might be well for me to present the bright side of the care of the cancerous poor.[57]

The article, replete with photographs of pleasant street scenes in the vicinity of Water Street, is clearly directed at a class of women who might regard life among the poor and dying as something alien and fearful—the type of readers who would have accepted without dismay the condescending tone in the *Times* announcement that Rose had begun "nursing the poor and lowly." Rose conceded, "There is, of course, some difficulty . . . in exchanging a style of living which is orderly and comparatively quiet for the turmoil of the pauper district." She assures her readers that this difficulty can be overcome, not so much because of the "picturesqueness [of] the pauper life itself," but because a woman is capable of changing her way of life to live in poverty among the poor. "It would seem," Rose wrote, "that the human frame is really a slave whom it is possible to subject at every point, and that the strength of the slave is herculean when once the creature is fully conquered."[58]

Rose sought to dispel prevalent fears about the disease whose victims she nursed: "There is very little torture even in this horrible disease when the treatments recommended at the New York Cancer Hospital are adopted. . . . [T]he sick have a great deal of comfort, if any one tries to give it to them." Rose concluded this article with a challenge to her female readers comparable to a "call to arms." What kind of women are suited to this work? Rose asked. "They are," she stated emphatically, "women . . . who have the good sense to realize that the life of an earnest woman, wherever she is, is one of suffering. They are the women who choose to do with less ameliorations of life to this good end of nursing destitute women, which I have stated to be, in my opinion, of equal importance with patriotism."[59]

57. R. H. Lathrop, "A Cheerful View," 659.
58. *Ibid.*, 663–67.
59. *Ibid.*

Rose's appeals for dedicated women did not meet with the same startling degree of success as did her appeals for money, though women continued to inquire and offer assistance. But Rose, Alice, and Cecelia formed a nucleus of women bound together in their commitment and making steady progress toward their goal of establishing a sisterhood. In September, 1899, Archbishop Corrigan consented to their request, supported by Father Thuente, that "they begin in a humble way and establish a Chapter in connection with the Church of the Dominican Fathers." Father Thuente immediately began giving formal instructions to the women in the conduct of their daily lives as tertiaries, and subsequently approved of their taking religious names and being called "Sister." On September 14, 1899, he received them into the Third Order of Saint Dominic. Alice became Sister Mary Rose, and Cecelia became Sister Mary Magdalen. Rose became Sister Mary Alphonsa, hoping that this name would, as she wrote, "be honored by holy living, instead of the one I have by no means honored."[60]

60. Rose Hawthorne Lathrop to Archbishop Michael Augustine Corrigan, September 9, 1899, in AANY; Rose Hawthorne Lathrop to Thomas Wentworth Higginson, October 13, 1899, in American Collection, BPL; Sister M. Joseph, *Out of Many Hearts,* 53–54.

VIII / *Mother Mary Alphonsa*

ONCE Rose, Alice, and Cecelia had been received as Dominican tertiaries, they made steady progress in turning their organization into a sisterhood. Archbishop Corrigan began to grant their requests with greater regularity. He permitted them to have Christmas mass celebrated in their home, and when they found a priest assigned to a church on nearby Pitts Street who would say mass for them on a weekly basis, Corrigan granted permission for this and the hearing of confession as well. The women's request to wear the full Dominican habit, however, was still being denied.[1]

Corrigan's refusal to allow the tertiaries fuller association with the Dominican order constituted something of a test of faith for Rose. During the summer of 1900, she made a retreat with the Dominicans in Caldwell, New Jersey, and wrote to her "dearest Sisters, and Sisters-to-be" on Cherry Street that it was "difficult to explain to [the Dominican] Sisters how one can be blessed by God in a work and not be blessed first by the Holy Father." Less-than-complete understanding by the Dominicans notwithstanding, Rose's experience with them helped her to clarify the way in which her own community of sisters should live. Fasting and rigorous mortification might be expected of nuns with less demanding work, but for her sisters this would be inappropriate. "These nuns eat

1. Sister Mary Alphonsa [Rose Hawthorne Lathrop] to Archbishop Michael Augustine Corrigan, December 10, 14, 28, 1899, January 25, Febraury 2, 11, 1900, all in AANY.

poorly," she noted, but "we should use nutritious [food] because we're nurses."[2]

The perseverance of Rose, Alice, and Cecelia, and the addition to their ranks of two others who wished to make work with terminally ill cancer patients their lifelong dedication, could not go unsanctioned by ecclesiastical authority forever. On December 8, 1900, Rose and her co-workers were invested with the full habit of the Dominicans. On January 24, 1901, they were incorporated by the state of New York under the title the Servants of Relief for Incurable Cancer.

Rose and Alice had originally considered calling their organization Daughters of the Puritans, possibly because, after the women became tertiaries, they wore what was described in one newspaper article as a "Puritan kerchief, close-fitting cap (over hair closely cropped for hygienic reasons), a snowy gown and an apron." Calling themselves "servants," however, suggests how fully Rose and her followers were determined to be identified with the poorest class of society. Although never affluent or even financially secure, Rose had been part of a class and an economic structure that permitted the employment of servants. When Rose and George had regarded their financial situation to be dire, they were forced to let their servant go, a circumstance that was remarked upon with dismay by George's mother. It was perhaps during that period that Rose drafted a poem in which the speaker, a society matron, is gently mocked for her inability to execute properly the tasks of her absent servant. The refrain of the poem establishes its tone: "Oh, bother the servants, say I, / (They are the plague of my life!)" The matron queries:

> Could Biddy know more than *I*?
> Yes, her fires were fine
> With a roar and a shine,—
> I'm choking with smoke! Oh-Oh, my!

Within the decade after this poem was probably drafted, Rose was referring to herself as a servant. She declined to visit Bessie, for example, because "I am a servant and a drudge and a sort of *mother,* and I cannot take any time from desperately sick people."[3]

2. Sister M. Alphonsa [Rose Hawthorne Lathrop] to Sisters of Saint Rose's Free Home for Incurable Cancer, n.d., July 29, [?], both in ASRIC.

3. "Mrs. Rose Hawthorne Lathrop," September 16, [1899?] (Clipping in Sophia Smith

As Rose ever more clearly defined the purpose and nature of her work, she saw the accomplishment of many of her goals. Her band of helpers was growing, she had ecclesiastical sanction for her organization as an affiliate of a recognized religious order, and her group had achieved, through her efforts, the legal status that facilitated its receiving gifts and accepting legacies as a corporate entity. But no sooner had she attained these objectives than she established new ones.

Rose was fully aware that cancer was a disease that did not discriminate according to sex. Men were victims, both of the disease and of the mistreatment of those dying from it. Thus Rose had begun saving money specifically for the purchase of a house that would accommodate both male and female patients. In the spring of 1901, the opportunity to obtain such a facility presented itself to her. She was approached by Father I. M. Cothonay, who was looking for a buyer for some property that his order owned in Sherman Park, a rural community north of New York City. Father Cothonay, a French Dominican, had some years before purchased what was then the Tecumseh Hotel and converted it into a monastery and a novitiate for his order. The rambling house had sixty rooms and was situated on nine acres of land studded with fruit trees, a garden, a grape arbor, and beehives. Father Cothonay was asking $28,000 for the property, and Rose immediately wrote to Archbishop Corrigan requesting permission for the Servants of Relief to purchase it.[4]

For a woman who had had little experience with financing—who had never had a stable income with which to learn about finances—Rose demonstrated remarkable acumen in money matters in her letter to Corrigan. Rose stated that Father Cothonay had been generous in his offer to sell the property at this price, considering that the home and its repairs had cost the priests around $50,000. She had already saved $1,000 for a home in which male patients could be cared for, she had been promised $2,000 from a gentleman when she had "definite plans for an annex for male cases," and she was expecting a legacy of $10,000 to be paid by June. As for discharging the rest of the debt and maintaining the new property as well as the Cherry Street home, Rose was confident that she could "appeal to the public

Collection, NL); Rose Hawthorne Lathrop, poem (MS in ASRIC); Rose Hawthorne Lathrop to Bessie Hunt, March 2, [1897?], in Sophia Smith Collection.

4. Sister M. Joseph, *Out of Many Hearts*, 99–100.

forcibly." Rose furthered her case for the purchase of the Sherman Park property by pointing out that a place "in the country would be self-supporting as regards food." Another significant consideration was that the purchase of the property would enable the sisters in the city to go to the country to restore their health and refresh their spirits.[5]

Corrigan was persuaded, an ample indication that his faith in Rose and in her endeavors was growing. On June 5, 1901, Rosary Hill Home in Sherman Park, New York, was formally opened to care for both male and female patients. The men who came to what Rose called "the beauties of the Hill" were often in hideous condition. One of the first male patients had cancers of the eye and nose, another had a cancer of the tongue, and another had a severely ulcerated cancer of the leg. No matter how deteriorated the condition of these men, Rosary Hill Home provided them with comfort. Some even experienced a temporary remission of their illness and could engage in minor farm labor and gardening. By August, 1902, Rose recorded that three of her male patients had died at the home, that one had returned to his family to die, and that another had run away in a "fit of insanity such as sometimes comes" right before death. "Great approval is often expressed in the service of these male cases by the charity, aside from their own approval and that of their friends," Rose wrote. "It seems to have been a sensible clause in the constitutions of the young endeavor," she concluded.[6]

In addition to providing plenty of room for both male and female patients, the property at Rosary Hill housed in one wing the novitiate for Rose's order. The aspiring Servants of Relief were supervised by Alice, who traveled from New York City each week to counsel and direct the postulants and novices. Rose assumed the title of mother superior, and as Mother Mary Alphonsa, she lived at Rosary Hill Home until the end of her life. The woman who had been itinerant for the first fifty years of her life had settled down for good.

Indeed, the remaining quarter century of Rose's life was remarkably devoid not only of travel (except for an occasional trip to Saint Rose's Free Home in New York City) but of personal incident. Her daily routine has been described by one of her current followers as

5. Sister M. Alphonsa to Archbishop Michael Augustine Corrigan, April 22, 23, 1901, both in AANY.

6. Mother M. Alphonsa [Rose Hawthorne Lathrop], *Christ's Poor,* II (August, 1902), 42–43.

"almost breathless . . . [and] strictly kept." The sisters arose at four-thirty every morning and went to the chapel. After prayers and mass, they commenced their tasks of cooking, caring for the sick, and even performing farm chores such as milking the cows. After breakfast the sisters would again visit the chapel and care for the sick. They recited the Psalms and traditional prayers of the Catholic church: the rosary, the angelus, and the little office of the Blessed Virgin Mary. After dinner they enjoyed a period of recreation, which during the winter might consist of indoor games. In the summer, the sisters would avail themselves of the nearby woods, where they might walk in search of wild flowers.[7]

Just as the daily routine gave Rose and the other sisters a common activity, their habit gave them a common appearance; but more than Rose's auburn hair had disappeared behind the veil she now wore. Julian later wrote: "The passions of her nature, doubtless as urgent as ever, centered no longer around her personal fate and interests, for in her own view she no longer existed. She lived, labored and prayed only for those incarnations of mortal misery which she had drawn about her."[8]

Rose saw Julian and his family from time to time, although she completely removed herself from the society of her former friends and literary acquaintances. In a letter to Bessie, she confided, "It has been quite hard to be utterly away from such intercourse." Nonetheless, she declined the invitation to participate in the celebration of Nathaniel's hundredth birthday at the Wayside. "I have no prospect whatever of being able to be present," she wrote to Margaret Mulford Lothrop, the current owner of the Wayside, who was planning the festivities. Rose continued:

> I have tried very hard for a couple of years to leave my work among the poor, to go to Concord, or its neighborhood, but have been prevented very imperatively. This is usually because taking care of the dying, and few of our patients living beyond expectation for some months or years, we are constantly thrown into extremely arduous situations, when every one must join in watching, laying out the dead, and seeing to the last rites; and, too, new patients are to be received, which entails much preliminary work, until they are refreshed and settled. We do all our own housework as well.[9]

7. Sister M. Joseph, *Out of Many Hearts,* 124–35.
8. *Ibid.,* 198.
9. Mother M. Alphonsa to Bessie Hunt, September 17, [1901?], in Sophia Smith Collection; Lothrop, *Wayside Home,* 14.

Living thus, Rose drew her emotional support not from relatives or past friends but from her relationship with her religious sisters, especially Alice. Because Alice headed Saint Rose's Free Home in New York City, she and Rose no longer lived together after the establishment of Rosary Hill Home. But their relationship, fostered largely through frequent correspondence (Rose never became comfortable using the telephone), grew and became more important to both women. "Your lovely letters," wrote Rose during the heat of her first summer at Rosary Hill, "are just as refreshing as lemonade." In the fall, Rose wrote again to Alice with similar whimsy, "Your letters and notes would keep life in a little dry toad, such as I sometimes find quite dead in our big house."[10]

In other letters Rose spoke directly and affectionately about her love for Alice, a love that was always subsumed within her concept of God's all-encompassing love.

> This letter contains a love for you that is growing more true than when you felt I loved you first, and which partakes more than ever of the light and security of God's love. But you see day by day how imperfect all that I do and feel still is, and you will have much occasion to instill generosity into your true and beautiful love for me. If I seem harsh, at times, it is the imperfect effort of a poor wretch to bring to your soul and mine, a greater share of God's truth, which will bless us, no matter how roughly we strive for it; for certainly our God must be willing to let us arrive at the truth according to our poor will and understanding since He gives us "free will" that our souls may come to paradise one of these days, hand in hand, and simple and gentle as two little doves that move shoulder to shoulder over the sword.[11]

With none of the other sisters did Rose seem to share such deep affection, and for none of the other sisters did Rose express such unstinted praise. Although she continually sought other women to join her order—Rose asked Corrigan's permission to allow three postulants to receive the habit of her order in September, 1901—she demanded extremely high standards of those whom she allowed to

10. Mother M. Alphonsa to Mother M. Rose [Alice Huber], August 22, September 29, 1901, both in ASRIC.

11. Mother M. Alphonsa to Mother M. Rose, August 29, 1901, *ibid.* The correspondence between Rose and Alice as well as the deeply affectionate relationship it fostered and expressed is not atypical of the expressions of intimacy between lifelong female friends and correspondents in nineteenth-century America. See Carroll Smith-Rosenberg, "The Female World of Love and Ritual: Relations Between Women in Nineteenth-Century America," in *The Signs Reader: Women, Gender and the Scholarship,* ed. Elizabeth Abel and Emily K. Abel (Chicago, 1983), 27–55.

stay. As she wrote to Alice on July 8, 1901, "[We] must refuse wicked crazy women who are too strong and interfere with the work of the houses." The next day Rose wrote to Corrigan requesting permission for Cecelia Higley, who, Rose said, "refuses obedience," to be dispensed from her vows so that she might depart from the community.[12]

To solicit both donations and dedicated co-workers, Rose began a new endeavor that she referred to as "the penwar . . . a warfare of love and humility."[13] Between September, 1901, and May, 1904, she published monthly, but with interruption during periods of illness in 1903, a magazine entitled *Christ's Poor.* The cost of a subscription, fifty cents a year, paid for the magazine's publication and provided some small revenue. In addition, the magazine attracted donations to the charity as well as women interested in devoting themselves to charity work, but possibly of greater significance is the fact that *Christ's Poor* records, in a variety of articles, the philosophical and theological basis for Rose's work.

Christ's Poor followed a regular format. The front page always featured an illustration, most frequently Jean François Millet's *The Man with the Hoe,* a mid-nineteenth-century painting of a laborer bent over a hoe in a field. Millet's painting had become the subject of considerable popular attention because it had been reprinted by Edwin Markham in his book *The Man with the Hoe and Other Poems,* which was a best seller for the year 1900. Rose thus deliberately connected her effort with Markham's lament for the suffering that various social institutions impose upon the common person. She even reprinted various groups of lines from "The Man with the Hoe" as the caption for Millet's picture, such as:

> O masters, lords and rulers in all lands,
> Is this the handiwork you give to God,
> This monstrous thing, distorted and soul-quenched?
> How will it be with kingdoms and with kings—
> With those who shaped him to the thing he is—
> When this dumb terror shall reply to God,
> After the silence of centuries?[14]

12. Mother M. Alphonsa to Archbishop Michael Augustine Corrigan, September 25, July 9, 1901, both in AANY; Mother M. Alphonsa to Mother M. Rose, July 8, 1901, in ASRIC.
13. Mother M. Alphonsa to Mother M. Rose, July 20, 1903, in ASRIC.
14. Edwin Markham, *The Man with the Hoe and Other Poems* (New York, 1899), 17.

Christ's Poor always included the imprimatur, in the early years of its publication given by "His Grace, Michael Augustine Corrigan, Archbishop of New York" and in later years by Corrigan's successor, the Reverend John M. Farley. The magazine contained lengthy articles and brief commentaries on issues of social justice, sometimes alluding to contemporary historical events or writers. Occasionally Rose documented the inception of her work and her difficulties in establishing it, and she printed replicas of her initial appeals that had appeared in the newspapers. She often related amusing narratives and anecdotes about the residents of the homes, focusing principally upon the male patients, to whose cause she wished to draw special attention.

Frequently Rose featured selections from writings of the saints or short biographies of them, especially when their lives reflected the very qualities of sacrifice and dedication to the poor and sick that she emulated in her own work. In particular, she recounted the lives of female saints, including Rose of Lima and Catherine of Siena. She also devoted several articles to Father Damien and his work with lepers. His life inspired her enormously, though she believed her task was inconsequential by comparison: "Cancer nursing bears to leprosy nursing somewhat the same relationship that a subaltern's duty bears to the responsibility of a colonel or general."[15]

From time to time Rose also published letters from her supporters. Among these admirers was Samuel Clemens, who addressed Rose as "Mrs. Lathrop."

> I have known about this lofty work of yours since long ago—indeed from the day you began it; I have known of its steady growth and progress step by step to its present generous development and assured position among those benefactions to which the reverent homage of all creeds and colors is due; I have seen it rise from seedling to tree with no endowment but the voluntary aid which your patient labor and faith have drawn from the purses of grateful and compassionate men; and I am glad in the prosperous issue of your work, and glad to know that this prosperity will continue, and be permanent—a thing which I do know, for that endowment is banked where it cannot fail until pity fails in the hearts of men. And that will never be.

Other, regular features of *Christ's Poor* were a statement entitled "The Objects of the Work," a list called "Needs of the Nurses for

15. Mother M. Alphonsa, *Christ's Poor,* III (June, 1904), 13.

Work Among the Poor," a form of bequest for those who wished to name the Servants of Relief as their heirs, an accounting of donations and expenditures, and a record of the patients who had died in the homes.[16]

This little periodical was popular among its subscribers and succeeded in calling attention to Rose's work and winning it friends and supporters. Nonetheless, there were occasional outbreaks of hostility toward Rose from "the dark side of the Catholic element" that "would array our patrons against us." The "bitter word[s] of the prelates" to which Rose was referring may, perhaps, have been triggered by the acerbic, even militant manner in which Rose criticized the shortcomings of established charities and prevailing attitudes toward the poor.[17] Not only was Rose engaged in a work no one else wanted to do, but she was saying things many people did not want to hear. She had aptly named her purpose in writing *Christ's Poor* as the waging of a "penwar."

Rose repeatedly attacked the experimental surgery performed upon terminally ill patients, believing that when there was no hope for recovery, the poor had the right to die as peacefully and comfortably as possible. Rose made no effort at diplomacy in stating her position in "The Objects of the Work."

> An important object of the charity is to look carefully to the interests of the poor, especially whenever the interests of science are held in autocratical estimation by persons of inferior judgment, as opposed to the enlightened and noble verdict of eminent physicians. Incurable cancer is now a matter of general and exhaustive study, and the poor supply the principal material used. This clause is of deepest concern to those who are really devoted to destitute misery. Reference cannot be made to policy or special approval of a human order, but to God's approval alone, notwithstanding the unfailing accompaniment of opposition from Pharisee and money-changer which such a course involves.

In an article in *Christ's Poor* entitled "The Real Case of the Cancerous Poor," Rose condemns the institutionalized neglect of cancer patients and their relegation to "cellar-holes or avoided corners" in hospitals, where "a feeling of courteous pity, and earnestness among doctors and nurses" was lacking. In another article, "What Econ-

16. *Ibid.*, I (December, 1901), 16.

17. Mother M. Alphonsa to Mother M. Rose, March 3, 1903, December 6, 1902, both in ASRIC.

omy Is Kind?," she attacks the inequity found in so-called charitable institutions in which administrators commanded high salaries but practiced false economy with regard to the needs of their charges. Posing a rhetorical question—"What shall we say of cold and scant meals for the very sick, while their care-takers are so well fed that their larders are a matter of delicate non-supervison?"—Rose responds, "It seems to me that economy should show itself above all in the manner of life of the care-takers. These persons should be fed, shod and harbored more roughly than the poor of the charity."[18]

Rose's solution to this problem of the institutionalized neglect of the poor and sick was a band of women who would give without remuneration both their lives and their service. Intrinsic to her mission was the belief that paid service would lead only to corruption because of the inevitable preference that would be shown toward those who could afford more attention. The sisters employed workers only in the case of male patients "who . . . sometimes require hired male help." Rose was, however, adamant, as she states in "The Objects of the Work," that "hired help . . . never be allowed in such force that the Sisters will lose personal control of cases."

Of equal importance in Rose's vision of this work was the fact that it was spearheaded by women. She wrote: "We women had better take hold of a problem that puzzles organizations and councils, when they face the poor; sufferers who are not heard, and are often forgotten in the general commotion about more interesting problems; and we can easily unravel this tangled mystery with our women's hands, if they are consecrated to work, nursing, prayer, courage and gentleness. When we place ourselves where poverty dwells, we see why our life must be given wholly, without weight of baggage or plans for self, to the arduous task."[19] Rose declared in "The Objects of the Work": "The only way to meet the great sufferings of the poor sick is to enlist the interest and personal service of the women of the different parishes, who could properly and fully attend to all cases of destitute incurables . . . if they would religiously devote a part of each week to them, at times never to be postponed or delegated."

Elsewhere, in her article "Nurses by Command," Rose employs a

18. Mother M. Alphonsa, *Christ's Poor,* I (August, 1901), 6, (November, 1901), 6–7.
19. *Ibid.* (December, 1901), 28.

decidedly feminist rhetoric to invoke the demonstrated power of women to form useful societies.

There is a tenacity about a woman's convictions, when she consents to have any, that holds better than her masculine rival's. I believe that a society established by American women can never become feeble, if it is simple, religiously painstaking, dauntless for the relief of the poor, and as strong in extent and support as an army. I believe that such a society would remain honorable and direct in usefulness in spite of size and time; in fact, become more so for these conditions. Feminine societies have indeed already steadily developed in this manner, with superlative integrity and unfading lustre.

Alluding here to the religious order cofounded by Jane de Chantel, whose life Rose had described with such admiration in *A Story of Courage,* she later refers to de Chantel as one who "began by bringing lepers into her chateau. She ended by stepping over the body of her prostrate son, who thus implored her not to leave flesh and blood that was very comfortably off, to befriend the destitute who daily suffered."[20]

Rose continually issued to women the challenge to exhibit the kind of heroism in charity that was typically attributed to men in military endeavors. Indeed, military metaphors pervade these articles about her work. On one occasion she wrote that "directors need to give the band of women hearty confidence, and as officers would keep cowards and awkward louts in the background of an army, so the directors do their best to make a Community represent training and capacity, or its heart fail in the advance."[21]

Believing that men were called to exercise heroism by means other than patriotic valor, she sought to disprove the tenet that "the masculine character cannot be depended upon to do duty in any field but those of brute courage and intellectual grasp," that the sacrifices attendant upon nursing were "beneath manly dignity." Rather, she was confident that men, who, she vowed, were "now capable of broader conscientiousness than the race ever knew before," would rally to the cause of caring for the sick poor when made aware of the sufferings of other men.[22]

Rose's optimism about "unraveling this tangled mystery with our

20. *Ibid.* (June, 1902), 10, 15.
21. *Ibid.* (January, 1902), 40.
22. *Ibid.* (February, 1902), 25, 27.

women's hands" and obtaining men's help in the process might appear naïve were it not grounded in a thoroughly realistic evaluation of the task. In "Some Reasons Why We Work," she bluntly addresses the motives for ignoring the poor and sick. "Why are we likely to look upon the question of the very poor, especially the sick poor, with contemptuous indifference?" she queries. Her answer is, "the poor are unattractive, the sick poor are nauseating."[23]

More fortunate people wish, said Rose elsewhere, to disassociate themselves from the poor, whom they regard as alien. Thus to the more comfortable classes the "distance up Fifth Avenue sometimes seems as far and as frozen as the road to the now famous mines of Alaska." But becoming poor and living with the poor, Rose assured her readers, quickly disabuses one of misconception: "After a few months of living among them one entirely abandons any idea of their being so different from other human beings." Rose believed that "if anyone wishes to know how extremely similar the poor are to friends and enemies up town, they may well give a week to studying them. It would take but a week more to sweep away all the carefully devised barriers placed between us and . . . the poor."[24]

In tones energetic and emphatic, Rose challenged her readers to accept her vision of a society in which barriers between individuals based on class and sex did not exist. Because the poor are ourselves, said Rose, we cannot ignore them. Because women are capable of heroic sacrifice and men are capable of great compassion, both sexes can give their lives to aid the good of society.

In June, 1904, the last issue of *Christ's Poor* made its appearance. The periodical had served its purpose, and Rose could no longer invest her precious time in its publication. Her daily routine of praying, nursing the dying, soliciting and administering funds, and attending to the growth of her order and the welfare of the sisters—who regarded her as their spiritual mother—clearly absorbed every moment of her time and every ounce of her energy.

Travel between Saint Rose's Free Home on Cherry Street and Rosary Hill Home in Sherman Park—soon renamed Hawthorne, in honor of Rose, its illustrious resident—was not easy and therefore not frequent for any of the sisters. Rose's abundant correspondence with

23. *Ibid.* (November, 1901), 23.
24. *Ibid.* (July, 1902), 5, 15, (October, 1901), 10.

Alice continued, and remained a source of great joy. Rose referred to herself in these letters variously, as "your mother famished for your companionship," "ever your loving, grateful, poor, funny, little mother," and "your loving Mary Alphonsa, and your devoted sister." Rose addressed Alice with affectionate titles such as "my dearest and best Friend and child," "my own, own, own sister," "my dearest pet and Tower of Strength," and "my darling daughter and captain." On one occasion Rose wrote, "I am trying to fit into the way of writing Mother M. Rose as it is correct," but this letter, dated some sixteen years after Alice's change of name, suggests that Rose never fully adjusted to thinking of her beloved friend in such formal terms.[25]

Rose regarded Alice as integral to the spiritual fabric of her life, a person with whom she felt a closeness that prefigured eternal union with God. "I love you," Rose wrote to Alice, "and believe that for your sake God will befriend this community, and I believe also that he has blessed the work." On another occasion she wrote, "Just think how infinitely happy we should be, if we were wholly united to Jesus, as little rivulets, bubbling and laughing along, in connection with a greater river than Niagara's St. Lawrence."[26]

Some letters suggest that Alice may have tempered the lack of subtlety that characterized Rose's zeal. "I am very well, my dove," wrote Rose, "and my notion of making everyone happy is already giving me the salubrious waves of sense and peace. . . . [T]he mule sense you prayed for . . . has come forward with its demure and contented expression and attentive ears." Alice clearly accepted Rose for exactly the person she was, and Rose was grateful: "I am thankful that you are safe and that you love me in spite of my being a porcupine."[27]

Perhaps the prickly side of Rose's nature showed itself most in her dealings with the aspirants to her order and the other sisters. Rose never ceased to solicit new members, but she was ceaseless as well in the rigorous demands she made of all who applied for entrance or succeeded in entering, notwithstanding Father Thuente's entreaty that she stop dismissing candidates so easily. Of one woman who expressed interest in the order, Rose wrote, "If she is odd or nervous I

25. Mother M. Alphonsa to Mother M. Rose [Alice Huber], 1901–1926 *passim,* November 16, 1916, in ASRIC.

26. Mother M. Alphonsa to Mother M. Rose, September 14, 1908, August 30, 1911, both *ibid.*

27. Mother M. Alphonsa to Mother M. Rose, September 14, 1908, and 1909, both *ibid.*

will send her away"; of another, Rose conceded a slight endorsement: "I like her—but of course you know we do not like any one too much any more."[28]

In her encounters with the other sisters, Rose could be playful at the same time she chastised. In one letter she conveyed through Alice "love to the good Sisters [at the New York home] and a bastinado for the naughty ones." The kinds of offenses Rose deemed deserving a "bastinado" were slight. The constraints imposed by the poverty of their lives demanded that each sister exercise the strictest economy, and Rose was therefore harsh with those who caused any kind of waste or desired anything beyond the basic necessities. One sister was criticized for spoiling food and not reporting it; another was faulted for requesting a pair of gold-rimmed eyeglasses. Rose demanded of her sisters hard work and the most complete self-discipline. "Self-indulgence" of any kind was condemned, and a sister who resorted to "sedatives" for a headache was considered to be less than completely self-sacrificing. Applying the same stringent standards to herself, Rose believed that she failed in the example she wished to set when recurrent pain in her heart, arm, and wrist required her to consider taking digitalis. "I commit the unpardonable sin," she wrote to Alice, "of falling out of the ranks when ill, and not being at my posts of various duties, when you yourself would die at your post."[29]

As strict as she was in her refusal to allow indulgence among the sisters, Rose was prodigal in her efforts to obtain any form of comfort for her patients. She continued to be adamant in her position that terminally ill patients should be allowed to die with dignity. One particularly pathetic patient had come to the sisters from a hospital in Newburgh. "Almost half of her face is eaten away," Rose wrote. "I suppose she is one of those whom they publish that they can 'cure.' . . . I wish somebody would stop those unstinted lies about cure which even that good hospital stoops to printing—for the sake of attracting subjects for experiment." Rose, on the other hand, sought to ease her patients' last moments with morphine, fresh air,

28. Mother M. Alphonsa to Mother M. Rose, 1908, June 19, 1922, August 15, 1908, all *ibid.*

29. Mother M. Alphonsa to Mother M. Rose, August 31, 1908, 1909, June 11, 1914, November 15, 1916, all *ibid.*

and whatever dainties they desired. Among the gifts for which she begged were always good foods, including fresh fruit, and an assortment of claret, sherry, and Bass's ale.[30]

Rose also refused to prohibit her patients, particularly the men, from smoking if it gave them pleasure. This decision necessitated considerable fortitude and vigilance on the part of all the sisters. The original structure of Rosary Hill Home was not fireproof, and situated as it was atop a windswept hill, smoking augmented the already-existing threat of fire in an era before electricity, when oil lamps illuminated dark hours and a coal-driven furnace kept residents warm. Fire during the winter, when water supplies might be frozen and exits icy, was especially fearful. One cold day in December, 1917, a local college had burned to the ground, and five years later, also in December, a fire had broken out in the furnace room of Rosary Hill Home. Luckily the fire occurred during the day; it was quickly discovered and was subdued by a bucket brigade formed by the sisters. Had the fire occurred at night, there would without doubt have been many lost lives. In light of these circumstances, raising $200,000 for a fireproof structure became one of Rose's major goals.[31]

When, in September, 1922, the editors at Houghton Mifflin approached Rose about reissuing *Memories of Hawthorne,* suggesting that she mention in a new preface that money derived from the sale of the book would be used to fund this fireproof structure, she readily agreed. The writing of this preface, which should have been completed by Christmas of that year, was delayed because of an illness from which, as she wrote to the editors, she had been "expected to succumb by the doctors." But she rallied and fulfilled her contractual obligation with Houghton Mifflin, and by the summer of 1923 was collecting revenue from the sale of the book to use for the fireproof building.[32]

The revenue from the reissue of *Memories of Hawthorne* provided but a small portion of the money needed for the new structure. Donations came from many sources—from large legacies as well as small

30. Mother M. Alphonsa to Mother M. Rose, June 8, 1914, *ibid.*

31. Sister M. Joseph, *Out of Many Hearts,* 187–93.

32. Mother M. Alphonsa to Sirs at Houghton and Mifflin, December 6, 1922, January 16, 17, August 1, 1923, Mother M. Alphonsa to Mr. Scaife, October 16, 1922, Mr. Scaife to Mother M. Alphonsa, September 16, October 18, 1922, January 19, 1923, all in Houghton Mifflin Papers, HL.

gifts. Rose, once again employing her proven method of direct appeals to the public through the newspapers, composed entreaties such as the following, which appeared in the *World* on February 18, 1923:

To the Editor of *The World:*
We are in need of great help from friends. There are thirty-five men and women harbored in the country Westchester County, N.Y. . . . home built of flimsy wood, who need a fireproof home. The work of the Servants of Relief for Incurable Cancer, for all creeds and nationalities, and for all parts of the United States, has been in danger of destruction by fire in its country branch for twenty-one years. The sister-nurses appeal for donations from readers of *The World,* for the patients are destitute and clearly wholly mendicant. A home on the adjacent ground for one hundred men and women is earnestly desired, and the sum needed is $400,000.00, as prices have doubled and only a modern building of excellent appointment is now permitted by law. We pray you to help our foundation for these sufferers.[33]

Rose was gratified by the response to such solicitations and by "prodigious results" in the form of five-, ten-, and fifty-dollar gifts; but as eager as she was to fund this project, she was always insistent that donors give to the charity as she conceived it. Of one potential benefactor who criticized the Catholic nature of her home, Rose wrote: "He can keep his old $10,000.00." With or without this particular donation, the fund drive resulted in the opening of a fireproof annex to Rosary Hill Home in April, 1924. This annex, called Saint Joseph's Home, served as a transitional structure where patients lived while funds for the new Rosary Hill Home were raised and that edifice was constructed. The following appeal, made in January, 1926, characterizes Rose's fund-raising method and describes the building that was eventually completed: "We and our patients only need to place upon a splendid lofty site among Westchester Hills a simple phalanx of Spanish mission quarters—a home for 100 cancerous poor; admirable in health devices and sensible conveniences, at the lowest cost consistent with wisdom, in place of an old wooden building inhabited by us for 25 years. Our patients, who are of all creeds and nationalities, pay nothing because their pockets are empty, and we are the connecting link with their friends among the public. Give us a fireproof Home."[34]

33. *World,* February 18, 1923 (Clipping in ASRIC).

34. Mother M. Alphonsa to Mother M. Rose, October 4, 1916, May 22, 1923, March 13, 1925, all in ASRIC; Sister M. Joseph, *Out of Many Hearts,* 194, 198.

Rose's fund-raising technique had resulted in a similar success more than a decade earlier with the opening of a new structure in New York. Saint Rose's Free Home, at first so spacious, had become obsolete with the growth of the work, and Rose had set her sights upon a piece of property on the corner of Front and Jackson streets. Facing the East River on one side and Corlears Park on the other, a new home in this location would, Rose believed, be ideal.

Rose had every hope that her New York City benefactors would continue to support her work in numerous ways. John Grant Coyle, a respected physician, provided free medical attention to the patients at Saint Rose's Free Home. Rose admired the respect and warmth he showed the patients; Dr. Grant did not disdain to bring his young daughter with him "to fraternize for a sociable hour with the dwellers in a corner of misery and disease." J. Warren Greene, an eminent attorney whose wife had died of cancer, provided legal aid to Rose's patients as well as monthly donations, sometimes as much as one thousand dollars. Another lawyer, James J. Walsh, was also a scholar who devised a series of annual Lenten lectures. These lectures, attended through subscriptions of ten dollars per person, were tremendously popular and produced hundreds of dollars each year for the Servants of Relief. Edward McGuire was legal counsel to the Emigrant Savings Bank and came to the rescue of Rosary Hill Home when its mortgage was due. Yet another benefactor was a retired pharmacist, Henry J. Reel, who created an auxiliary association to provide free medication for Rose's patients.[35]

The largest donations received during the acquisition of the new Saint Rose's Free Home came from Cornelius Cronin and Edward J. Smith who contributed $25,000 each in May, 1911. Rose and the other sisters then engaged in a massive campaign of newspaper appeals to obtain the remaining funds needed. Against Rose's better judgment, a fund drive was also established, and although it was startlingly successful, the methods used did not meet Rose's high standards. She therefore terminated the drive and relied upon slower means, including a large mortgage, to discharge the debt on the new structure. But even these less spectacular methods of fund raising proved to be remarkably successful, for by mid-December, 1912, the

35. *Report: Dominican Cancer Homes for the Destitute,* January, 1908–October, 1912, pp. 6–21 (Clipping *ibid.*).

building was ready to be dedicated. On January 13, 1913, mass was celebrated in the new home for the first time.[36]

The testimony of Rose's work provided the indisputable inspiration for numerous donations. She was scrupulous in her keeping of accounts, which demonstrated that all money raised went exclusively to the care of those dying of cancer and to the construction of residential facilities for them. In a report for the period that included her fund drive for the new Saint Rose's Free Home (January 1, 1908, through October 1, 1912), Rose demonstrated a balance of $324.32 after expenses of $137,587.81—for everything from food to funeral expenses—had been deducted from total revenues of $137,912.13. Donations accounted for $87,558.95 of these receipts, and legacies for the other $50,353.18. Rose also demonstrated that her charity, which had been founded for a specific and heretofore-neglected class, was not confined to a specific sex, religion, or race. In a report on the first sixteen years of nursing cancer patients, she documented the care of 1,045 patients, of whom 652 were Catholics, 363 were Protestants, and 30 were "Hebrews." In a report on the 340 patients cared for in Saint Rose's Free Home during 1916, she classified her patients by sex (120 male and 220 female), by race (325 white, 14 "colored," and 1 "Chinese"), and by religion (247 Catholics, 81 Protestants, 11 "Hebrews," and 1 "Chinese").[37]

Along with the meticulous reporting of accounts and patients, Rose was pleased to announce that one of her original goals—the demonstration that cancer was not contagious—had been met. "Constant care and cleanliness, rather than the skeleton effects of furniture and the unconcealed desire to relegate the cancer patient to the level of an animal, are the means by which the Sisters keep well, and counteract the horrors of the disease. In fifteen years of labor," Rose proudly proclaimed, "there has been no disaster to the Sisters from cancer-nursing." This had been accomplished, Rose declared emphatically, without the use of protective gloves. "If a person wearing rubber gloves were to enter the humble Homes of the Servants of Relief it is not easy to say how they would be expelled, but that would not take long. The Sisters also cut short any exhibition of disgust

36. Sister M. Joseph, *Out of Many Hearts,* 154–59.

37. *Report: Dominican Cancer Homes,* January, 1908–October, 1912, pp. 34, 39, October, 1915–October, 1916, p. 19.

in the presence of a patient. These people are not dehumanized by the misfortune which they bravely endure, of disease and poverty combined."[38]

The New York newspapers had covered all events connected with the acquisition of the property for Saint Rose's Free Home on Front and Jackson streets, the appeals for funds for the building, and the celebration of its dedication. During precisely the same period, the New York presses also covered the events surrounding Julian's indictment and subsequent trial for fraudulent use of the United States Postal Service. In October, 1912, a federal grand jury began its investigation into a venture Julian had undertaken with several other men, acquaintances from his days at Harvard. They were accused of advertising through the mail stock in worthless mines in Ontario. All the men went to trial. Invariably, however, the papers reported on the "Hawthorne Case," and for many days during December, the New York *Times* published the evidence mounted against Julian in the form of letters he had signed. The prosecution continued its examination throughout December, and Julian's defense began in January. The trial dragged on almost until the spring. On March 13, 1913, under the headline "Wise Flays Hawthorne," the *Times* related the district attorney's summation. Henry A. Wise called the defendants "bunko steerers" and "swindlers." When the presiding judge objected to Wise's language, the district attorney retorted: "We all know some of these men bear honored names. Theirs is the greater crime for they have prostituted them."[39]

On March 15, 1913, the *Times* ran as its front page headline: "Convict Three Men in Hawthorne Case / Jury Finds Son of Novelist . . . Guilty." The judge sentenced Julian to a term of imprisonment in the federal penitentiary in Atlanta of a year and a day, dating from the first day of the trial. Julian's attorney, Herbert C. Smyth, made a plea for clemency, asserting that Julian's "fault was one of judgment rather than evil intent." Smyth declared to the court that

38. *Ibid.*, January, 1908–October, 1912, p. 29.

39. The New York *Times* for 1912: October 24, p. 22; October 26, p. 5; November 26, p. 24; November 27, p. 7; November 28, p. 20; November 30, p. 9; December 3, p. 8; December 4, pp. 2, 3; December 5, p. 5; December 7, p. 9; December 10, p. 10; December 11, p. 8; December 13, p. 9; December 17, p. 24; December 18, p. 10; December 20, p. 12; December 27, p. 14. The New York *Times* for 1913: January 8, p. 3; January 10, p. 20; January 11, p. 16; January 16, p. 1; March 13, p. 3.

"[Julian] bears an honored name, and surely to a man of his age it should be sufficient punishment that he has knowledge that he has sullied that name in the eyes of the world." The judge was unmoved, however, and on March 23, after a brief imprisonment in the Tombs, Julian set out for the Atlanta penitentiary. On March 26, the *Times* ran, again on the front page, the headline "Hawthorne is No. 41,435."[40]

Julian's disgrace did not estrange him from Rose's affection. She had written to Hildegarde Hawthorne, of whom she continued to be especially fond, to commend her bravery upon "being hurt by your father's great difficulties." Rose told her, "I wish I could help you in some way, niece of mine, but I can in no way and I think you are equal to your problems." But if Rose saw no way to assist Hildegarde in January, 1913, by the summer of that year she had devised a plan that she thought might help Julian. She traveled to Washington, D.C., where she attempted to see President Wilson and plead for her brother's pardon. Although Wilson's secretary assured her that she would have an interview with the president, nothing ever came of her effort. Julian was not granted a pardon, nor was he granted a parole when that was requested in July.[41]

Rose had not been able to help Julian in any material way, but her love and the example of her life affected him profoundly. Years after this unfortunate incident, he wrote her, "You and your work are never out of my mind: it is a vision of Jacob's ladder, by which angels descend to earth, and mortals climb to heaven."[42]

Rose's sortie into the public sphere in behalf of Julian was her one departure from the daily round of praying and caring for the dying this last third of her life. Not only did she refrain from activities in the outside world, but the events of the world seem not to have encroached at all upon her life at Rosary Hill. As involved as she and her sisters were with the suffering and death of cancer patients, Rose seems not to have remarked in any of her writings upon the global suffering and death caused by World War I or the great influenza pandemic of 1918–1919.

However unaware Rose may have been of the outside world, the

40. New York *Times,* March 15, 1913, p. 1, March 26, 1913, p. 1.

41. Mother M. Alphonsa to Hildegarde Hawthorne, January 21, [?], in Henry W. and Albert A. Berg Collection, NYPL; Bassan, *Hawthorne's Son,* 215.

42. Julian Hawthorne to Rose Hawthorne Lathrop, December 11, 1923, in ASRIC.

world had taken note of her. By the end of her life, circles of respect and love for Rose had enlarged beyond her blood relatives and her religious sisters. She was loved by the poor whom she nursed and comforted, one of whom attempted to convey his gratitude in a humble letter. "Reverend Mother," wrote James Spearing, "we takes this opportunity of congratulating you on the grand work you are doing for us poor men and women that the great All Mighty Seen fit to afflict with a Terrible disease of plage." Spearing concluded this letter with a wish that "God may prosper your work and that when the great Almighty calls you home to that home beyond the Clouds He will have Bright Crowns of gold waiting for you there where their is no more pain or Trouble but all happiness for ever."[43]

The woman whose work had at first been greeted with caution now commanded the admiration of ecclesiastical authorities as the head of a recognized and growing religious order. Rose had also won the respect of the National Institute of Social Sciences, and in 1914 she was awarded its medal for "notable achievement in the field of Social Service." Bowdoin College conferred upon her the degree of honorary master of arts in 1925, and shortly before her death, on April 18, 1926, the Rotary Club of New York presented her with its service medal, praising her as a "soldier of love, a friend of the poor, organizer of rare ability, hope of the hopeless."[44]

Thus Pessima's fear that she should "never come off well in the world" had not been realized. In her teens, Rose had exhibited typical adolescent shortcomings: egocentrism, superficiality, and an uncritical adoption of cultural mores. She had dreamed of a "little niggar girl" whose deformity had repelled her: the girl "kept taking hold of my hand and making me perfectly miserable." When Rose became an adult, however, egocentrism gave way to altruism. Rose transcended the constraints of culture and embraced as equals persons of all races whose illnesses had disfigured them and cast them beyond the pale of social institutions. Therein public recognition had come to Rose—not for the art with which Rösl had once hoped to "send a thrill of pleasure through anyone," nor for the writing about

43. Sister M. Joseph, *Out of Many Hearts,* 169.

44. Council and the Medal Committee of the National Institute of Social Sciences to Mother M. Alphonsa, January 1, 1914, Rotary Club of New York Presentation to Mother Alphonsa (Award Program), April 18, 1928, both in ASRIC.

which Rose Hawthorne Lathrop had acknowledged, "I do not expect to be a fine writer, though I *mean* to be." Her stories about the war between the sexes and her poems satirizing young coquettes armored with parasols did not succeed as did her "penwar" for the poor. This had made her a victorious "soldier of love." Indeed, the letter with which Sophia had celebrated her younger daughter's seventeenth birthday contained an insight into Rose's character that was truly prophetic. Rose did indeed have a desire for "beauty and order and right" that sometimes made her "pettish and unreasonable"; but she also had a "religious principle and sentiment" that rendered her finally "gentle and charitable." "You have to suffer," Sophia had told her daughter, "because GOD has given you the perilous gift of genius. With it you are to become greater and lovelier than your less gifted fellow beings."[45]

If Rose's mother had precisely foretold the nature of her daughter's genius, it was to her father that Rose attributed her particular inspirations. As a child, Rose had felt guilty about her imaginative productions because her father had forbidden her to write stories. Nonetheless, by reading *his* stories she had felt his guidance, and in his brief narrative of the gentleman in the English almshouse, she saw an emblem of the work she must do. Veiling the autobiographical element in his account, Nathaniel described a man of more than "customary reserve, shy of actual contact with human beings, afflicted with a peculiar distaste for whatever was ugly, and furthermore, accustomed to that habit of observation from an insulated stand-point which is said . . . to have the tendency of putting ice into the blood." He described how a "sickly, humor-eaten infant . . . prowled about him like a pet kitten" until he "took up the loathesome child and caressed it as tenderly as if he had been its father." This embrace became a sign "that he was responsible, in his degree, for all the sufferings and misdemeanors of the world in which he lived, and was not entitled to look upon a particle of its dark calamity as if it were none of his concern."[46]

While Rose often cited this incident as the catalyst of her concern for the poor and sick, she never expressed any awareness that her fa-

45. Sophia Peabody Hawthorne to Rose Hawthorne Lathrop, May 20, 1868, in Hawthorne and Lathrop Collections, MA 3400, PML.

46. N. Hawthorne, *Our Old Home,* 300–301.

ther's response was very different from her own. In Nathaniel's description, he both disguises his own identity and dehumanizes the child; the embrace, which he manages in spite of his revulsion, constitues but a momentary and uncharacteristic gesture. Rose, who was intolerant of those who would reduce the poor and sick to the "level of an animal," would never have described a patient as "a pet kitten." Her embrace was not the gesture of a moment but the thirty-year-long witness—in word and in deed—that "these people are not dehumanized by the misfortune which they bravely endure, of disease and poverty combined." Rose, who instructed her sisters to "cut short any [visitor's] exhibition of disgust in the presence of a patient," saw beyond the disfigurement when she embraced the dying, for she saw the diseased poor not as "the offspring of a brother's iniquity," as had her father, but as Christ himself.[47]

Rose spent July 8, 1926, engaged in the activities that had occupied her last twenty-six years. Content with the life she had chosen, she prayed, she nursed the dying, she nurtured the spirituality of her sisters and aspiring postulants. She wrote, until almost ten o'clock that night, letters soliciting donations for her charity. And then Rose, no longer a stranger to herself, went to bed. The next morning, when the sisters went to awaken Mother Mary Alphonsa, they discovered that she had died peacefully in her sleep.

47. *Ibid.*, 301.

Selected Bibliography

Published Works by Rose Hawthorne Lathrop

BOOKS

Along the Shore. Boston, 1888.

Memories of Hawthorne. Boston, 1897. New ed., Boston, 1923.

A Story of Courage: Annals of the Georgetown Convent of the Visitation of the Blessed Mary. With George Parsons Lathrop. Boston, 1894.

SHORT FICTION

"Browning the Meerschaum." *Harper's Bazar,* 1874. Clipping file, Archives of the Servants of Relief for Incurable Cancer, Hawthorne, N.Y.

"For a Lord." *Harper's Bazar,* July 30, 1892, pp. 613–15.

"Fun Beams." *St. Nicholas Magazine,* XI (1884), 225–31.

"Huff and Tiff." *Harper's Weekly,* September 2, 1882, p. 554.

"Lindie's Portrait." *St. Nicholas Magazine,* XIV (1887), 512–14.

"The Owl That Stared." *St. Nicholas Magazine,* IV (1876), 16–18.

"Princess Roundabout." *Independent,* 1875. Clipping file, Archives of the Servants of Relief for Incurable Cancer, Hawthorne, N.Y.

"Prisoners!" *Harper's New Monthly Magazine,* LXVII (1883), 503–11, 696–705.

"Saagenfreed." *Appleton's Journal,* June 10, 1876, pp. 741–45.

"Toy Mysteries." *Independent.* Clipping file, Archives of the Servants of Relief for Incurable Cancer, Hawthorne, N.Y.

"Troth." *Harper's New Monthly Magazine,* LXXXV (1892), 341–50.

"An Up Country Titania." July 12, 1879. Clipping file, Archives of the Servants of Relief for Incurable Cancer, Hawthorne, N.Y.

POETRY NOT APPEARING IN *Along the Shore*

"At the Breakfast Table: Our Modern Amazon." July 20, 1891. Clipping file, Archives of the Servants of Relief for Incurable Cancer, Hawthorne, N.Y.
"The Choice." *Catholic World,* LVI (October, 1892), 17.
"The Fault-Demon." *New Century Magazine,* V (1883–84), 798.
"The Greater World." *Scribner's Magazine,* V (1889), 536.
"Just Bloomed." *Century,* XXXVIII (1889), 480.
"The Lover's Fate." *Appleton's Journal,* XIX (January, 1878), 50.
"The World Runs On." *Harper's New Monthly Magazine,* LXXXI (1890), 845.

ARTICLES

"A Cheerful View of a Hard Problem." *Catholic World,* LXVIII (February, 1899), 659–69.
"Hawthorne as Worker." *Cambridge Magazine,* II (June, 1896), 68–79.
"My Father's Literary Methods." *Ladies' Home Journal,* XI (March, 1894), 371–75.
"Some Memories of Hawthorne." *Atlantic Monthly,* LXXVII (1896), 173–86, 373–87, 492–507, 649–60.

Biographical and Historical Sources

ARCHIVAL MATERIALS

Archives of the Archdiocese of New York, Yonkers
Archives of the Grey Nuns of Montreal
Archives of the Servants of Relief for Incurable Cancer, Hawthorne, N.Y.
Beinecke Rare Book and Manuscript Library, Yale University, New Haven, Conn.
  Collection of American Literature.
Boston Public Library
  American Collection.
Bowdoin College Library, Brunswick, Maine
  Bridge-Maurice Papers.
Concord Free Public Library, Concord, Mass.
  Rose Hawthorne Lathrop Correspondence.
Essex Institute Library, Salem, Mass.
  Hawthorne-Manning Collection.
Houghton Library, Harvard University, Cambridge, Mass.
  Thomas Bailey Aldrich Collection.
  Thomas Wentworth Higginson Collection.
  H. O. Houghton Collection.
  Houghton Mifflin Papers.
  William Dean Howells Collection.

Henry Wadsworth Longfellow Collection.
James Russell Lowell Collection.
Thomas B. Mosher Collection.
J. R. Osgood Collection.
Massachusetts Historical Society, Boston
Norcross Papers.
Perry-Clarke Papers.
Neilson Library, Smith College, Northampton, Mass.
Sophia Smith Collection.
New York Public Library, New York City
Henry W. and Albert A. Berg Collection.
Rare Books and Manuscripts Division
Alfred Williams Anthony Collection.
R. R. Bowker Papers.
Century Company Papers.
William Conant Church Papers.
Owen D. Young Library, St. Lawrence University, Canton, N.Y.
Ulysses S. Milburn Collection.
Pierpont Morgan Library, New York City
Hawthorne and Lathrop Collections, MA 3400.

PUBLISHED SOURCES

Bassan, Maurice. *Hawthorne's Son: The Life and Literary Career of Julian Hawthorne*. Columbus, Ohio, 1970.

Bucknell, John Charles, and Daniel Hack Tuke. *A Manual for Psychological Medicine: Containing the History and Nosology, Description, Statistics, Diagnosis, Pathology, and Treatment of Insanity*. Philadelphia, 1859.

Burrows, George M. *Commentaries on the Causes, Forms, Symptoms, and Treatment, Moral and Medical, of Insanity*. 1828; rpr. New York, 1976.

Burton, Katherine. *Sorrow Built a Bridge*. New York, 1937.

Cantab, M. B., and J. Thompson Dickson. "A Contribution to the Study of the So-Called Puerperal Insanity." *Journal of Mental Science,* XVI (October, 1870), 379–90.

Cantwell, Robert. *Nathaniel Hawthorne: The American Years*. Ann Arbor, 1979.

Conot, Robert. *A Streak of Luck*. New York, 1979.

Cook, George Willis. *Unitarianism in America*. Boston, 1902.

Eliot, T. S. "The Hawthorne Aspect." *Little Review,* V (August, 1918), 47–53.

Gordon, Lyndall. *Eliot's Early Years*. Oxford, 1977.

Hawthorne, Edith Garrigues, ed. *The Memoirs of Julian Hawthorne*. New York, 1938.

Hawthorne, Julian. *Hawthorne and His Circle*. New York, 1903.

———. *Nathaniel Hawthorne and His Wife*. 2 vols. Boston, 1884. Vols. XIV and XV of *The Works of Nathaniel Hawthorne.* [Edited by George Parsons Lathrop.] 15 vols.

Hawthorne, Nathaniel. *Doctor Grimshawe's Secret.* Boston, 1882. Vol. XIII of *The Works of Nathaniel Hawthorne.* [Edited by George Parsons Lathrop.] 15 vols.

———. *The English Note-Books.* 2 vols. Boston, 1883. Vols. VII and VIII of *The Works of Nathaniel Hawthorne.* [Edited by George Parsons Lathrop.] 15 vols.

———. *The Letters, 1843–1853.* Edited by Thomas Woodson, L. Neal Smith, and Norman Holmes Pearson. Columbus, Ohio, 1985. Vol. XVI of *The Centenary Edition of the Works of Nathaniel Hawthorne.* Edited by William Charvat, Roy Harvey Pearce, and Claude M. Simpson. 22 vols. projected.

———. *The Letters, 1853–1856.* Edited by Thomas Woodson, James A. Rubino, L. Neal Smith, and Norman Holmes Pearson. Columbus, Ohio, 1987. Vol. XVII of *The Centenary Edition of the Works of Nathaniel Hawthorne.* Edited by William Charvat, Roy Harvey Pearce, and Claude M. Simpson. 22 vols. projected.

———. *Our Old Home.* Edited by William Charvat, Roy Harvey Pearce, Claude M. Simpson, and Matthew J. Bruccoli. Columbus, Ohio, 1970. Vol. V of *The Centenary Edition of the Works of Nathaniel Hawthorne.* Edited by William Charvat, Roy Harvey Pearce, and Claude M. Simpson. 22 vols. projected.

Hawthorne, Sophia. *Notes in England and Italy.* New York, 1870.

Hennesey, James. *American Catholics: A History of the Roman Catholic Community in the United States.* New York, 1981.

Higginson, Thomas Wentworth. "Una Hawthorne." *Outlook,* LXXVII (1904), 517–24.

Hull, Raymona. *Nathaniel Hawthorne: The English Experience, 1853–1864.* Pittsburgh, 1980.

———. "Una Hawthorne: A Biographical Sketch." *Nathaniel Hawthorne Journal,* VI (1976), 87–119.

Jacob, Heinrich E. *The World of Emma Lazarus.* New York, 1949.

Joseph, Sister M. *Out of Many Hearts: Mother Alphonsa Lathrop and Her Work.* Hawthorne, N.Y., 1965.

Kolmer, Sister Elizabeth. "Catholic Women Religious and Women's History: A Survey of Literature." In *Women in American Religion,* edited by Janet Wilson James. Philadelphia, 1980.

Lathrop, George Parsons. *A Study of Hawthorne.* Boston, 1876.

———. *Dreams and Days.* New York, 1892.

Loggins, Vernon. *The Hawthornes: The Story of Seven Generations of an American Family.* New York, 1951.

Lothrop, Margaret Mulford. *Wayside Home of Authors.* New York, 1940.

Markham, Edwin. *The Man with the Hoe and Other Poems.* New York, 1899.

Maynard, Theodore. *A Fire Was Lighted.* Milwaukee, 1948.

Mellow, James R. *Nathaniel Hawthorne in His Times.* Boston, 1980.

A Memorial of American Authors, [Autographs of American citizens . . . who . . . urge the passage by Congress of an International Copyright law.]. N.p., [1884?]. Copy in Main Reading Room, New York Public Library.

Newman, Barbara. *Sister of Wisdom: St. Hildegard's Theology of the Feminine.* Berkeley, 1987.

Parkes, Henry Bamford. *The Pragmatic Test: Essays on the History of Ideas.* San Francisco, 1941.

Rosenberg, Charles. *The Care of Strangers: The Rise of the American Hospital System.* New York, 1987.

Sanborn, Franklin Benjamin. *Memorabilia of Hawthorne, Alcott, and Concord.* Hartford, 1970.

Shimkin, Michael Boris. *Contrary to Nature.* Washington, D.C., 1977.

Smith-Rosenberg, Carroll. "The Female World of Love and Ritual: Relations Between Women in Nineteenth-Century America." In *The Signs Reader: Women, Gender and the Scholarship,* edited by Elizabeth Abel and Emily K. Abel. Chicago, 1983.

Stewart, Randall. *Nathaniel Hawthorne: A Biography.* New Haven, 1948.

Vance, Marguerite. *On the Wings of Fire: The Story of Nathaniel Hawthorne's Daughter Rose.* New York, 1955.

Welter, Barbara. *Dimity Convictions: The American Woman in the Nineteenth Century.* Athens, Ohio, 1979.

Wyman, Morrill. *The Early History of the McLean Asylum for the Insane: A Criticism of the Report of the Massachusetts State Board of Health for 1877.* Cambridge, 1877.

Index